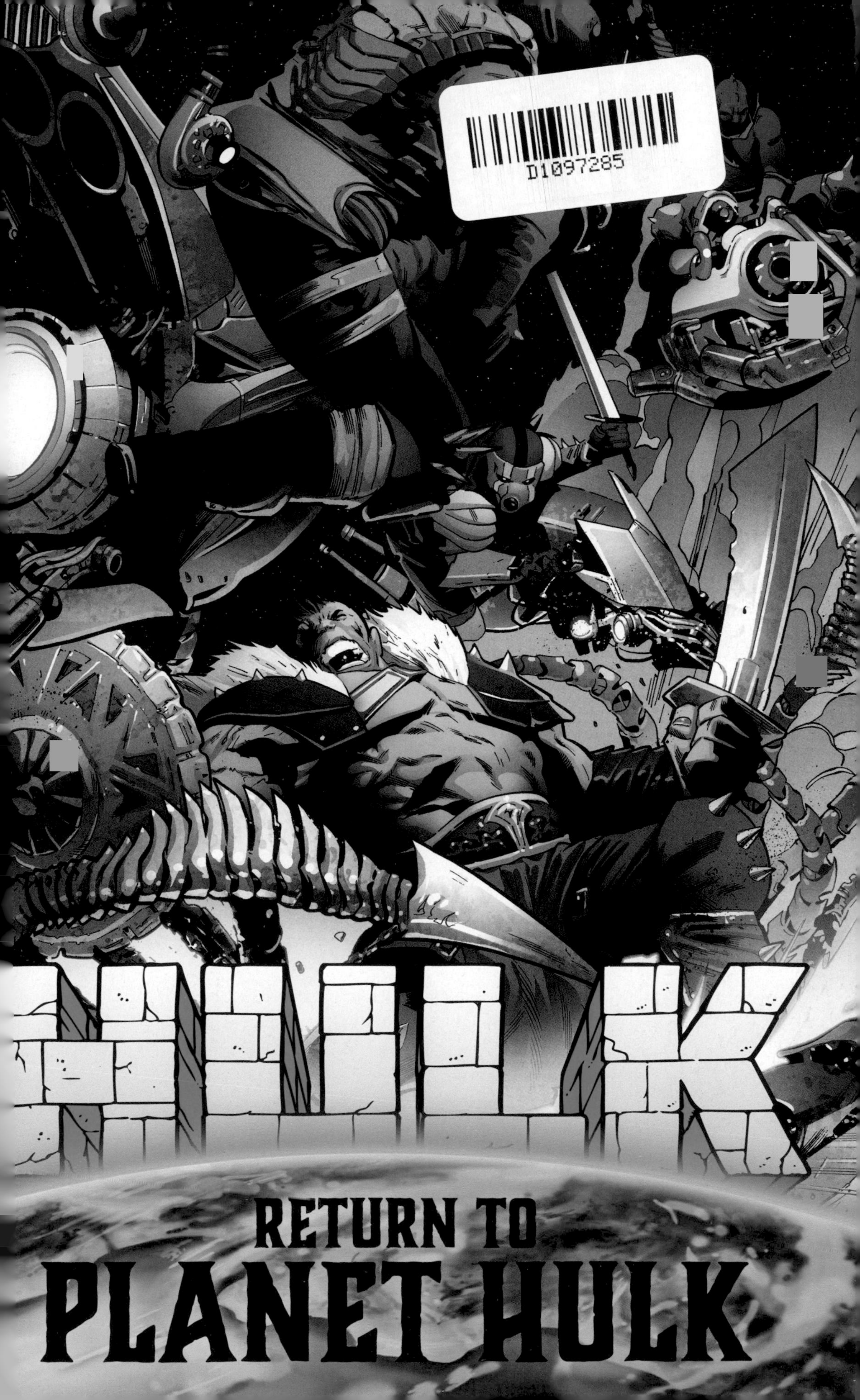
HULK
RETURN TO
PLANET HULK

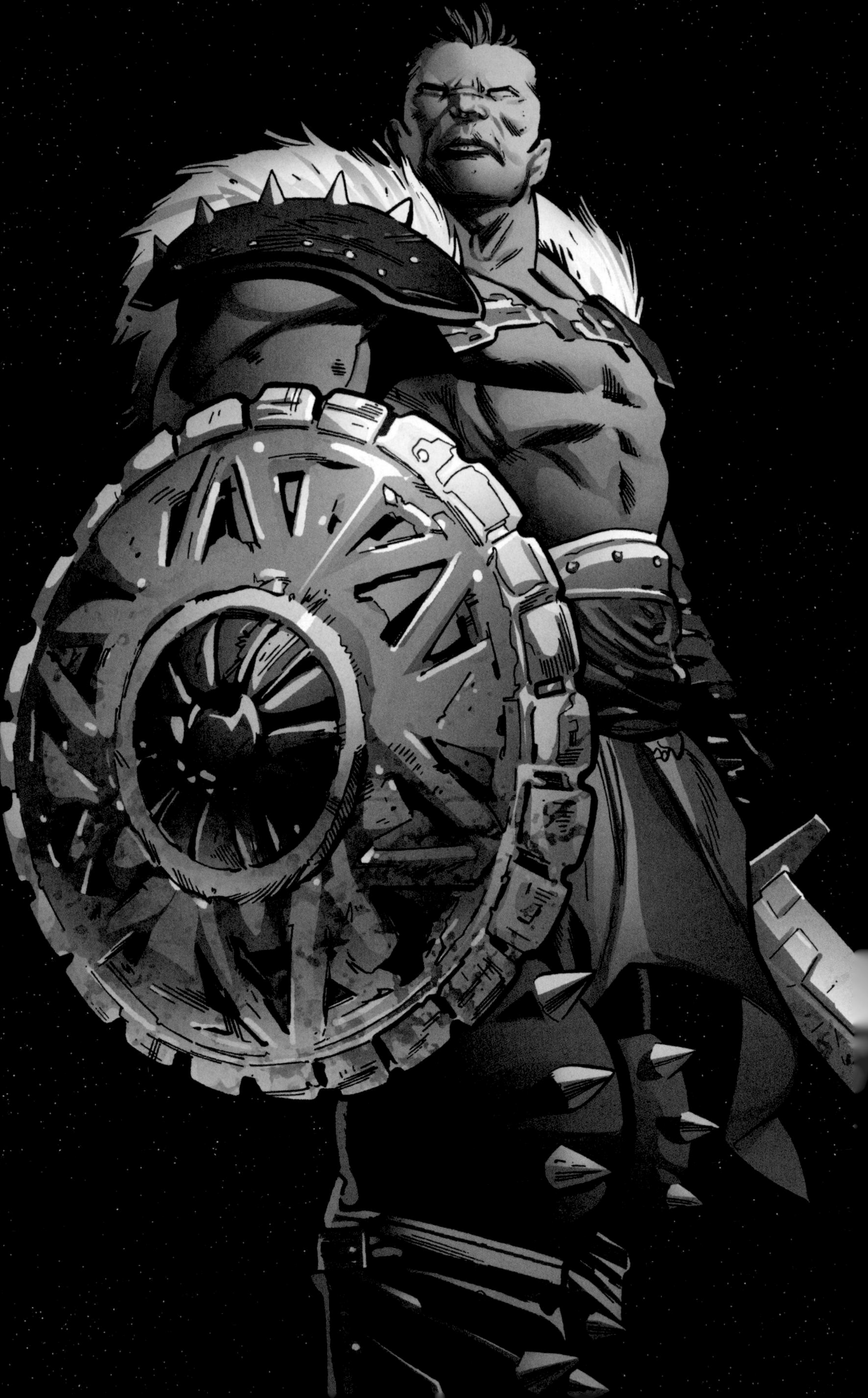

RETURN TO PLANET HULK

GREG PAK
WRITER

GREG LAND
PENCILER

JAY LEISTEN
INKER

FRANK D'ARMATA
COLOR ARTIST

VC's CORY PETIT
LETTERER

GREG LAND, JAY LEISTEN & FRANK D'ARMATA
COVER ART

CHRIS ROBINSON
ASSISTANT EDITOR

MARK PANICCIA
EDITOR

HULK CREATED BY **STAN LEE** & **JACK KIRBY**

COLLECTION EDITOR: **MARK D. BEAZLEY**
ASSISTANT EDITOR: **CAITLIN O'CONNELL**
ASSOCIATE MANAGING EDITOR: **KATERI WOODY**
EDITOR, SPECIAL PROJECTS: **JENNIFER GRÜNWALD**

VP PRODUCTION & SPECIAL PROJECTS: **JEFF YOUNGQUIST**
SVP PRINT, SALES & MARKETING: **DAVID GABRIEL**
BOOK DESIGNER: **ADAM DEL RE**

EDITOR IN CHIEF: **C.B. CEBULSKI**
CHIEF CREATIVE OFFICER: **JOE QUESADA**
PRESIDENT: **DAN BUCKLEY**
EXECUTIVE PRODUCER: **ALAN FINE**

HULK: RETURN TO PLANET HULK. Contains material originally published in magazine form as INCREDIBLE HULK #709-713. First printing 2018. ISBN 978-1-302-90996-3. Published by MARVEL WORLDWIDE, INC., a subsidiary of MARVEL ENTERTAINMENT, LLC. OFFICE OF PUBLICATION: 135 West 50th Street, New York, NY 10020. Copyright © 2018 MARVEL. No similarity between any of the names, characters, persons, and/or institutions in this magazine with those of any living or dead person or institution is intended, and any such similarity which may exist is purely coincidental. **Printed in the U.S.A.** DAN BUCKLEY, President, Marvel Entertainment; JOHN NEE, Publisher; JOE QUESADA, Chief Creative Officer; TOM BREVOORT, SVP of Publishing; DAVID BOGART, SVP of Business Affairs & Operations, Publishing & Partnership; DAVID GABRIEL, SVP of Sales & Marketing, Publishing; JEFF YOUNGQUIST, VP of Production & Special Projects; DAN CARR, Executive Director of Publishing Technology; ALEX MORALES, Director of Publishing Operations; SUSAN CRESPI, Production Manager; STAN LEE, Chairman Emeritus. For information regarding advertising in Marvel Comics or on Marvel.com, please contact Vit DeBellis, Custom Solutions & Integrated Advertising Manager, at vdebellis@marvel.com. For Marvel subscription inquiries, please call 888-511-5480. **Manufactured between 3/23/2018 and 4/24/2018 by LSC COMMUNICATIONS INC., KENDALLVILLE, IN, USA.**

10 9 8 7 6 5 4 3 2 1

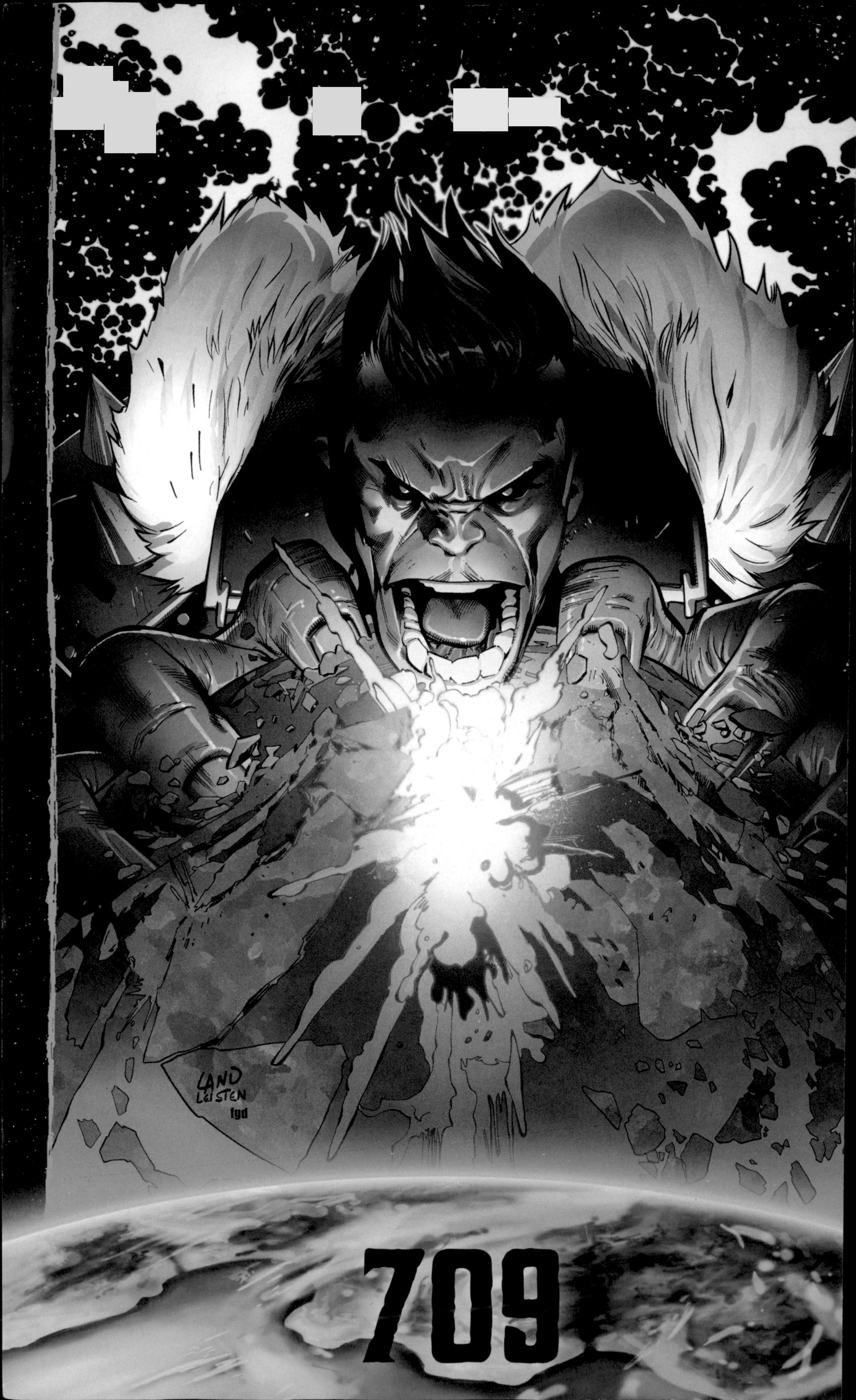
LAND
LEISTEN
fgd
709

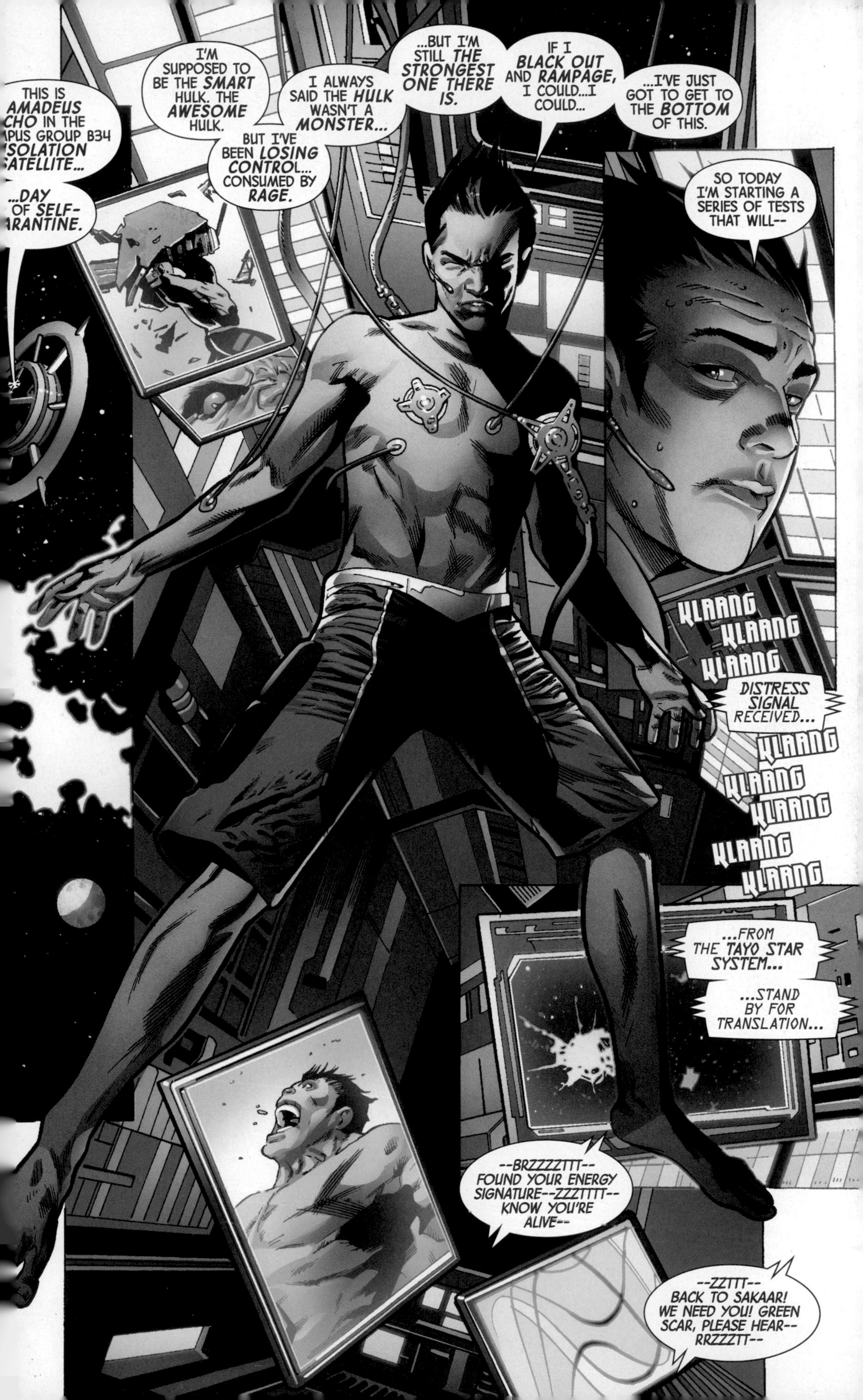
THIS IS AMADEUS CHO IN THE [T]APUS GROUP B34 [I]SOLATION [S]ATELLITE...
...DAY OF SELF-[QU]ARANTINE.
I'M SUPPOSED TO BE THE SMART HULK. THE AWESOME HULK.
BUT I'VE BEEN LOSING CONTROL... CONSUMED BY RAGE.
I ALWAYS SAID THE HULK WASN'T A MONSTER...
...BUT I'M STILL THE STRONGEST ONE THERE IS.
IF I BLACK OUT AND RAMPAGE, I COULD...I COULD...
...I'VE JUST GOT TO GET TO THE BOTTOM OF THIS.
SO TODAY I'M STARTING A SERIES OF TESTS THAT WILL--
KLAANG KLAANG KLAANG
DISTRESS SIGNAL RECEIVED...
KLAANG KLAANG KLAANG KLAANG KLAANG
...FROM THE TAYO STAR SYSTEM...
...STAND BY FOR TRANSLATION...
--BRZZZZTTT-- FOUND YOUR ENERGY SIGNATURE--ZZZTTTT-- KNOW YOU'RE ALIVE--
--ZZTTT-- BACK TO SAKAAR! WE NEED YOU! GREEN SCAR, PLEASE HEAR-- RRZZZTT--

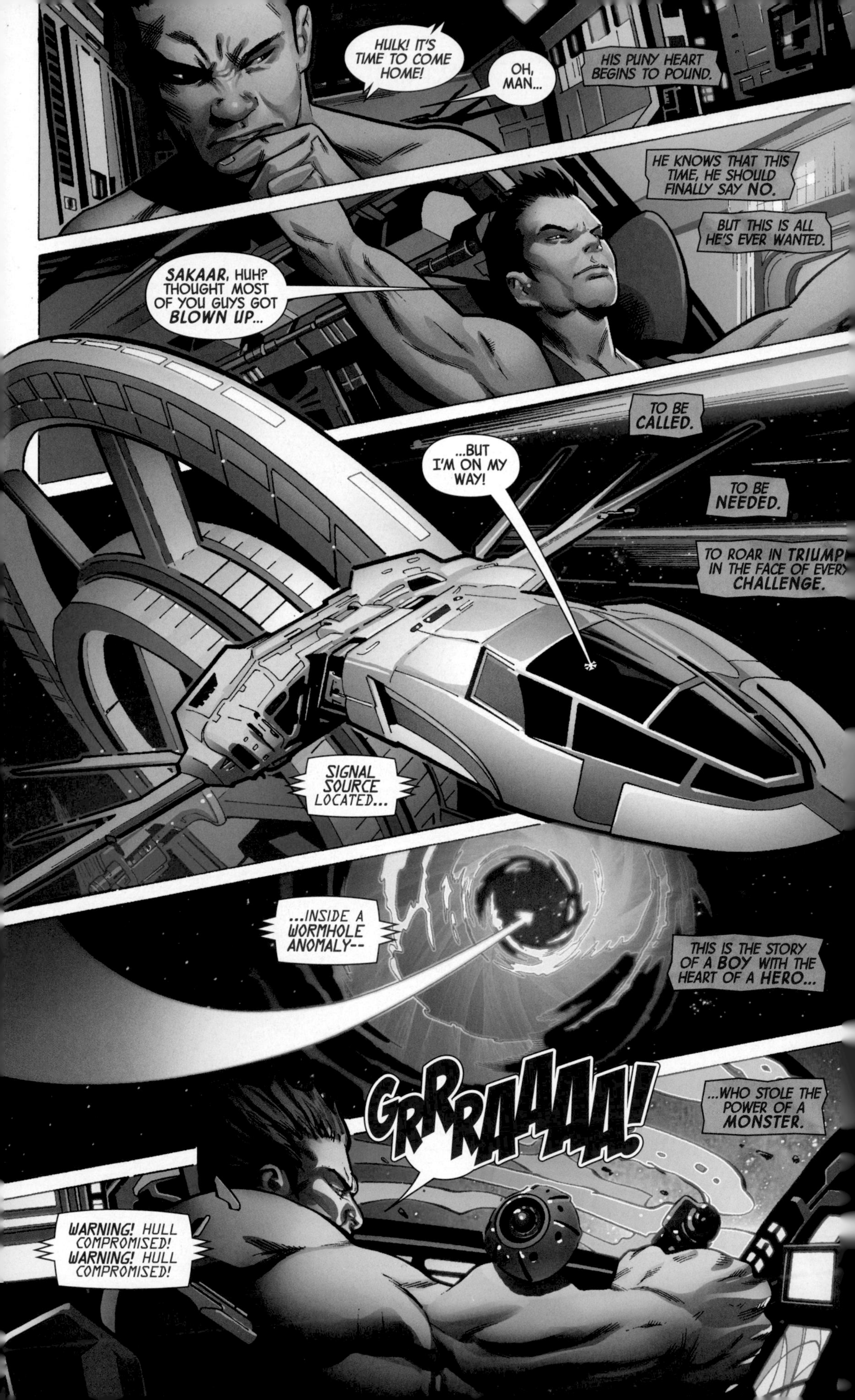
HULK! IT'S TIME TO COME HOME!
OH, MAN...
HIS PUNY HEART BEGINS TO POUND.
HE KNOWS THAT THIS TIME, HE SHOULD FINALLY SAY NO.
BUT THIS IS ALL HE'S EVER WANTED.
SAKAAR, HUH? THOUGHT MOST OF YOU GUYS GOT BLOWN UP...
TO BE CALLED.
...BUT I'M ON MY WAY!
TO BE NEEDED.
TO ROAR IN TRIUMP IN THE FACE OF EVERY CHALLENGE.
SIGNAL SOURCE LOCATED...
...INSIDE A WORMHOLE ANOMALY--
THIS IS THE STORY OF A BOY WITH THE HEART OF A HERO...
GRRRAAAAA!
...WHO STOLE THE POWER OF A MONSTER.
WARNING! HULL COMPROMISED! WARNING! HULL COMPROMISED!

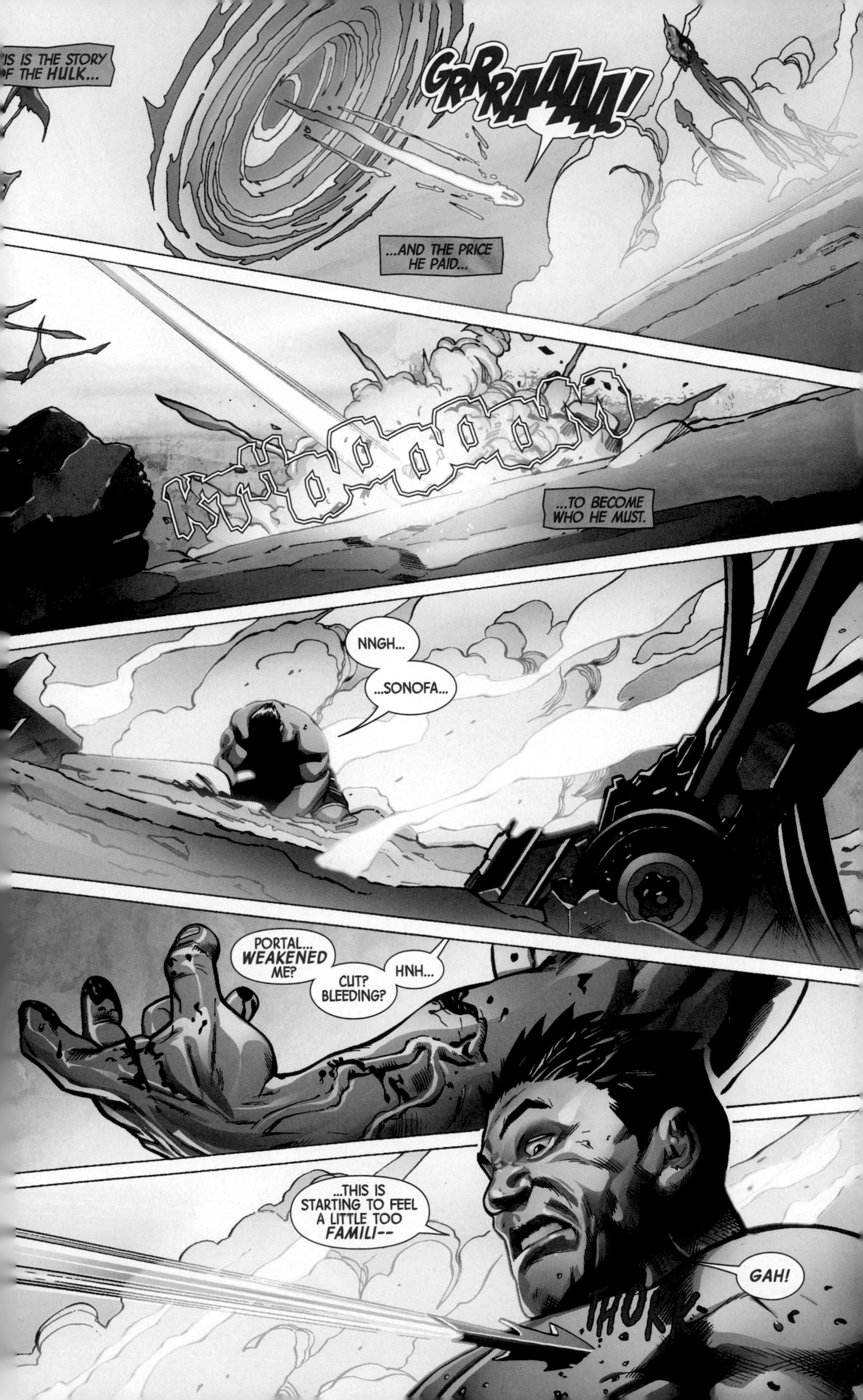

IS IS THE STORY OF THE HULK...
GRRRAAAAA!
...AND THE PRICE HE PAID...
KRUOOOOOOOOM
...TO BECOME WHO HE MUST.
NNGH...
...SONOFA...
PORTAL... WEAKENED ME?
CUT? BLEEDING?
HNH...
...THIS IS STARTING TO FEEL A LITTLE TOO FAMILI--
GAH!
THORK

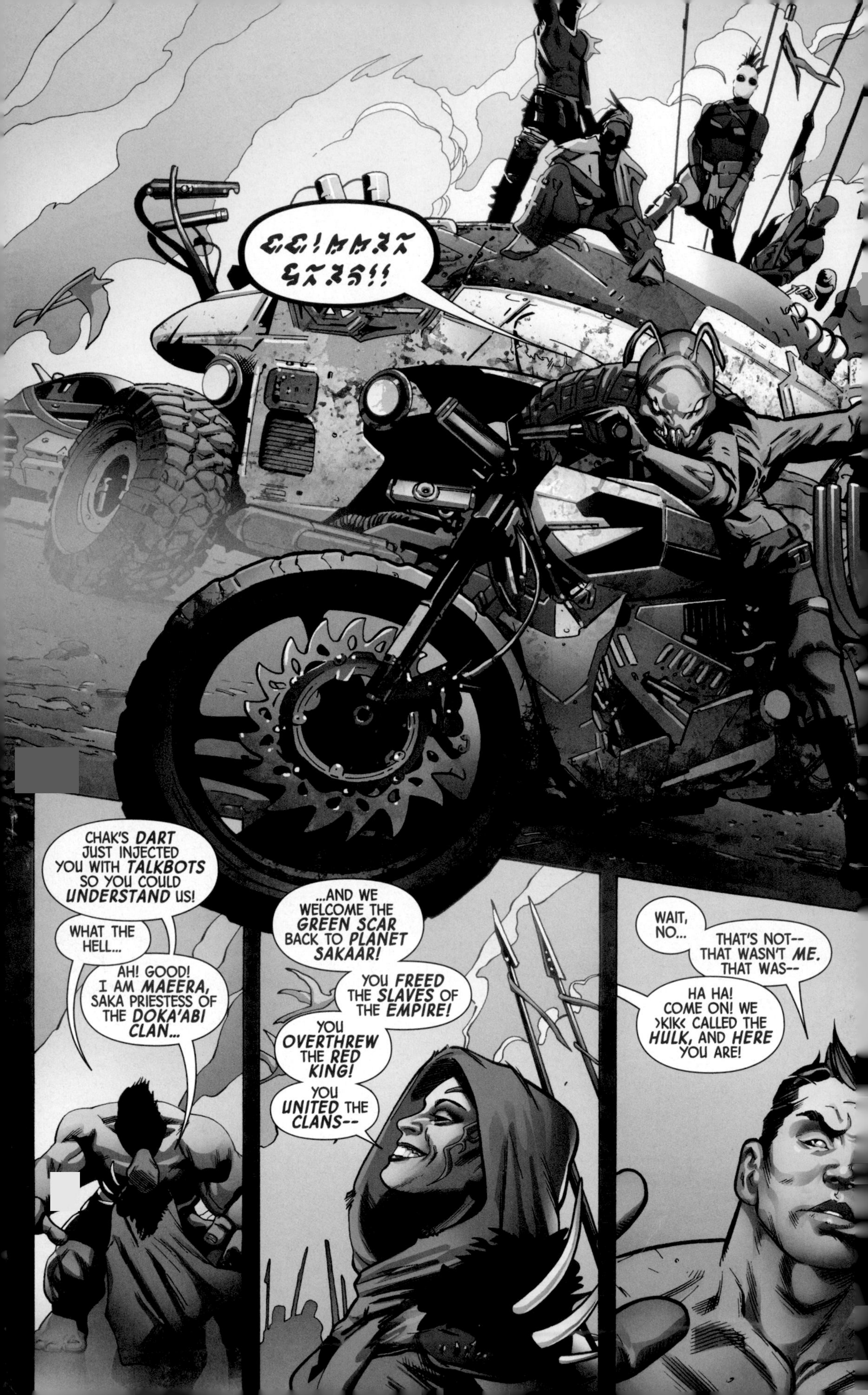
CHAK'S DART JUST INJECTED YOU WITH TALKBOTS SO YOU COULD UNDERSTAND US!
WHAT THE HELL...
AH! GOOD! I AM MAEERA, SAKA PRIESTESS OF THE DOKA'ABI CLAN...
...AND WE WELCOME THE GREEN SCAR BACK TO PLANET SAKAAR!
YOU FREED THE SLAVES OF THE EMPIRE!
YOU OVERTHREW THE RED KING!
YOU UNITED THE CLANS--
WAIT, NO...
THAT'S NOT-- THAT WASN'T ME. THAT WAS--
HA HA! COME ON! WE ›KIK‹ CALLED THE HULK, AND HERE YOU ARE!

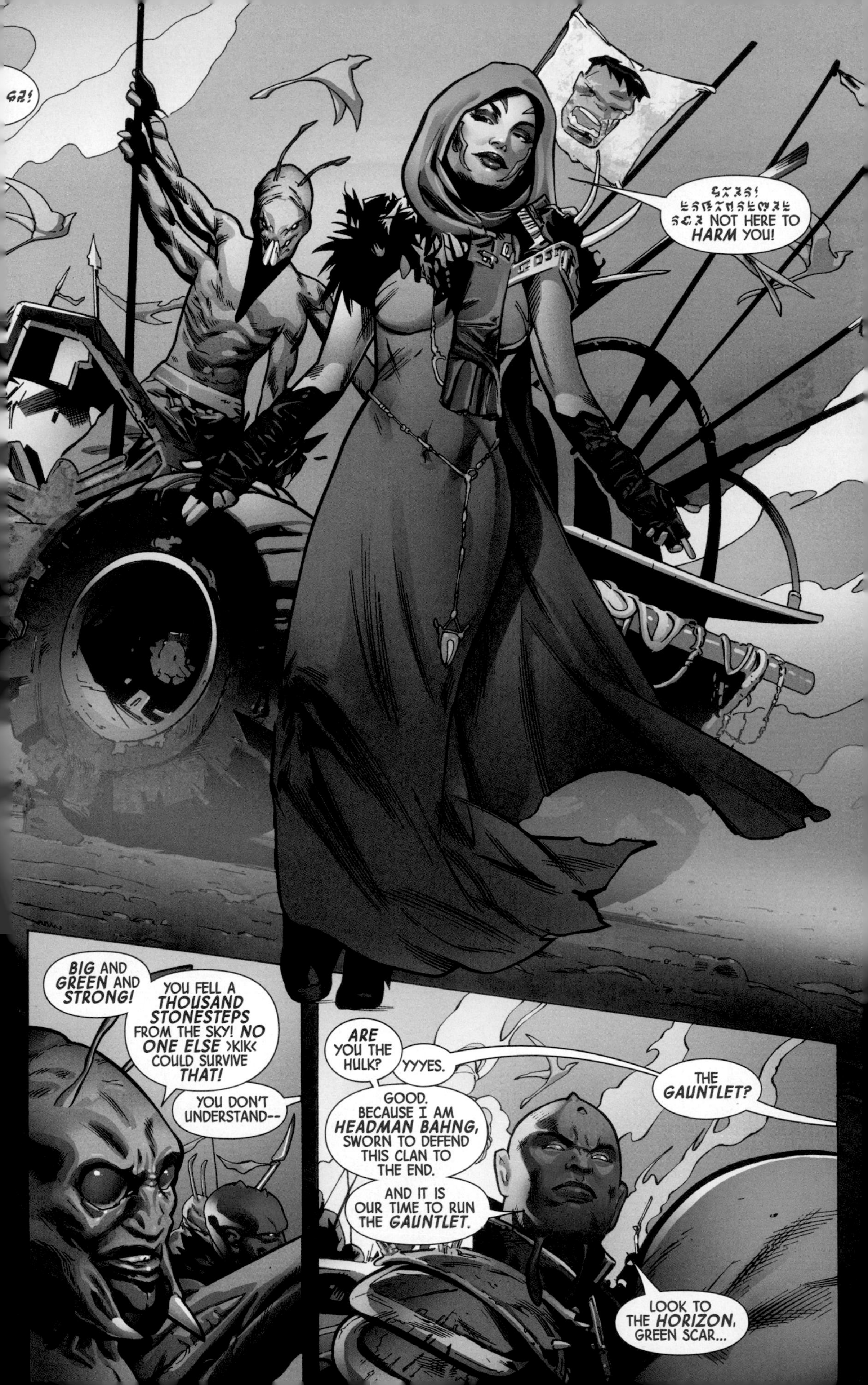
NOT HERE TO HARM YOU!
BIG AND GREEN AND STRONG!
YOU FELL A THOUSAND STONESTEPS FROM THE SKY! NO ONE ELSE >KIK< COULD SURVIVE THAT!
YOU DON'T UNDERSTAND--
ARE YOU THE HULK?
YYYES.
GOOD. BECAUSE I AM HEADMAN BAHNG, SWORN TO DEFEND THIS CLAN TO THE END.
AND IT IS OUR TIME TO RUN THE GAUNTLET.
THE GAUNTLET?
LOOK TO THE HORIZON, GREEN SCAR...

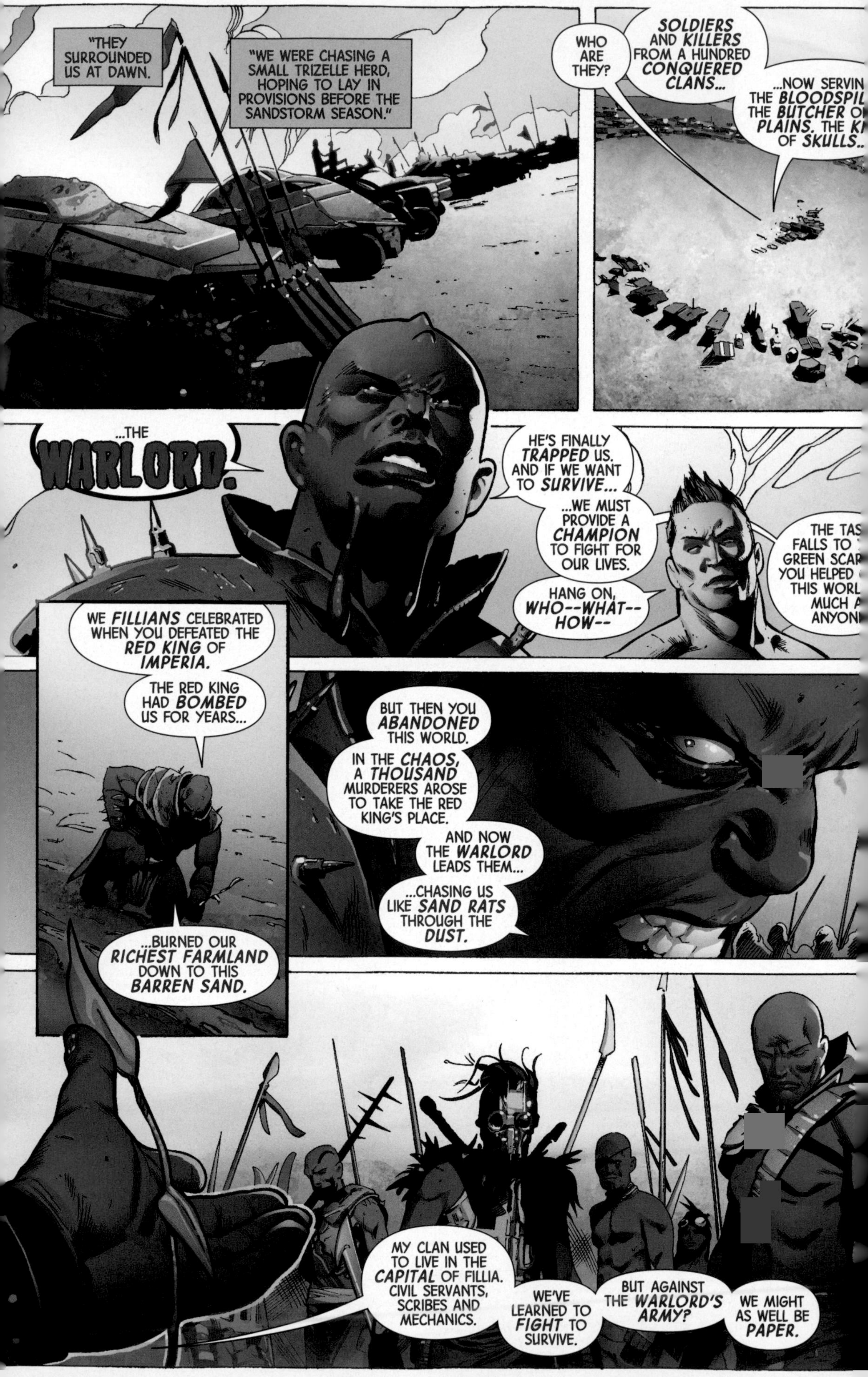
"THEY SURROUNDED US AT DAWN.
"WE WERE CHASING A SMALL TRIZELLE HERD, HOPING TO LAY IN PROVISIONS BEFORE THE SANDSTORM SEASON."
WHO ARE THEY?
SOLDIERS AND KILLERS FROM A HUNDRED CONQUERED CLANS...
...NOW SERVIN THE BLOODSPIL THE BUTCHER O PLAINS. THE KI OF SKULLS..
...THE WARLORD.
HE'S FINALLY TRAPPED US. AND IF WE WANT TO SURVIVE...
...WE MUST PROVIDE A CHAMPION TO FIGHT FOR OUR LIVES.
HANG ON, WHO--WHAT--HOW--
THE TAS FALLS TO GREEN SCAR YOU HELPED THIS WORL MUCH A ANYON
WE FILLIANS CELEBRATED WHEN YOU DEFEATED THE RED KING OF IMPERIA.
THE RED KING HAD BOMBED US FOR YEARS...
...BURNED OUR RICHEST FARMLAND DOWN TO THIS BARREN SAND.
BUT THEN YOU ABANDONED THIS WORLD.
IN THE CHAOS, A THOUSAND MURDERERS AROSE TO TAKE THE RED KING'S PLACE.
AND NOW THE WARLORD LEADS THEM...
...CHASING US LIKE SAND RATS THROUGH THE DUST.
MY CLAN USED TO LIVE IN THE CAPITAL OF FILLIA. CIVIL SERVANTS, SCRIBES AND MECHANICS.
WE'VE LEARNED TO FIGHT TO SURVIVE.
BUT AGAINST THE WARLORD'S ARMY?
WE MIGHT AS WELL BE PAPER.

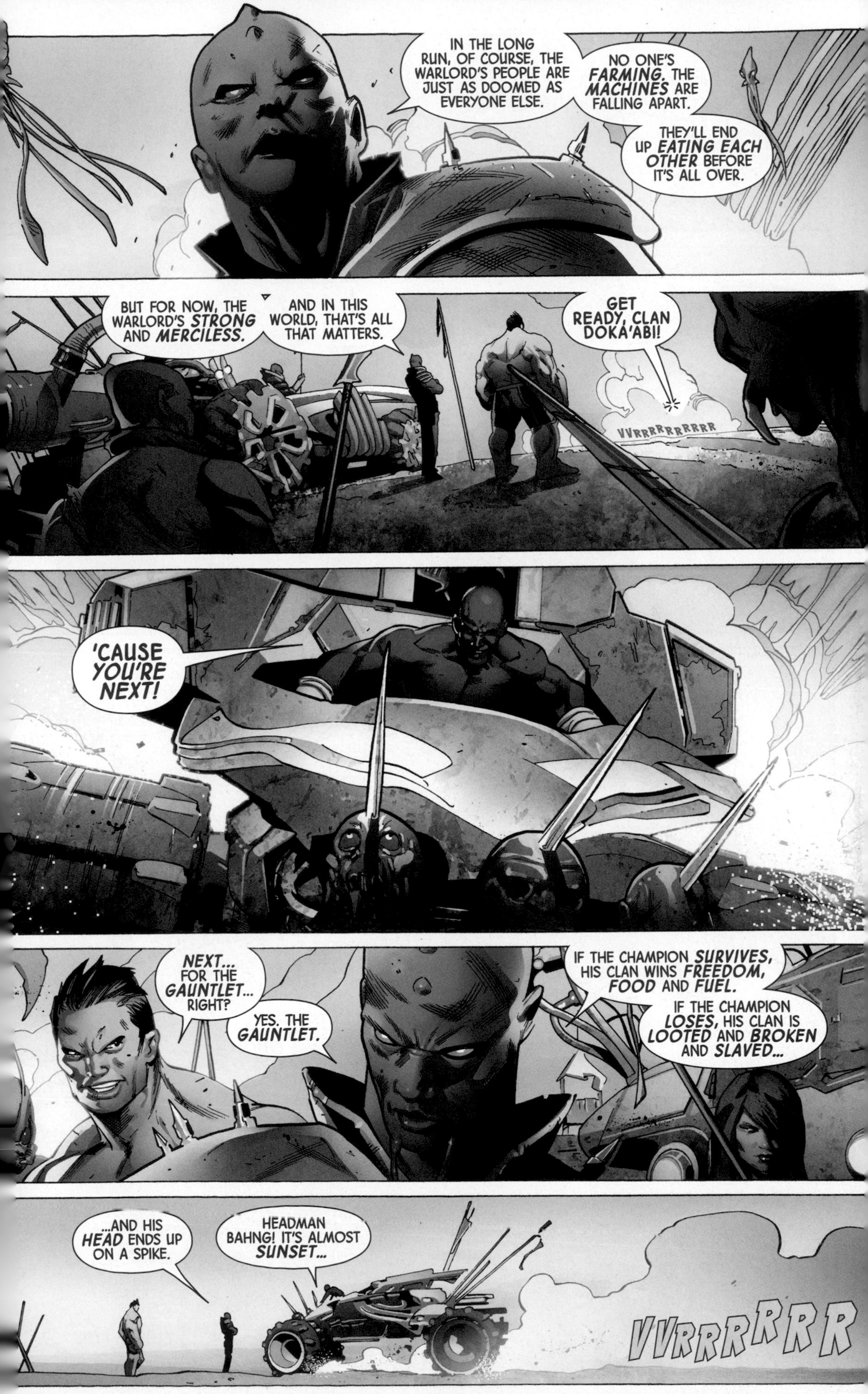
IN THE LONG RUN, OF COURSE, THE WARLORD'S PEOPLE ARE JUST AS DOOMED AS EVERYONE ELSE.
NO ONE'S FARMING. THE MACHINES ARE FALLING APART.
THEY'LL END UP EATING EACH OTHER BEFORE IT'S ALL OVER.
BUT FOR NOW, THE WARLORD'S STRONG AND MERCILESS.
AND IN THIS WORLD, THAT'S ALL THAT MATTERS.
GET READY, CLAN DOKA'ABI!
VVRRRRRRRRRR
'CAUSE YOU'RE NEXT!
NEXT... FOR THE GAUNTLET... RIGHT?
YES. THE GAUNTLET.
IF THE CHAMPION SURVIVES, HIS CLAN WINS FREEDOM, FOOD AND FUEL.
IF THE CHAMPION LOSES, HIS CLAN IS LOOTED AND BROKEN AND SLAVED...
...AND HIS HEAD ENDS UP ON A SPIKE.
HEADMAN BAHNG! IT'S ALMOST SUNSET...
VVRRRRRRR

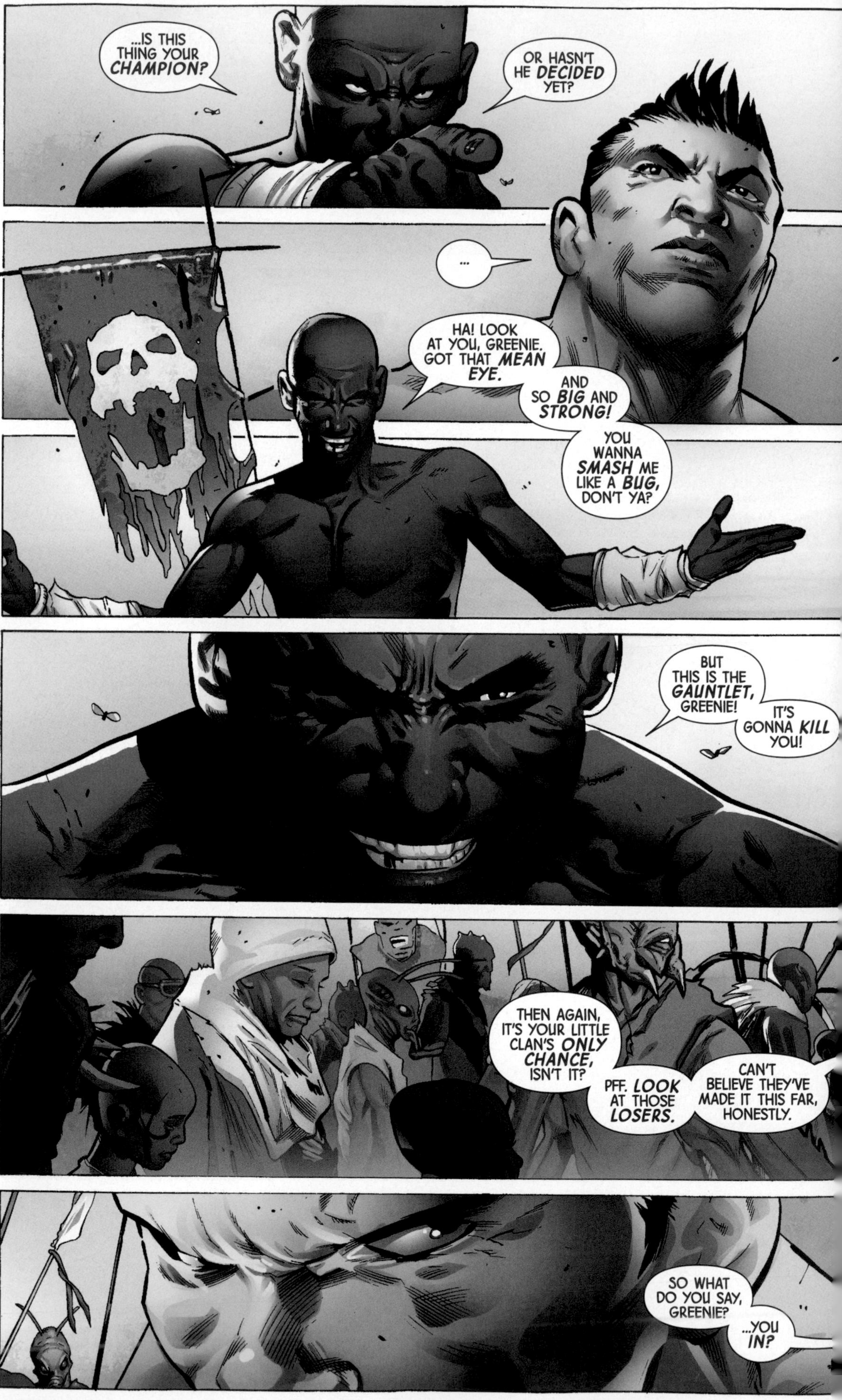
...IS THIS THING YOUR CHAMPION?
OR HASN'T HE DECIDED YET?
...
HA! LOOK AT YOU, GREENIE. GOT THAT MEAN EYE.
AND SO BIG AND STRONG!
YOU WANNA SMASH ME LIKE A BUG, DON'T YA?
BUT THIS IS THE GAUNTLET, GREENIE!
IT'S GONNA KILL YOU!
THEN AGAIN, IT'S YOUR LITTLE CLAN'S ONLY CHANCE, ISN'T IT?
PFF. LOOK AT THOSE LOSERS.
CAN'T BELIEVE THEY'VE MADE IT THIS FAR, HONESTLY.
SO WHAT DO YOU SAY, GREENIE?
...YOU IN?

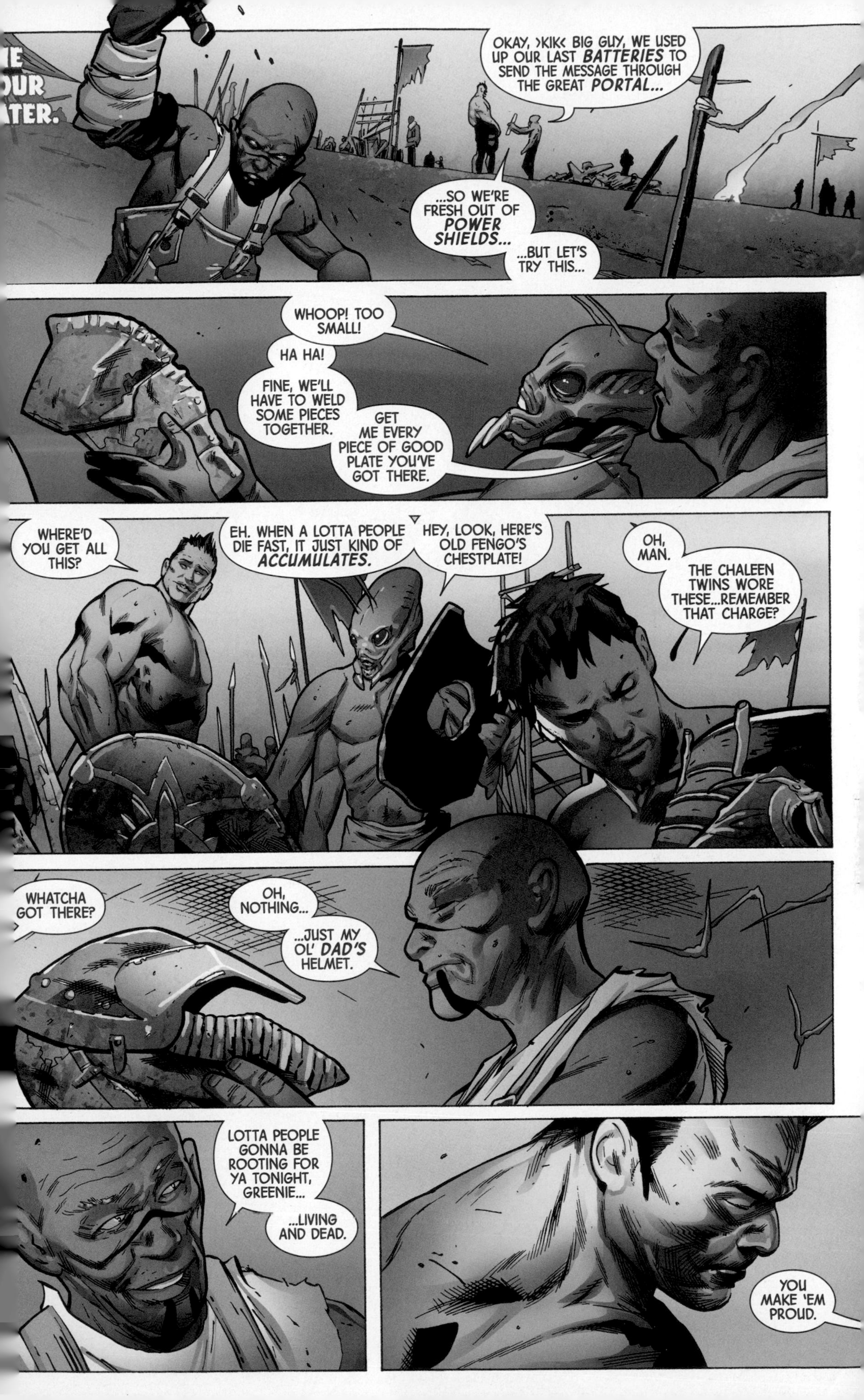
OKAY, >KIK< BIG GUY, WE USED UP OUR LAST BATTERIES TO SEND THE MESSAGE THROUGH THE GREAT PORTAL...
...SO WE'RE FRESH OUT OF POWER SHIELDS...
...BUT LET'S TRY THIS...
WHOOP! TOO SMALL!
HA HA!
FINE, WE'LL HAVE TO WELD SOME PIECES TOGETHER.
GET ME EVERY PIECE OF GOOD PLATE YOU'VE GOT THERE.
WHERE'D YOU GET ALL THIS?
EH. WHEN A LOTTA PEOPLE DIE FAST, IT JUST KIND OF ACCUMULATES.
HEY, LOOK, HERE'S OLD FENGO'S CHESTPLATE!
OH, MAN.
THE CHALEEN TWINS WORE THESE...REMEMBER THAT CHARGE?
WHATCHA GOT THERE?
OH, NOTHING...
...JUST MY OL' DAD'S HELMET.
LOTTA PEOPLE GONNA BE ROOTING FOR YA TONIGHT, GREENIE...
...LIVING AND DEAD.
YOU MAKE 'EM PROUD.

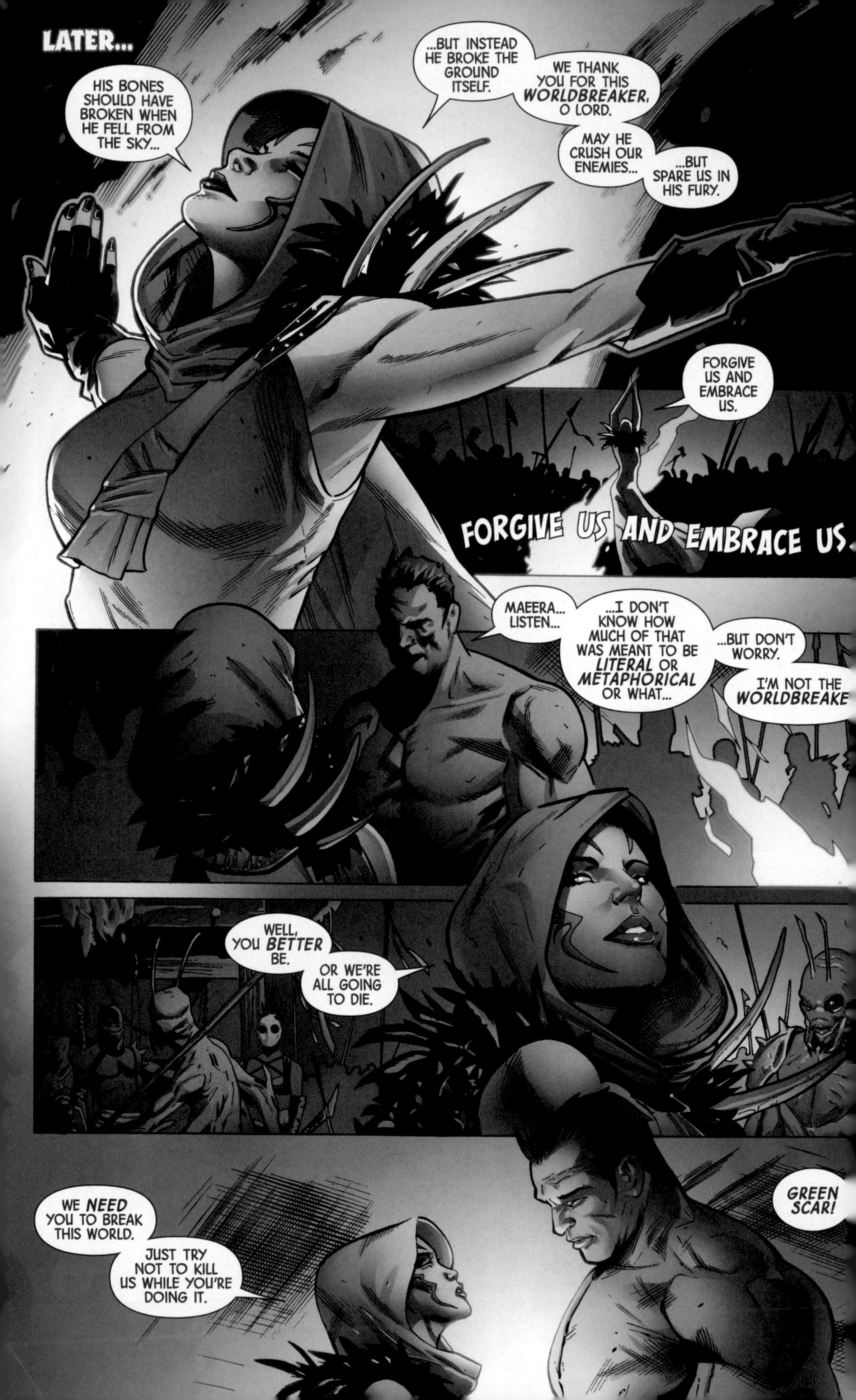
LATER...
HIS BONES SHOULD HAVE BROKEN WHEN HE FELL FROM THE SKY...
...BUT INSTEAD HE BROKE THE GROUND ITSELF.
WE THANK YOU FOR THIS WORLDBREAKER, O LORD.
MAY HE CRUSH OUR ENEMIES...
...BUT SPARE US IN HIS FURY.
FORGIVE US AND EMBRACE US.
FORGIVE US AND EMBRACE US.
MAEERA... LISTEN...
...I DON'T KNOW HOW MUCH OF THAT WAS MEANT TO BE LITERAL OR METAPHORICAL OR WHAT...
...BUT DON'T WORRY.
I'M NOT THE WORLDBREAKE
WELL, YOU BETTER BE.
OR WE'RE ALL GOING TO DIE.
WE NEED YOU TO BREAK THIS WORLD.
JUST TRY NOT TO KILL US WHILE YOU'RE DOING IT.
GREEN SCAR!

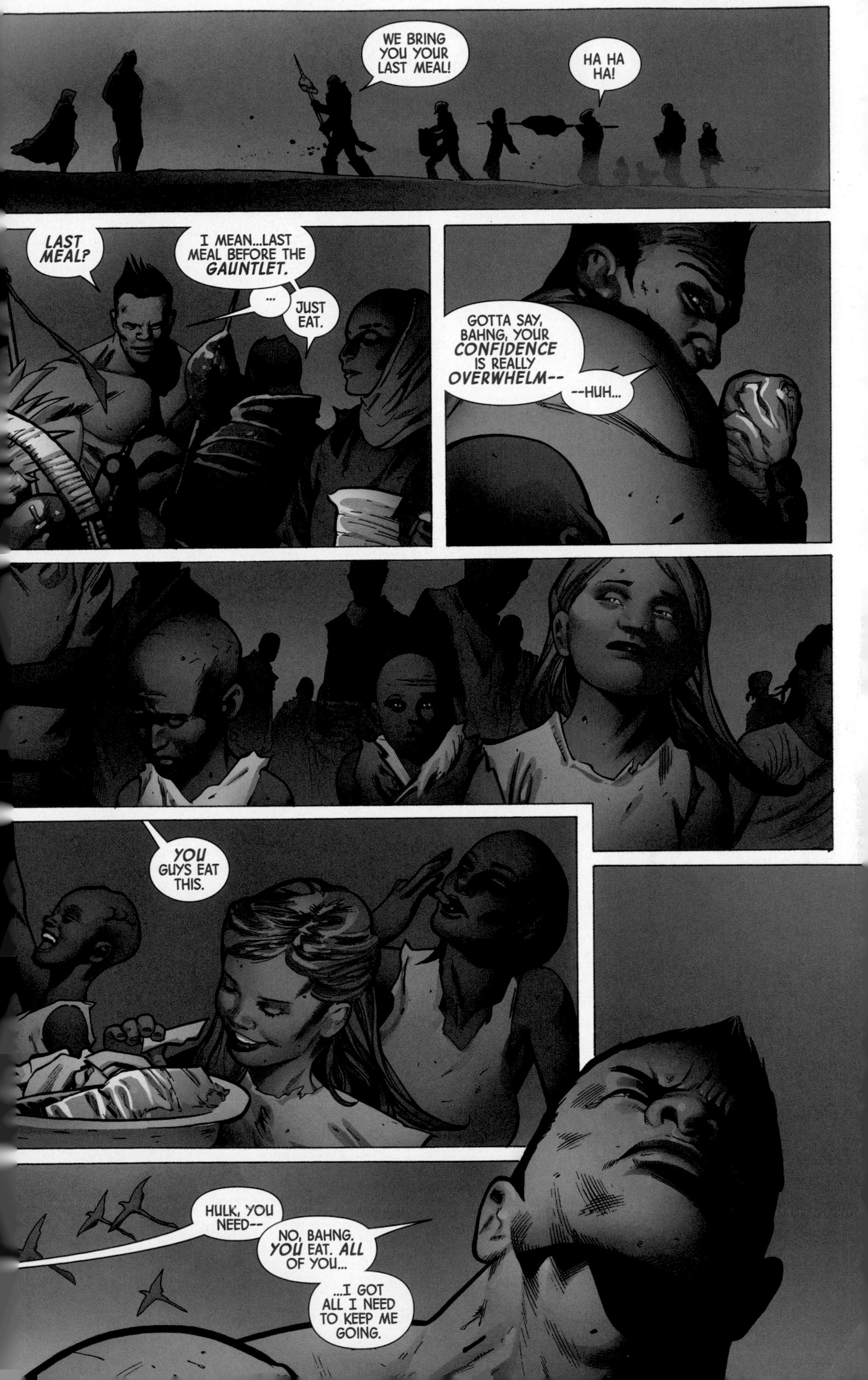
WE BRING YOU YOUR LAST MEAL!
HA HA HA!
LAST MEAL?
I MEAN...LAST MEAL BEFORE THE GAUNTLET.
...
JUST EAT.
GOTTA SAY, BAHNG, YOUR CONFIDENCE IS REALLY OVERWHELM--
--HUH...
YOU GUYS EAT THIS.
HULK, YOU NEED--
NO, BAHNG. YOU EAT. ALL OF YOU...
...I GOT ALL I NEED TO KEEP ME GOING.

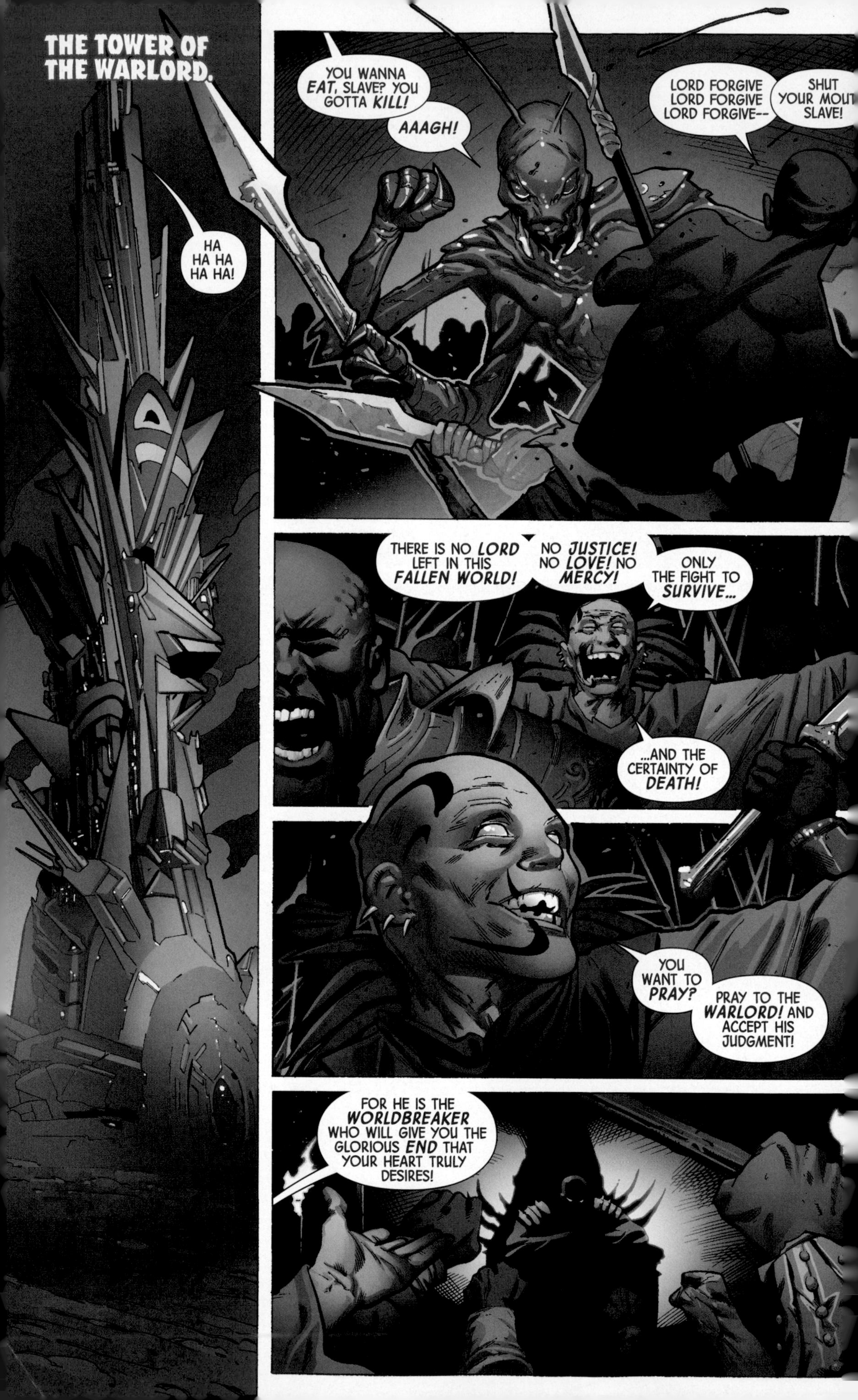
THE TOWER OF THE WARLORD.
HA HA HA HA HA!
YOU WANNA EAT, SLAVE? YOU GOTTA KILL!
AAAGH!
LORD FORGIVE LORD FORGIVE LORD FORGIVE--
SHUT YOUR MOUT SLAVE!
THERE IS NO LORD LEFT IN THIS FALLEN WORLD!
NO JUSTICE! NO LOVE! NO MERCY!
ONLY THE FIGHT TO SURVIVE...
...AND THE CERTAINTY OF DEATH!
YOU WANT TO PRAY?
PRAY TO THE WARLORD! AND ACCEPT HIS JUDGMENT!
FOR HE IS THE WORLDBREAKER WHO WILL GIVE YOU THE GLORIOUS END THAT YOUR HEART TRULY DESIRES!

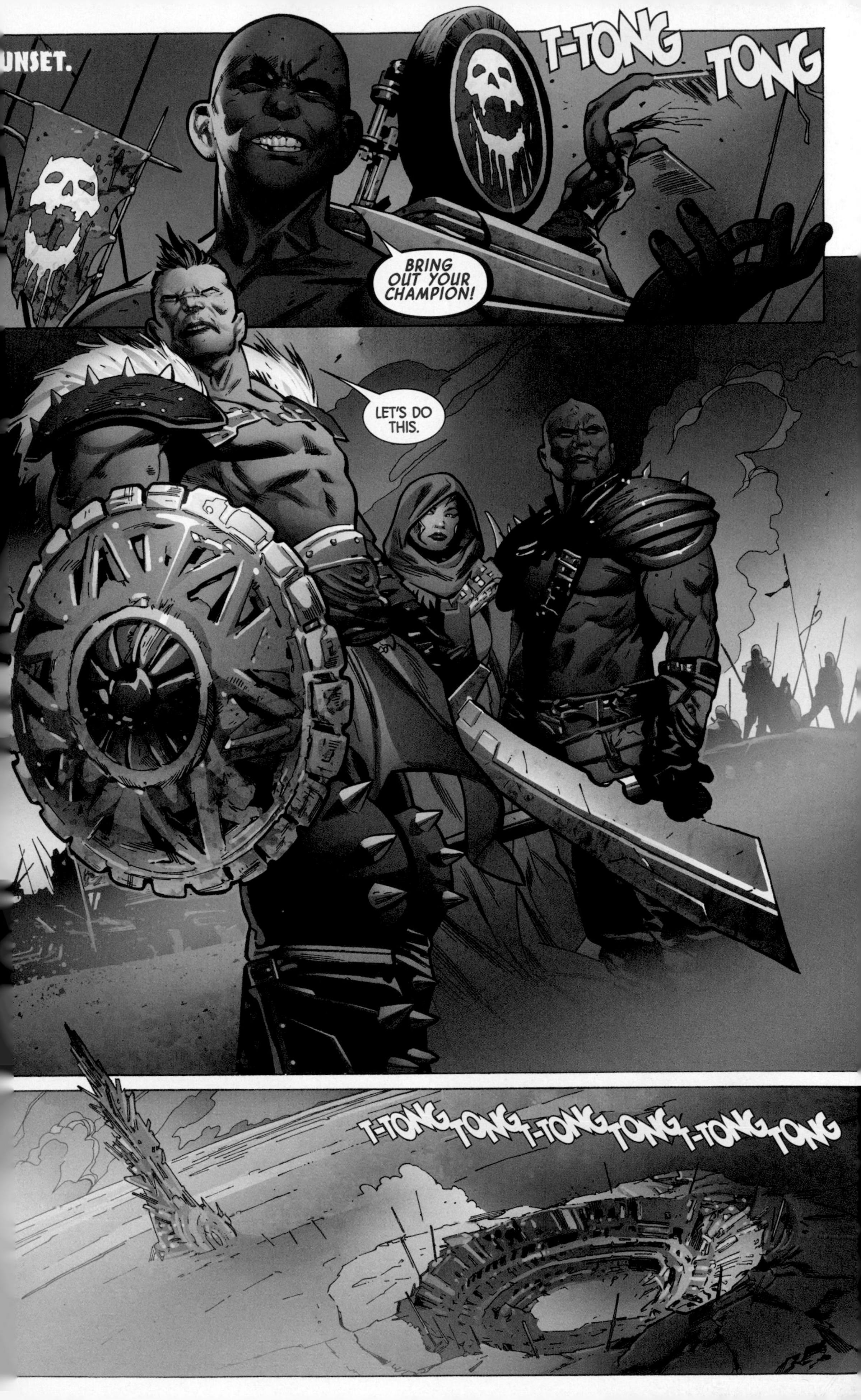
UNSET.
T-TONG
TONG
BRING OUT YOUR CHAMPION!
LET'S DO THIS.
T-TONG TONG T-TONG TONG T-TONG TONG

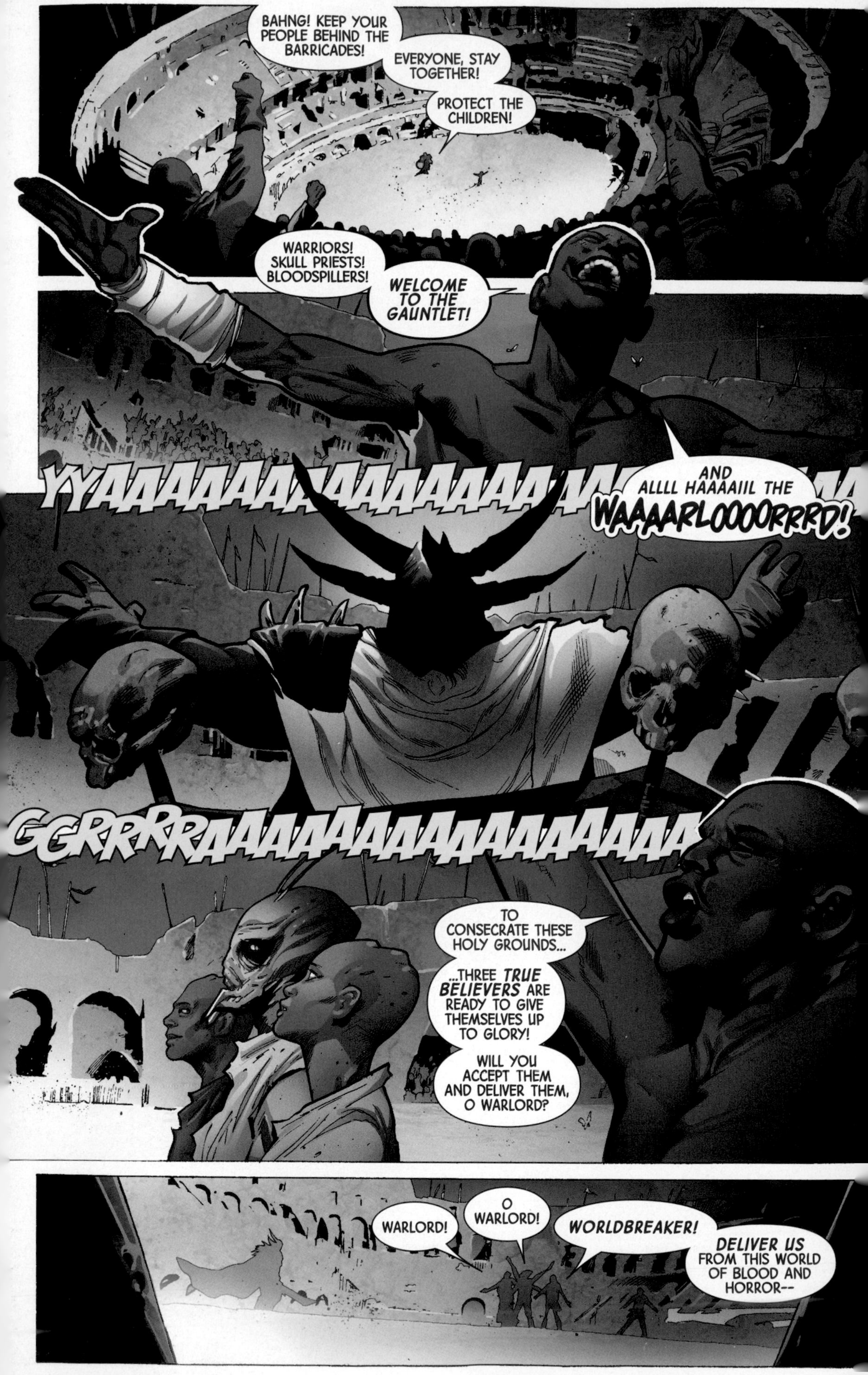
BAHNG! KEEP YOUR PEOPLE BEHIND THE BARRICADES!
EVERYONE, STAY TOGETHER!
PROTECT THE CHILDREN!
WARRIORS! SKULL PRIESTS! BLOODSPILLERS!
WELCOME TO THE GAUNTLET!
YYAAAAAAAAAAAAAAAAA
AND ALLLL HAAAAIIL THE WAAAARLOOOORRRD!
GGRRRRAAAAAAAAAAAAAAAAA
TO CONSECRATE THESE HOLY GROUNDS...
...THREE TRUE BELIEVERS ARE READY TO GIVE THEMSELVES UP TO GLORY!
WILL YOU ACCEPT THEM AND DELIVER THEM, O WARLORD?
WARLORD!
O WARLORD!
WORLDBREAKER!
DELIVER US FROM THIS WORLD OF BLOOD AND HORROR--

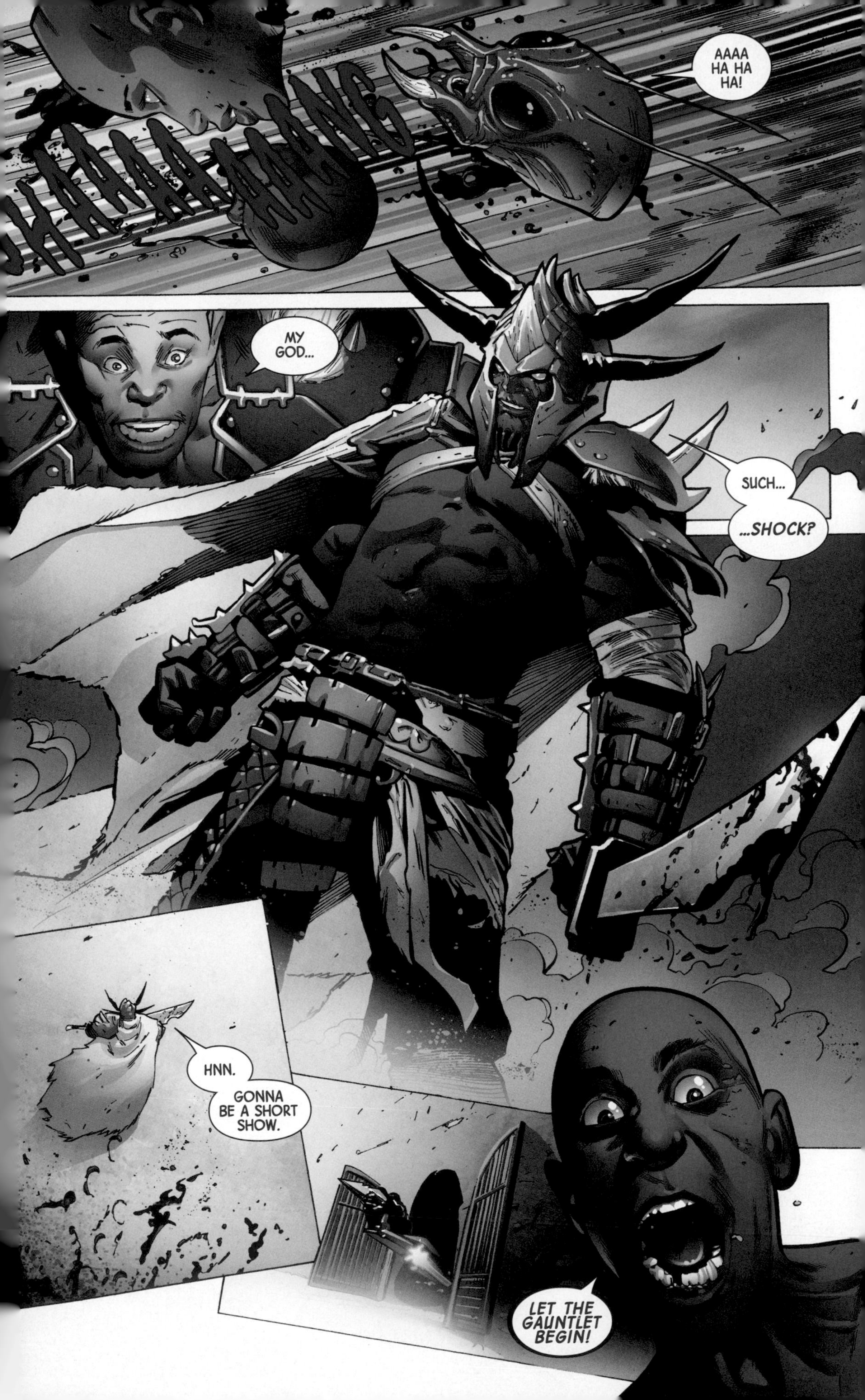
SHHAAAAAANG
AAAA HA HA HA!
MY GOD...
SUCH...
...SHOCK?
HNN. GONNA BE A SHORT SHOW.
LET THE GAUNTLET BEGIN!

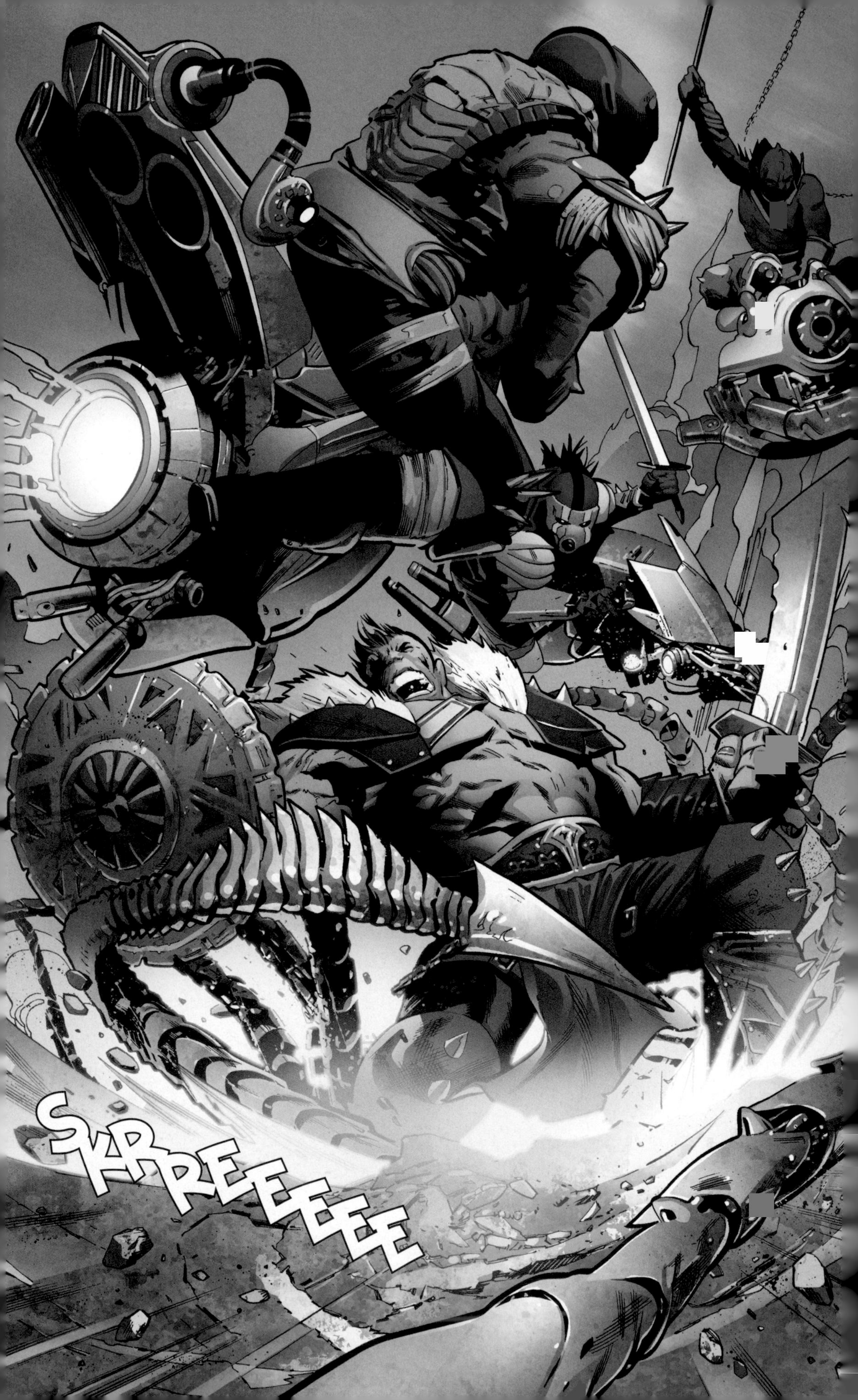
SKREEEEEEE

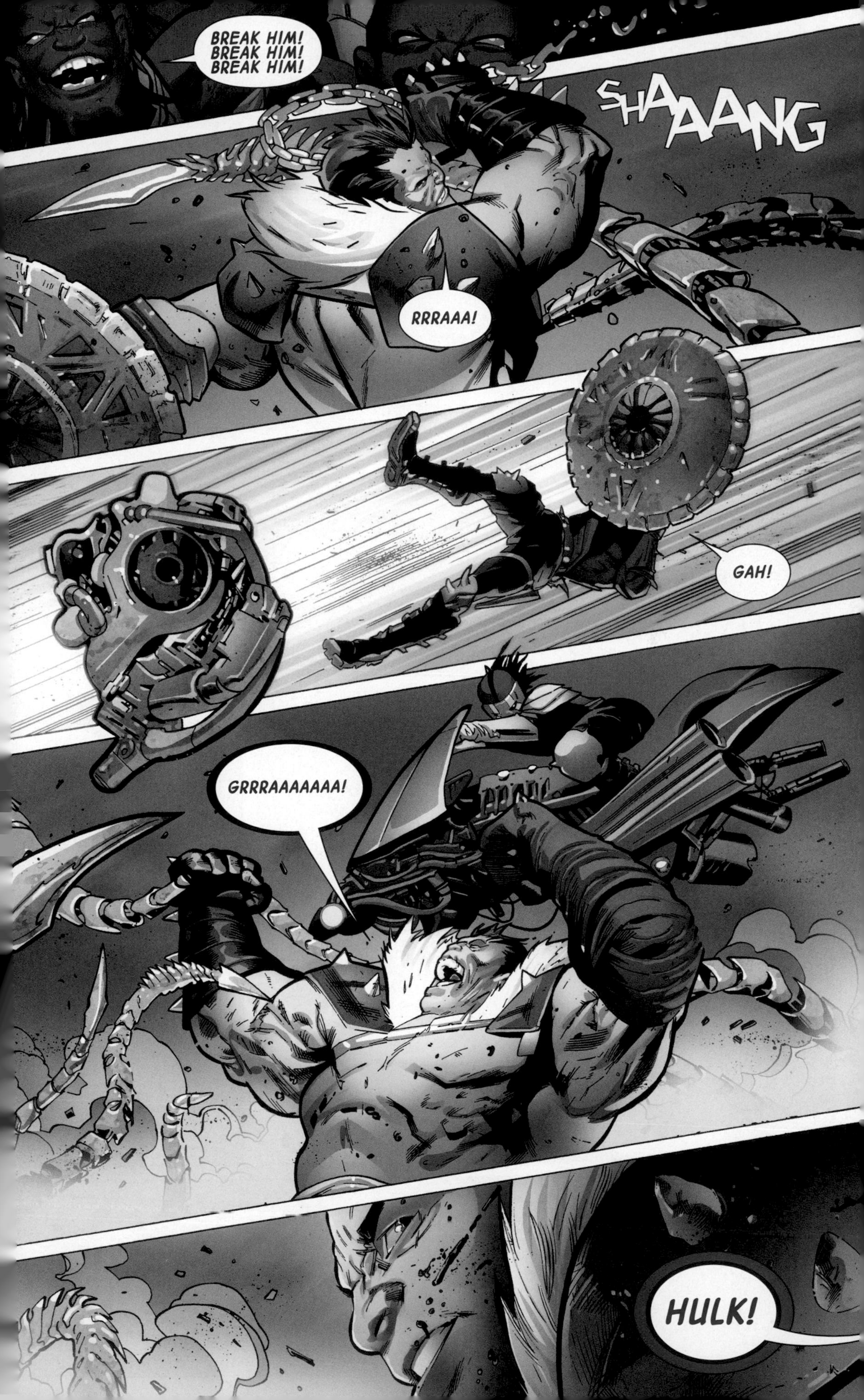
BREAK HIM! BREAK HIM! BREAK HIM!
SHAAANG
RRRAAA!
GAH!
GRRRAAAAAAA!
HULK!

HEEEELP!

HUUULK!

AAAAAAAH!

KREEEEEE!

SHAAAANG

NO! THEY'RE JUST SPECTATORS!

I'M THE ONE YOU'RE SUPPOSED TO BE FIGHTING!

EVERYONE, GET BACK! I'LL HOLD THEM OFF AS LONG AS I--

HA HA HA HA!

KILL THEM! KILL THEM ALL!

GAH!

SHUNK

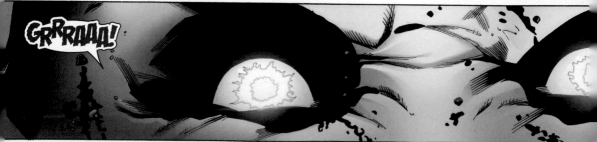

GRRRAAA!

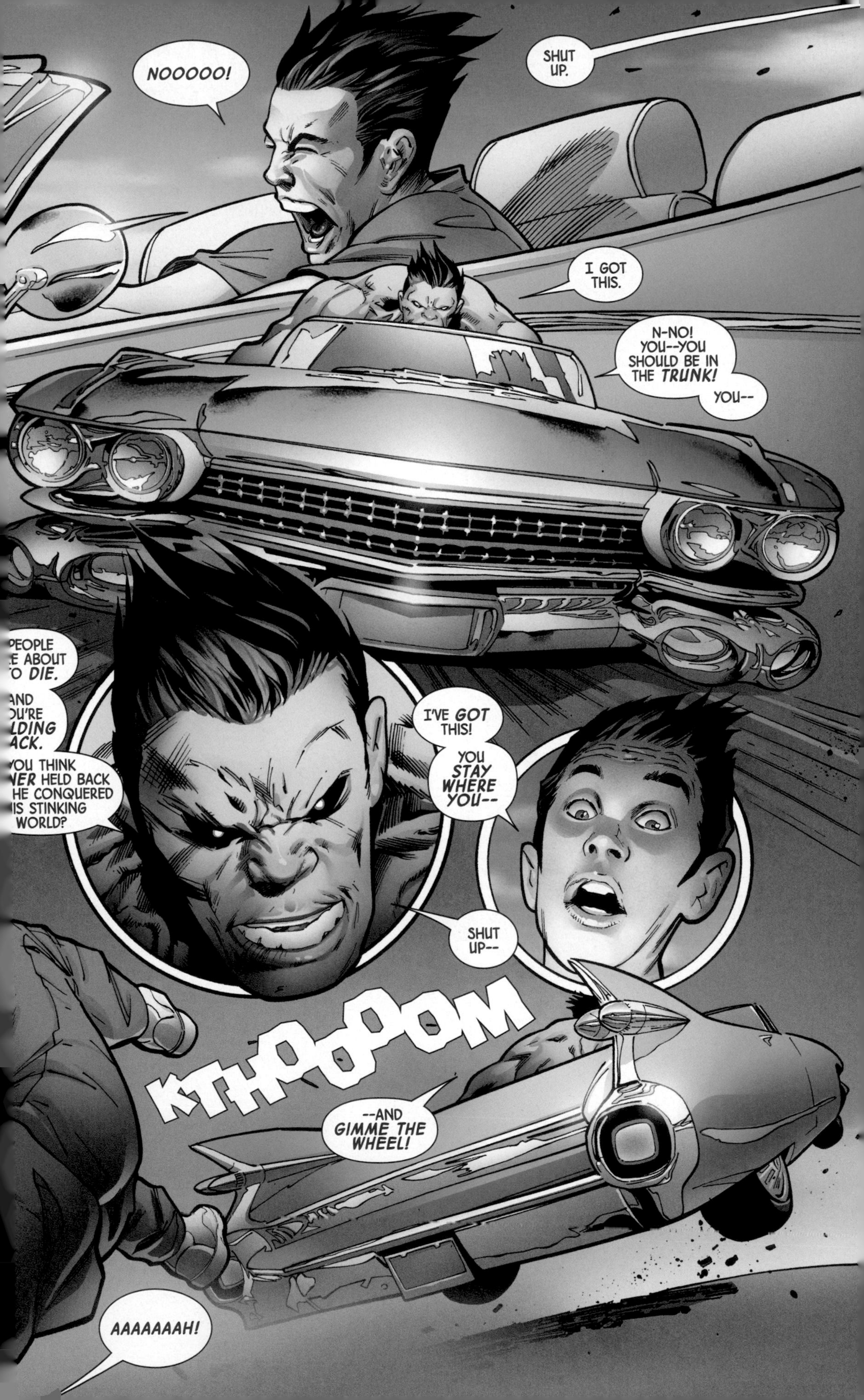

NOOOOO!
SHUT UP.
I GOT THIS.
N-NO! YOU--YOU SHOULD BE IN THE TRUNK!
YOU--
PEOPLE E ABOUT O DIE.
AND OU'RE LDING ACK.
YOU THINK NER HELD BACK HE CONQUERED IS STINKING WORLD?
I'VE GOT THIS!
YOU STAY WHERE YOU--
SHUT UP--
KTHOOOOM
--AND GIMME THE WHEEL!
AAAAAAAH!

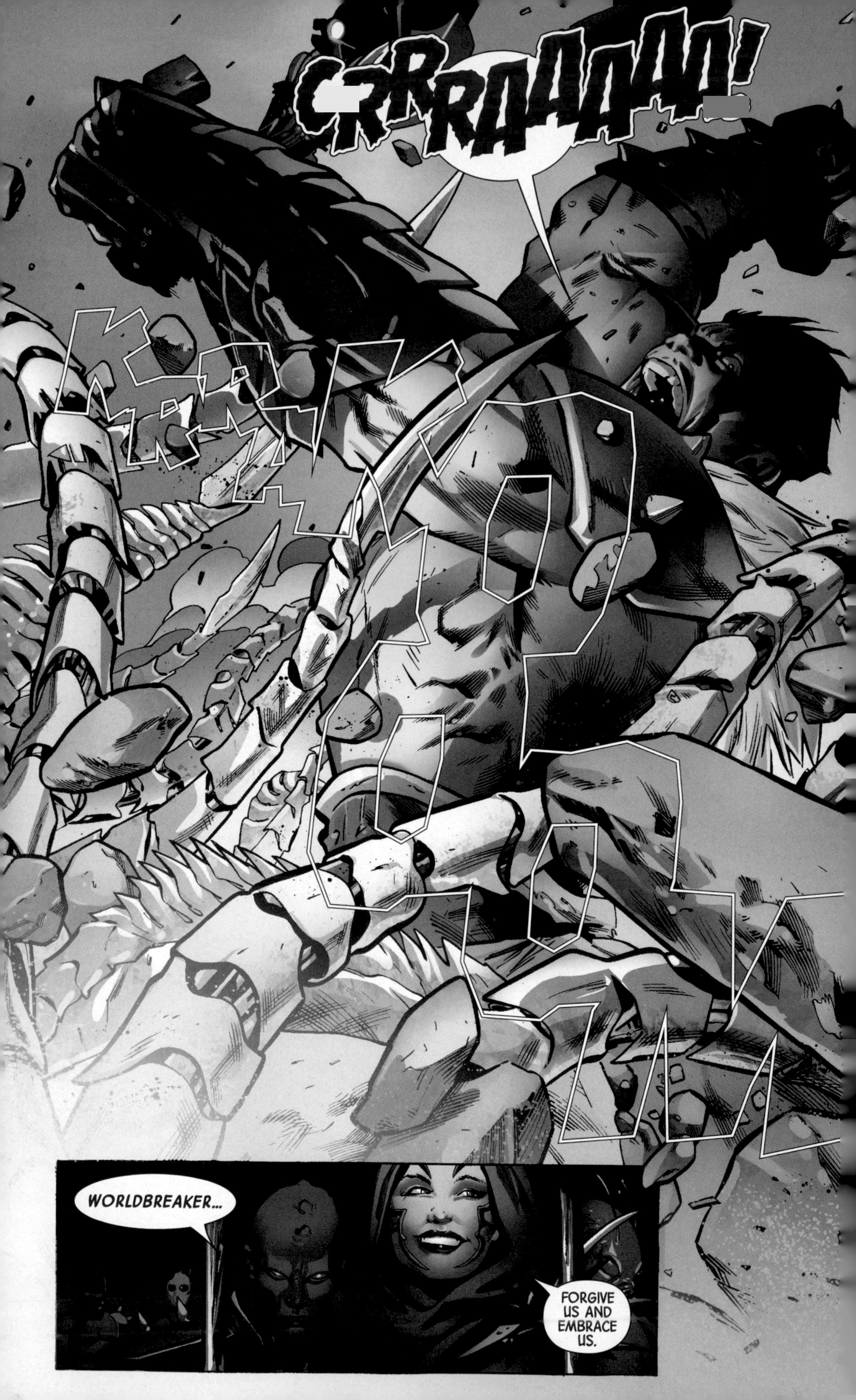
CRRAAAAAA!
WORLDBREAKER...
FORGIVE US AND EMBRACE US.

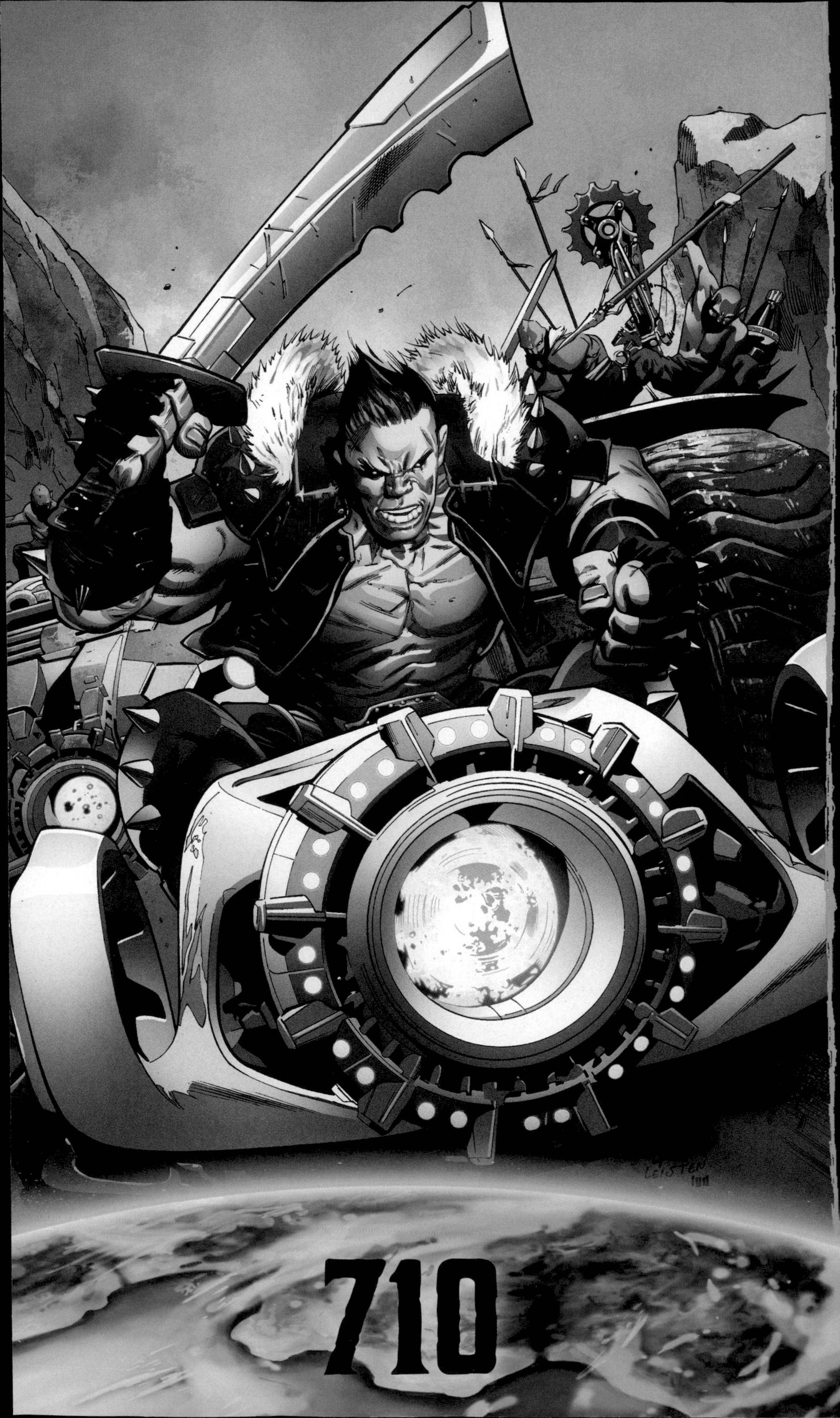
LEISTEN
710

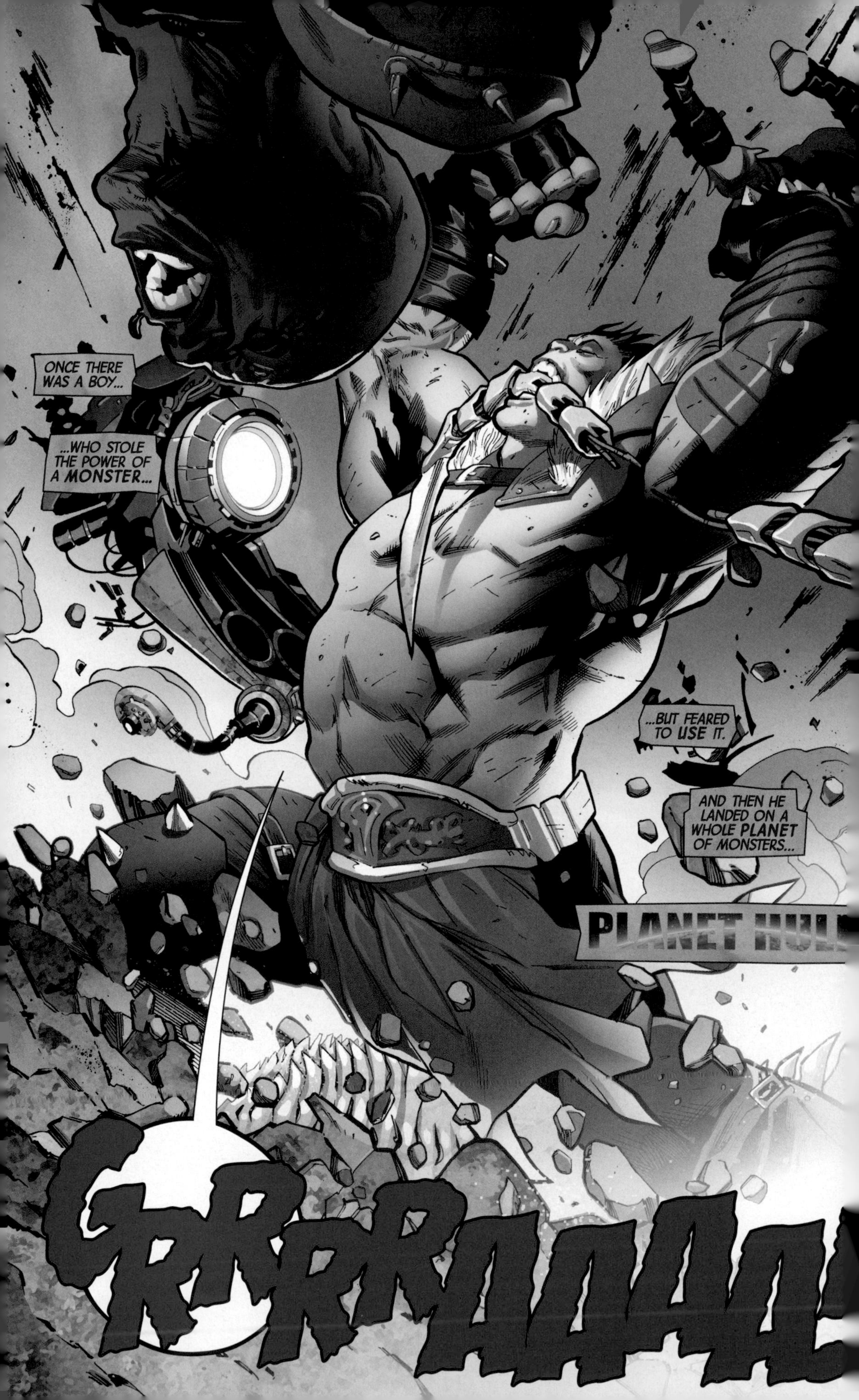
ONCE THERE WAS A BOY...
...WHO STOLE THE POWER OF A MONSTER...
...BUT FEARED TO USE IT.
AND THEN HE LANDED ON A WHOLE PLANET OF MONSTERS...
PLANET HULK
GRRRAAAAAL

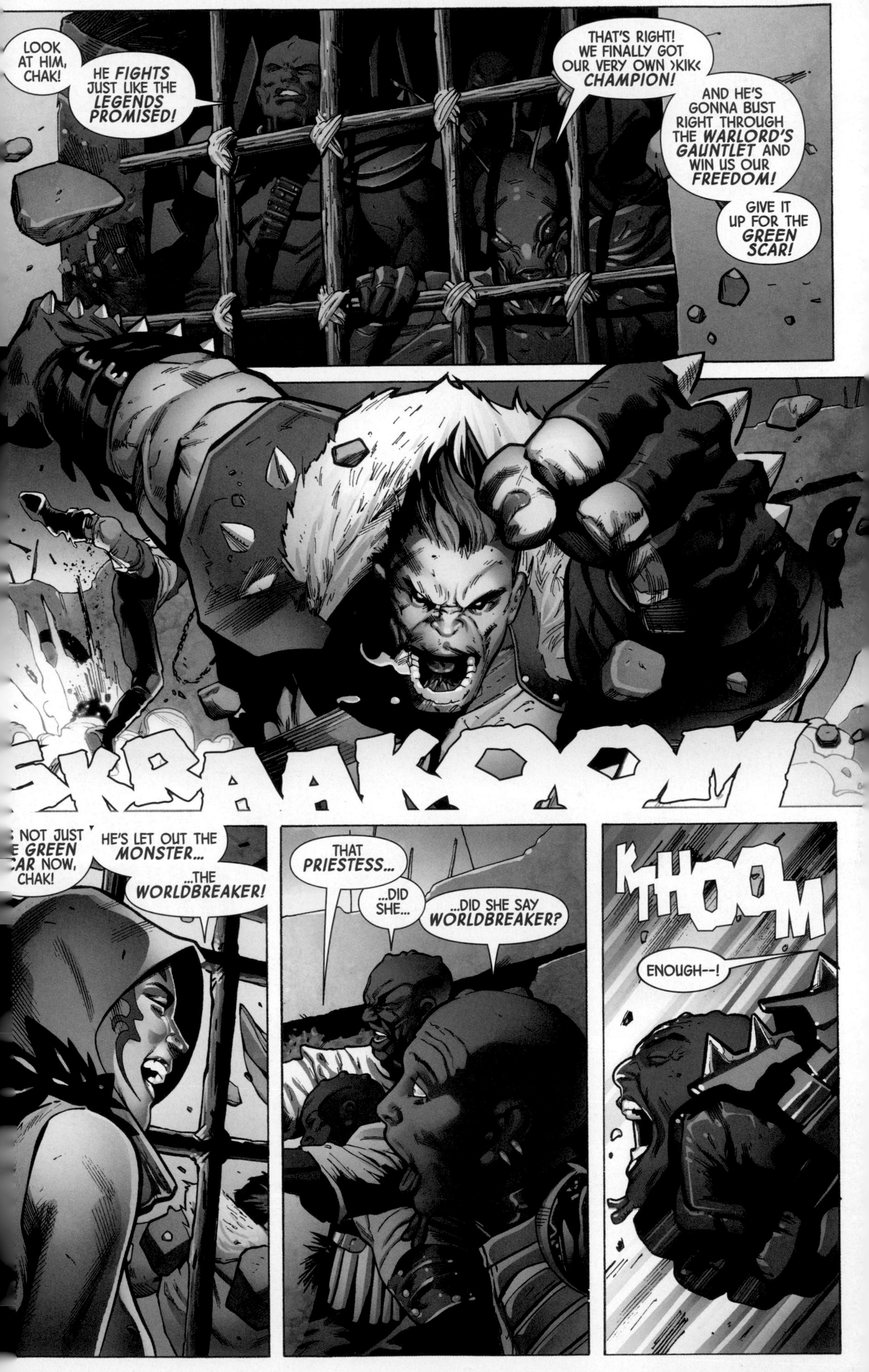
LOOK AT HIM, CHAK!
HE FIGHTS JUST LIKE THE LEGENDS PROMISED!
THAT'S RIGHT! WE FINALLY GOT OUR VERY OWN ›KIK‹ CHAMPION!
AND HE'S GONNA BUST RIGHT THROUGH THE WARLORD'S GAUNTLET AND WIN US OUR FREEDOM!
GIVE IT UP FOR THE GREEN SCAR!
KRAAKOOM
S NOT JUST E GREEN CAR NOW, CHAK!
HE'S LET OUT THE MONSTER...
...THE WORLDBREAKER!
THAT PRIESTESS...
...DID SHE...
...DID SHE SAY WORLDBREAKER?
KTHOOOM
ENOUGH--!

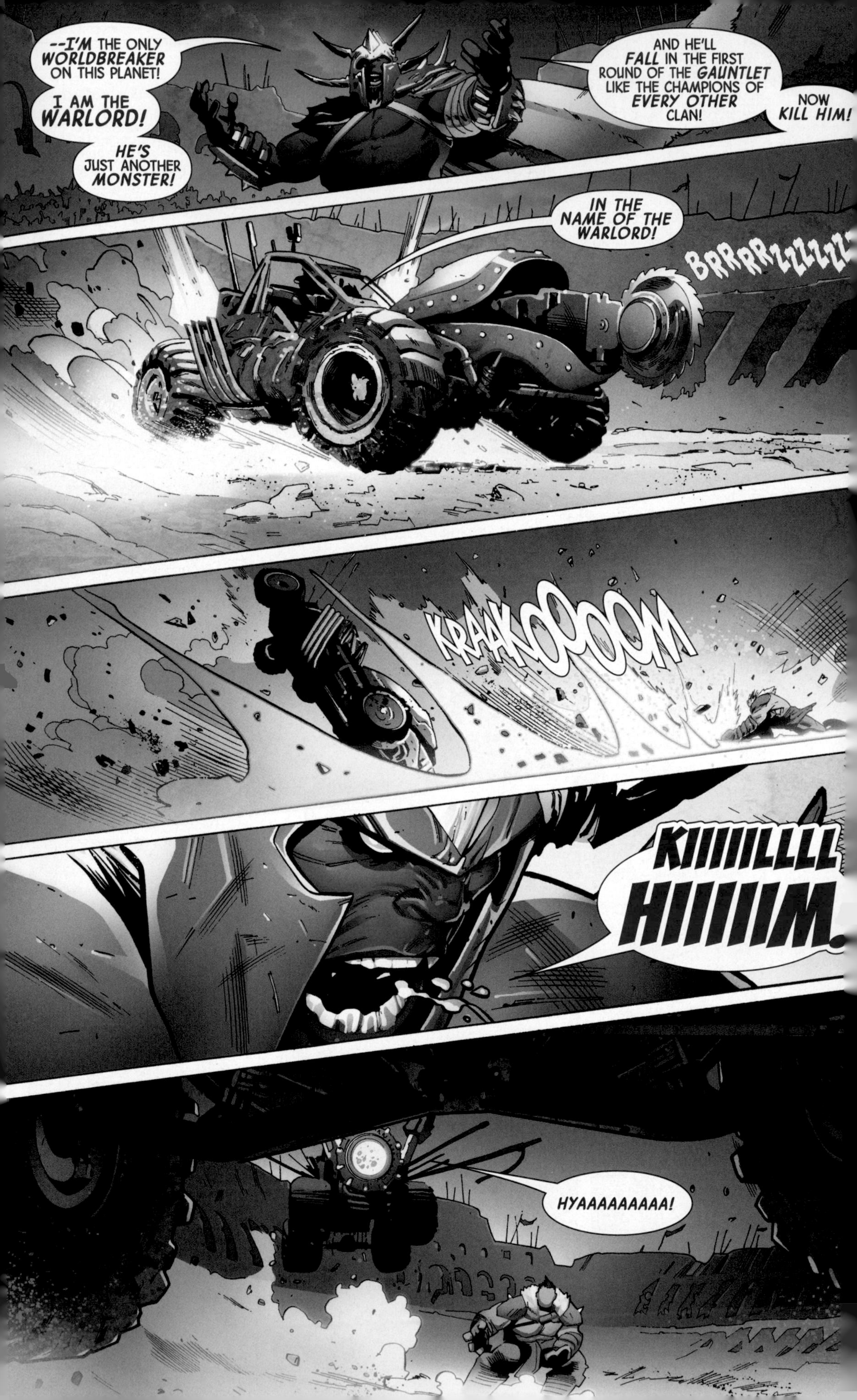
--I'M THE ONLY WORLDBREAKER ON THIS PLANET!
I AM THE WARLORD!
HE'S JUST ANOTHER MONSTER!
AND HE'LL FALL IN THE FIRST ROUND OF THE GAUNTLET LIKE THE CHAMPIONS OF EVERY OTHER CLAN!
NOW KILL HIM!
IN THE NAME OF THE WARLORD!
BRRRRZZZZZZ
KRAAKOOOOM
KIIIIILLLL HIIIIIM.
HYAAAAAAAAA!

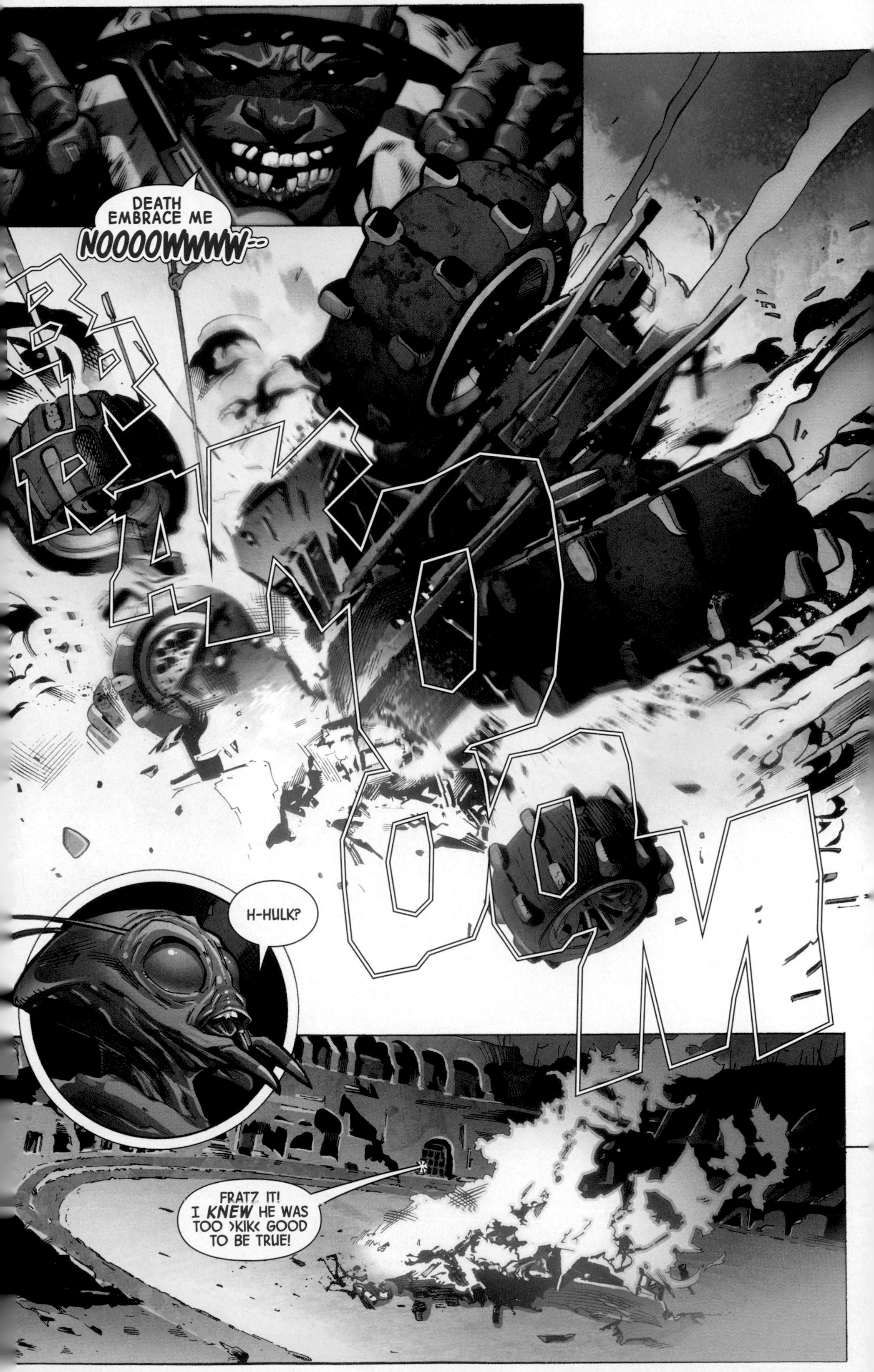
DEATH EMBRACE ME NOOOOWWWW--
H-HULK?
FRATZ IT! I *KNEW* HE WAS TOO ›KIK‹ GOOD TO BE TRUE!

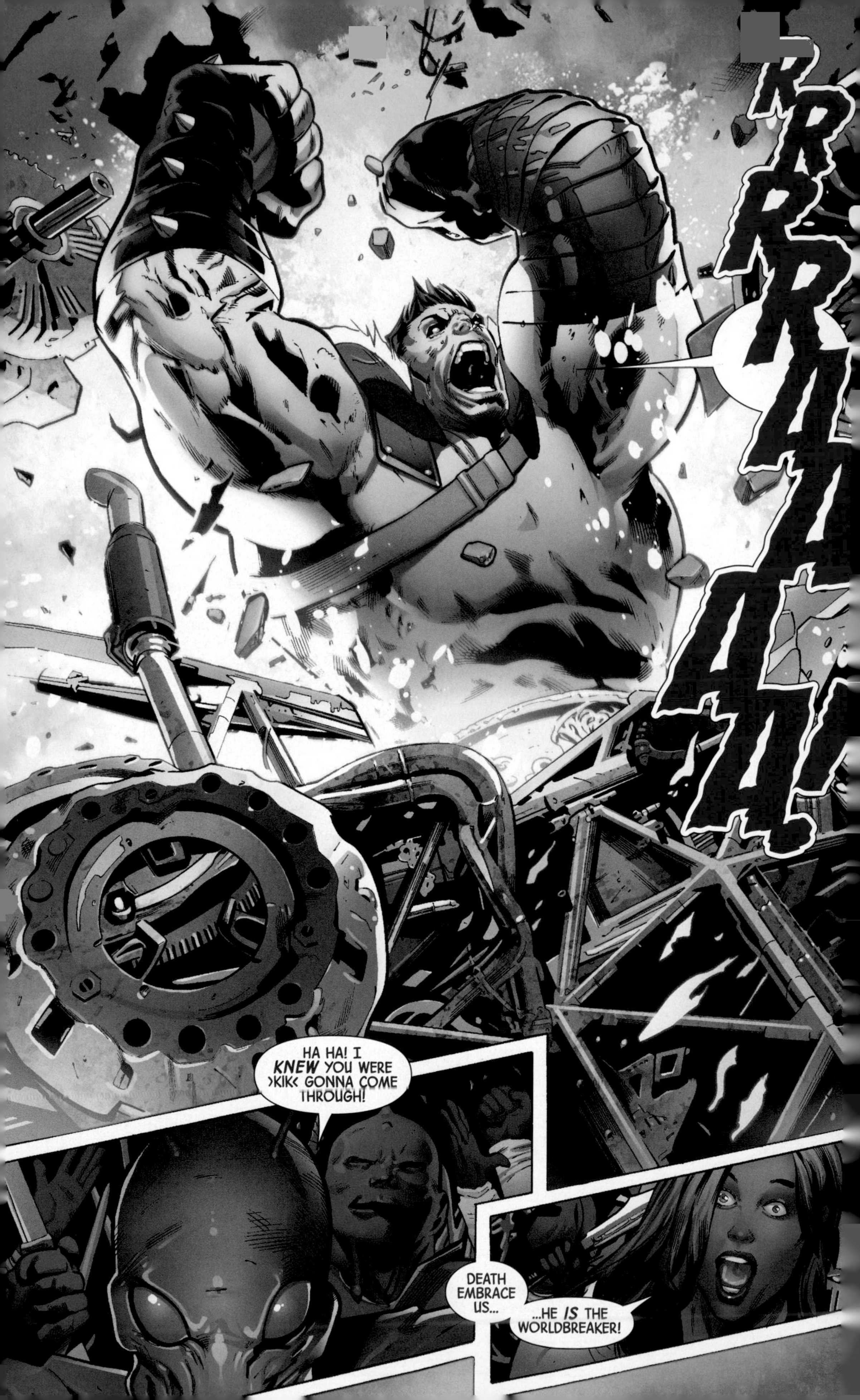
HA HA! I KNEW YOU WERE ›KIK‹ GONNA COME THROUGH!
DEATH EMBRACE US...
...HE IS THE WORLDBREAKER!

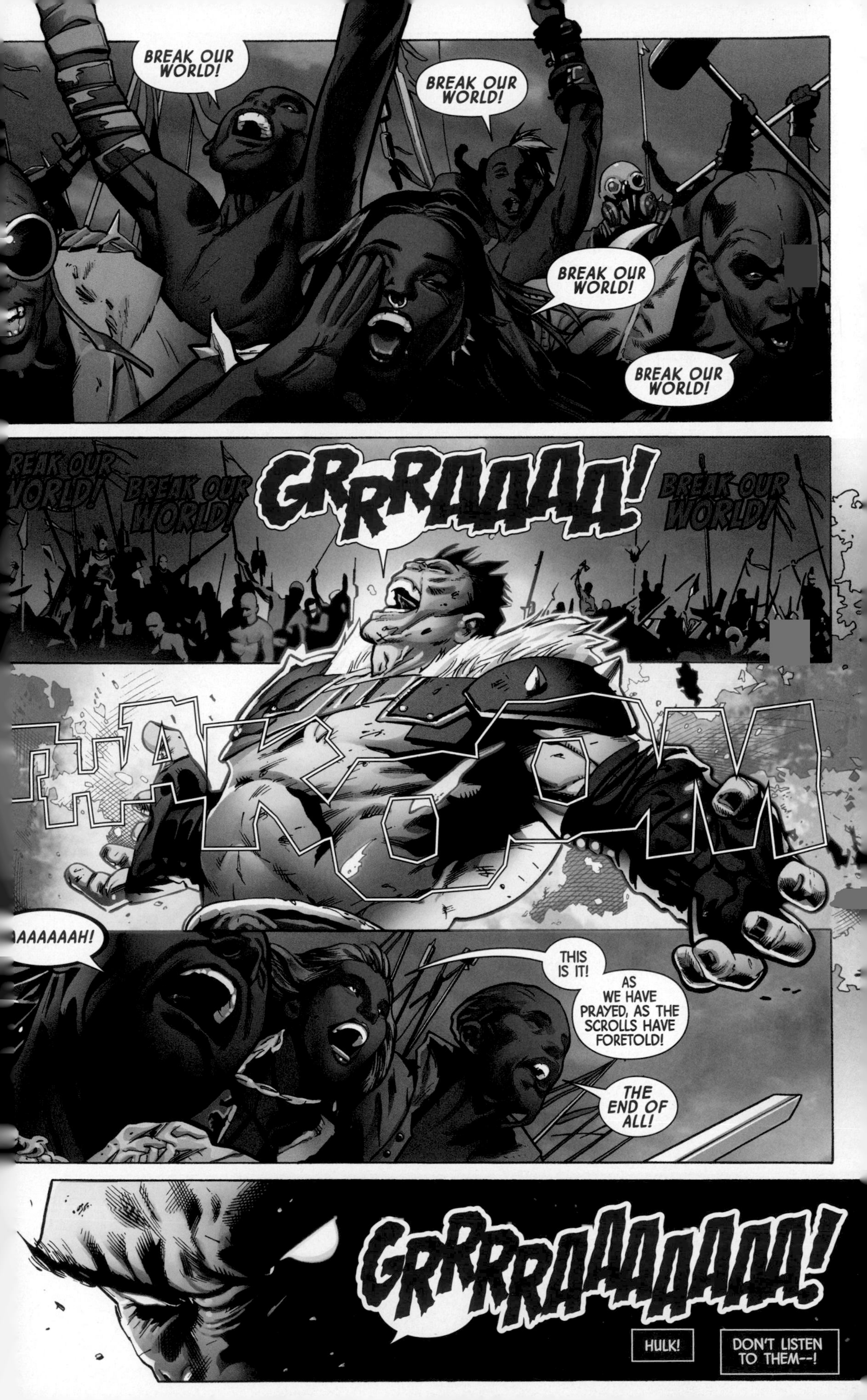
BREAK OUR WORLD!
BREAK OUR WORLD!
BREAK OUR WORLD!
BREAK OUR WORLD!
BREAK OUR WORLD!
BREAK OUR WORLD!
GRRRAAAAA!
BREAK OUR WORLD!
THAKOOM
AAAAAAAH!
THIS IS IT!
AS WE HAVE PRAYED, AS THE SCROLLS HAVE FORETOLD!
THE END OF ALL!
GRRRRAAAAAAAA!
HULK!
DON'T LISTEN TO THEM--!

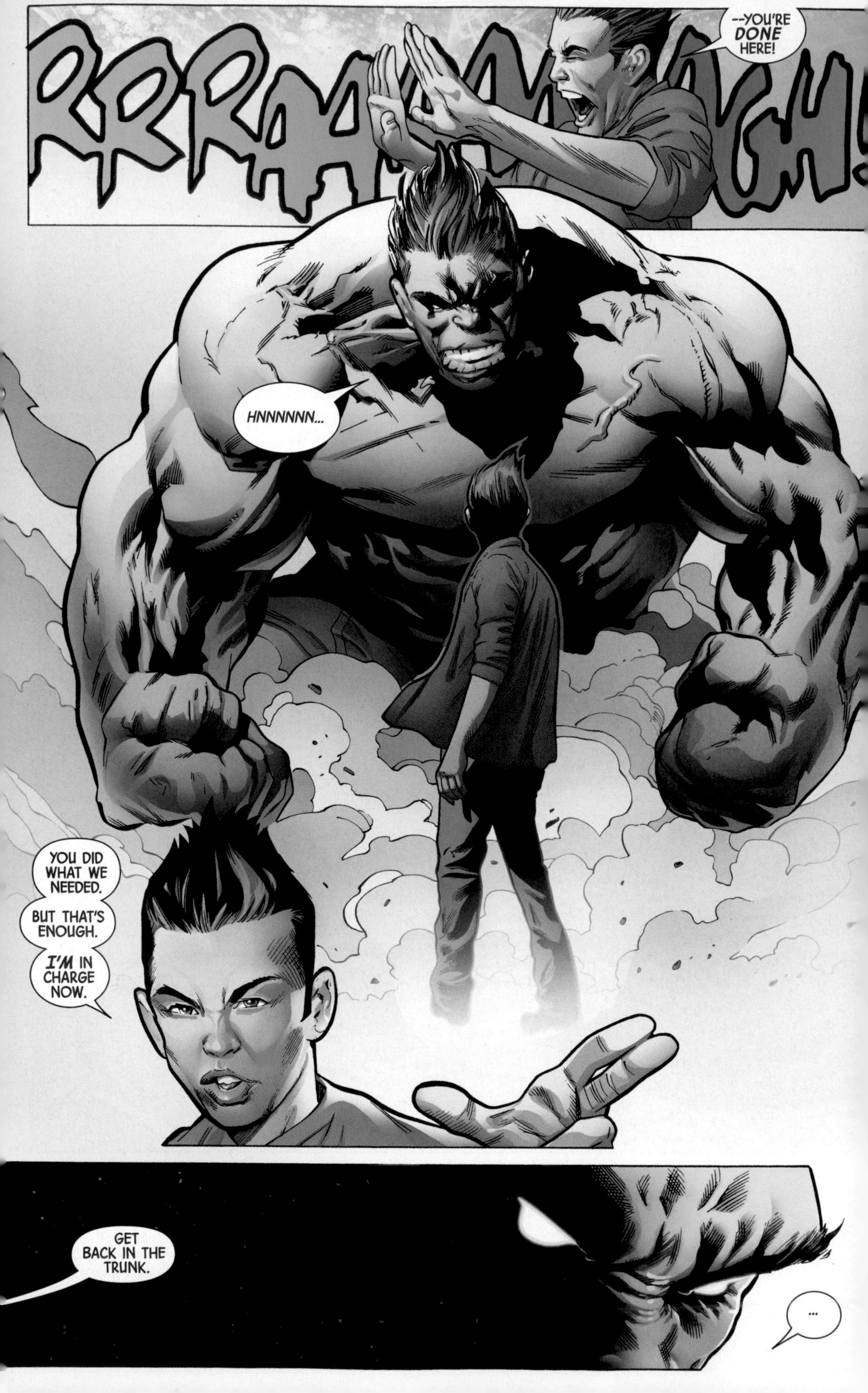
RRRAAAAAAAGH!
--YOU'RE DONE HERE!
HNNNNNN...
YOU DID WHAT WE NEEDED.
BUT THAT'S ENOUGH.
I'M IN CHARGE NOW.
GET BACK IN THE TRUNK.
...

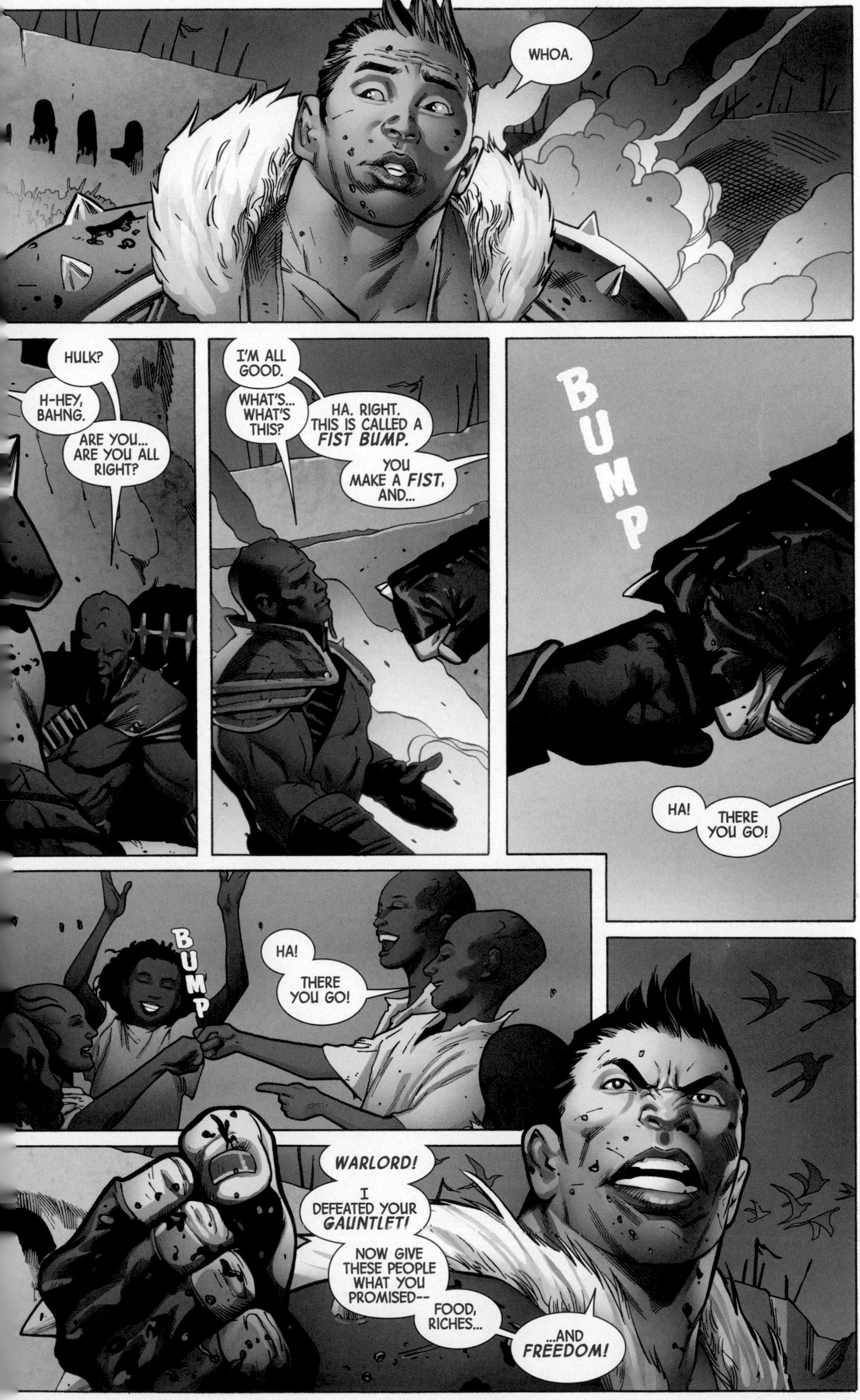

WHOA.
HULK?
H-HEY, BAHNG.
ARE YOU... ARE YOU ALL RIGHT?
I'M ALL GOOD.
WHAT'S... WHAT'S THIS?
HA. RIGHT. THIS IS CALLED A *FIST BUMP.*
YOU MAKE A *FIST,* AND...
BUMP
HA!
THERE YOU GO!
BUMP
HA!
THERE YOU GO!
WARLORD!
I DEFEATED YOUR *GAUNTLET!*
NOW GIVE THESE PEOPLE WHAT YOU PROMISED--
FOOD, RICHES...
...AND *FREEDOM!*

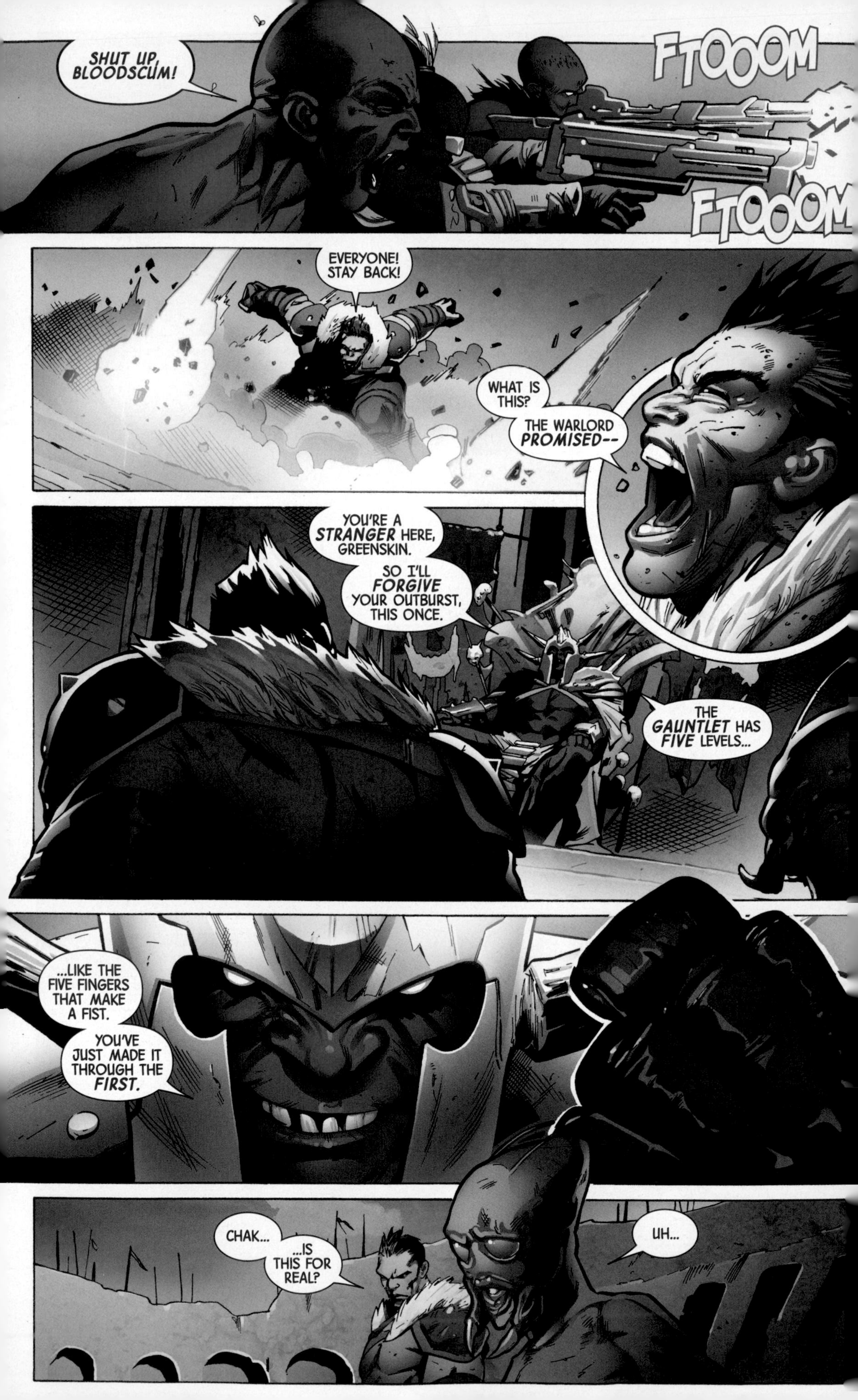
SHUT UP BLOODSCUM!
FTOOOM
FTOOOM
EVERYONE! STAY BACK!
WHAT IS THIS?
THE WARLORD PROMISED--
YOU'RE A STRANGER HERE, GREENSKIN.
SO I'LL FORGIVE YOUR OUTBURST, THIS ONCE.
THE GAUNTLET HAS FIVE LEVELS...
...LIKE THE FIVE FINGERS THAT MAKE A FIST.
YOU'VE JUST MADE IT THROUGH THE FIRST.
CHAK...
...IS THIS FOR REAL?
UH...

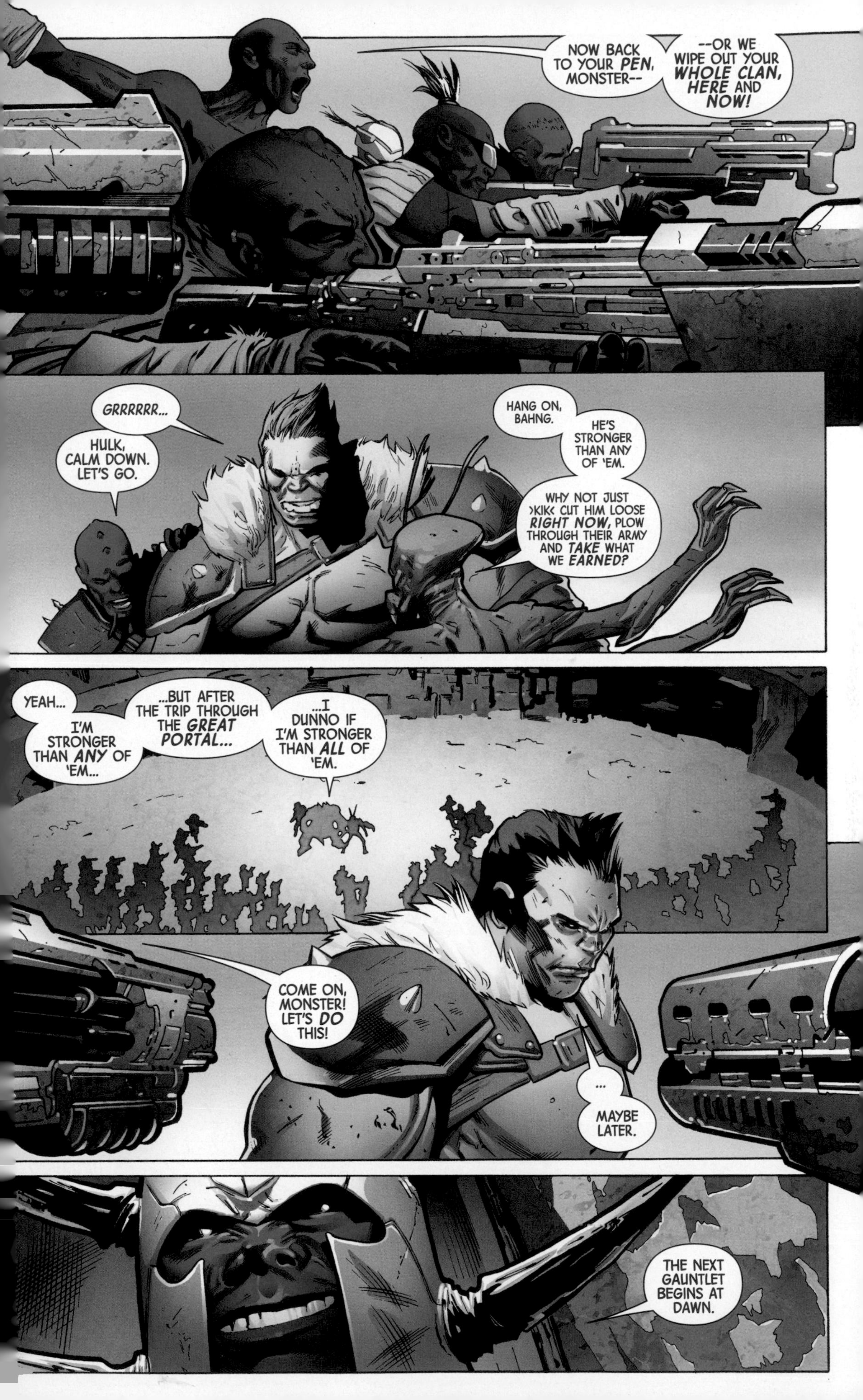
NOW BACK TO YOUR PEN, MONSTER--
--OR WE WIPE OUT YOUR WHOLE CLAN, HERE AND NOW!
GRRRRRR...
HULK, CALM DOWN. LET'S GO.
HANG ON, BAHNG.
HE'S STRONGER THAN ANY OF 'EM.
WHY NOT JUST >KIK< CUT HIM LOOSE RIGHT NOW, PLOW THROUGH THEIR ARMY AND TAKE WHAT WE EARNED?
YEAH...
I'M STRONGER THAN ANY OF 'EM...
...BUT AFTER THE TRIP THROUGH THE GREAT PORTAL...
...I DUNNO IF I'M STRONGER THAN ALL OF 'EM.
COME ON, MONSTER! LET'S DO THIS!
...
MAYBE LATER.
THE NEXT GAUNTLET BEGINS AT DAWN.

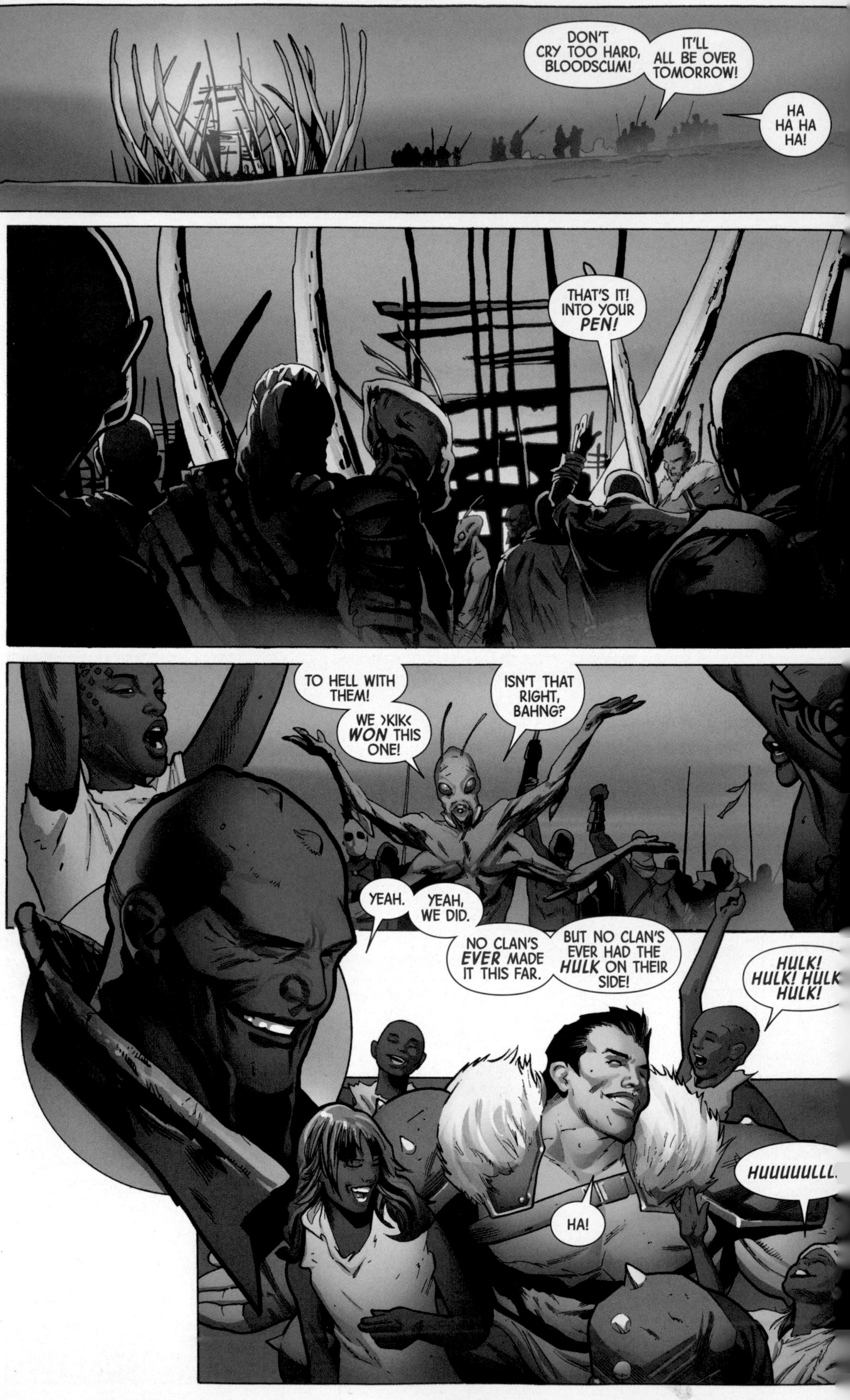
DON'T CRY TOO HARD, BLOODSCUM!
IT'LL ALL BE OVER TOMORROW!
HA HA HA HA!
THAT'S IT! INTO YOUR PEN!
TO HELL WITH THEM!
WE >KIK< WON THIS ONE!
ISN'T THAT RIGHT, BAHNG?
YEAH.
YEAH, WE DID.
NO CLAN'S EVER MADE IT THIS FAR.
BUT NO CLAN'S EVER HAD THE HULK ON THEIR SIDE!
HULK! HULK! HULK HULK!
HUUUUULLL.
HA!

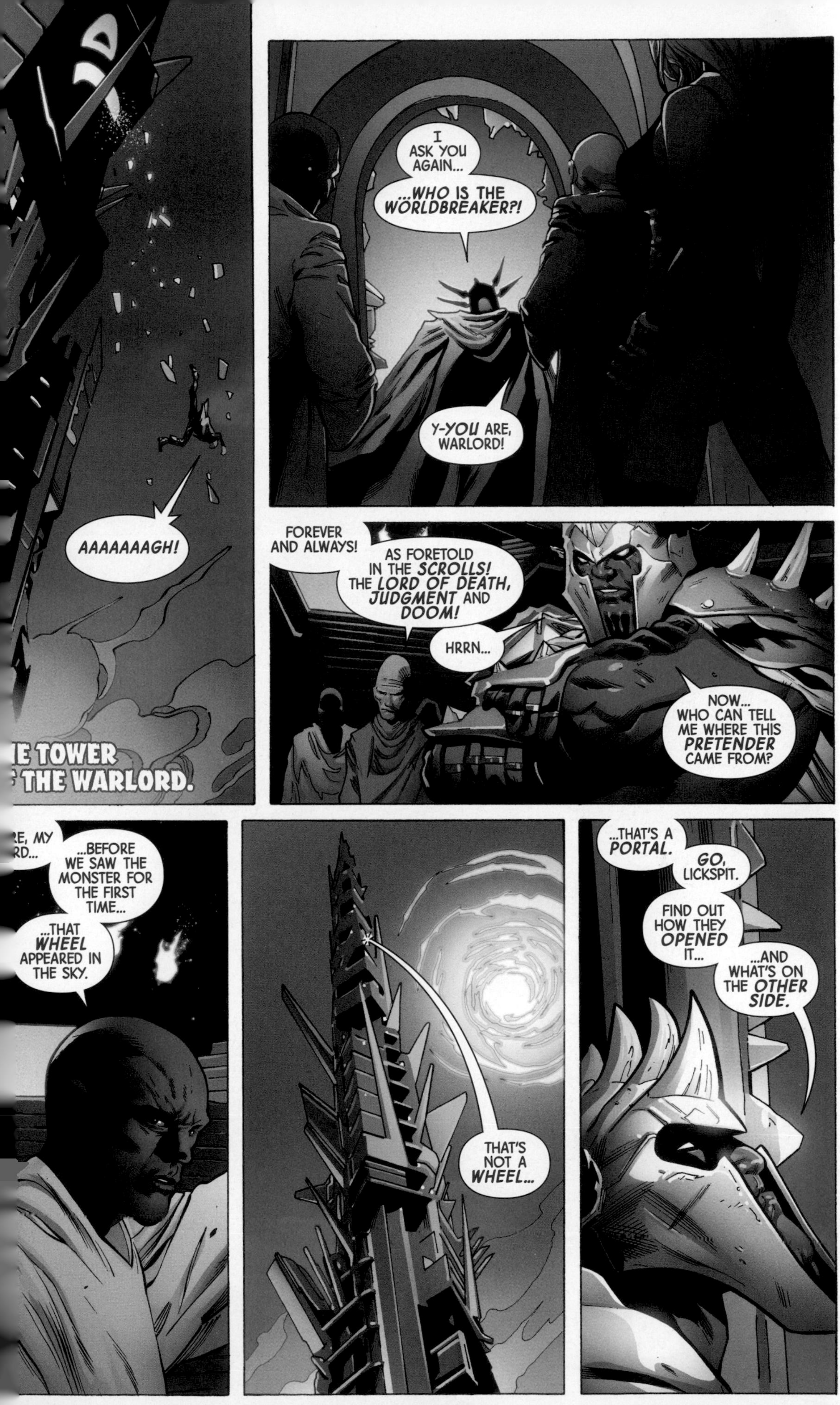
AAAAAAAGH!
...E TOWER
...THE WARLORD.
I ASK YOU AGAIN...
...WHO IS THE WORLDBREAKER?!
Y-YOU ARE, WARLORD!
FOREVER AND ALWAYS!
AS FORETOLD IN THE SCROLLS! THE LORD OF DEATH, JUDGMENT AND DOOM!
HRRN...
NOW... WHO CAN TELL ME WHERE THIS PRETENDER CAME FROM?
...RE, MY ...RD...
...BEFORE WE SAW THE MONSTER FOR THE FIRST TIME...
...THAT WHEEL APPEARED IN THE SKY.
THAT'S NOT A WHEEL...
...THAT'S A PORTAL.
GO, LICKSPIT.
FIND OUT HOW THEY OPENED IT...
...AND WHAT'S ON THE OTHER SIDE.

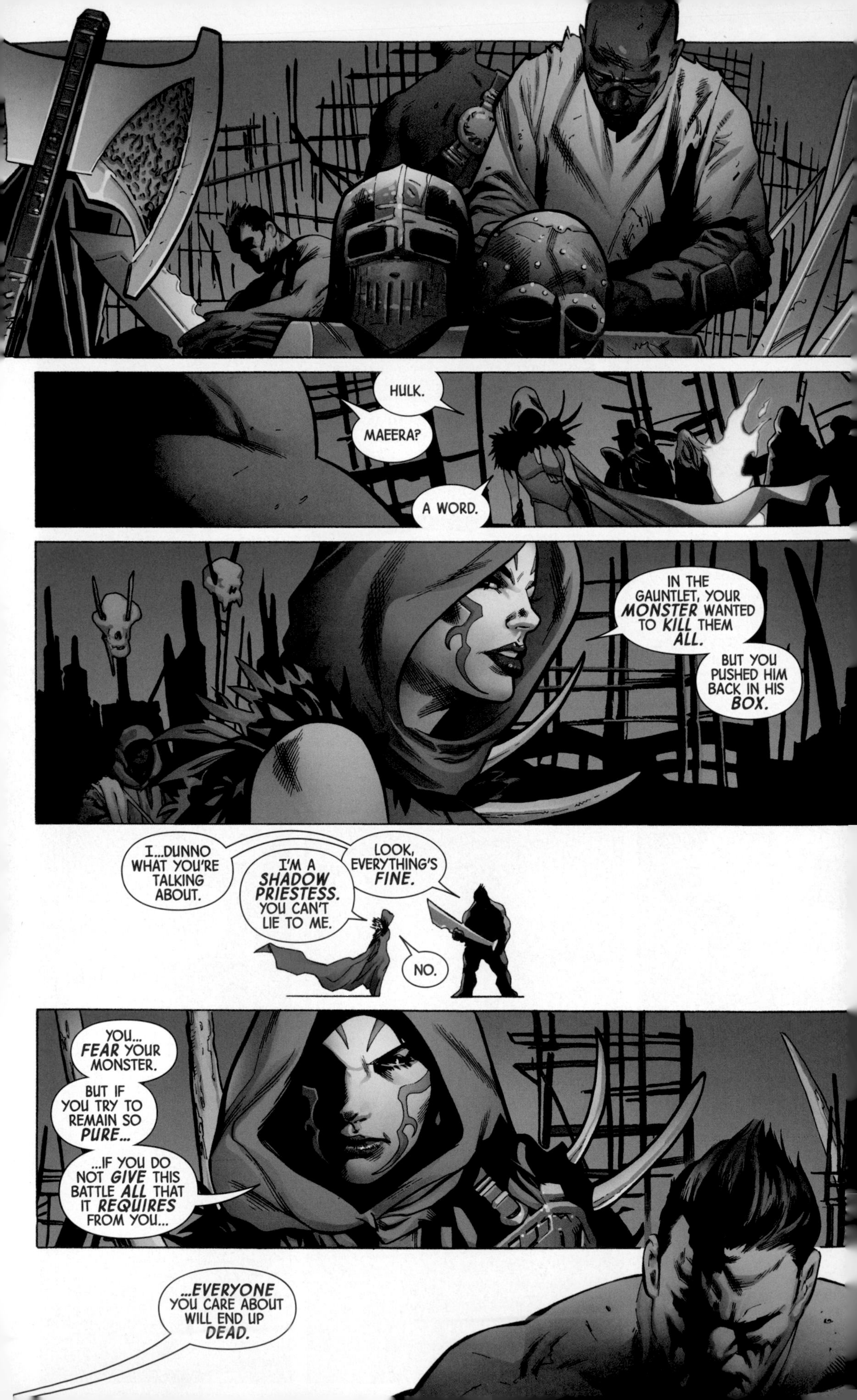
HULK.
MAEERA?
A WORD.
IN THE GAUNTLET, YOUR MONSTER WANTED TO KILL THEM ALL.
BUT YOU PUSHED HIM BACK IN HIS BOX.
I...DUNNO WHAT YOU'RE TALKING ABOUT.
LOOK, EVERYTHING'S FINE.
I'M A SHADOW PRIESTESS. YOU CAN'T LIE TO ME.
NO.
YOU... FEAR YOUR MONSTER.
BUT IF YOU TRY TO REMAIN SO PURE...
...IF YOU DO NOT GIVE THIS BATTLE ALL THAT IT REQUIRES FROM YOU...
...EVERYONE YOU CARE ABOUT WILL END UP DEAD.

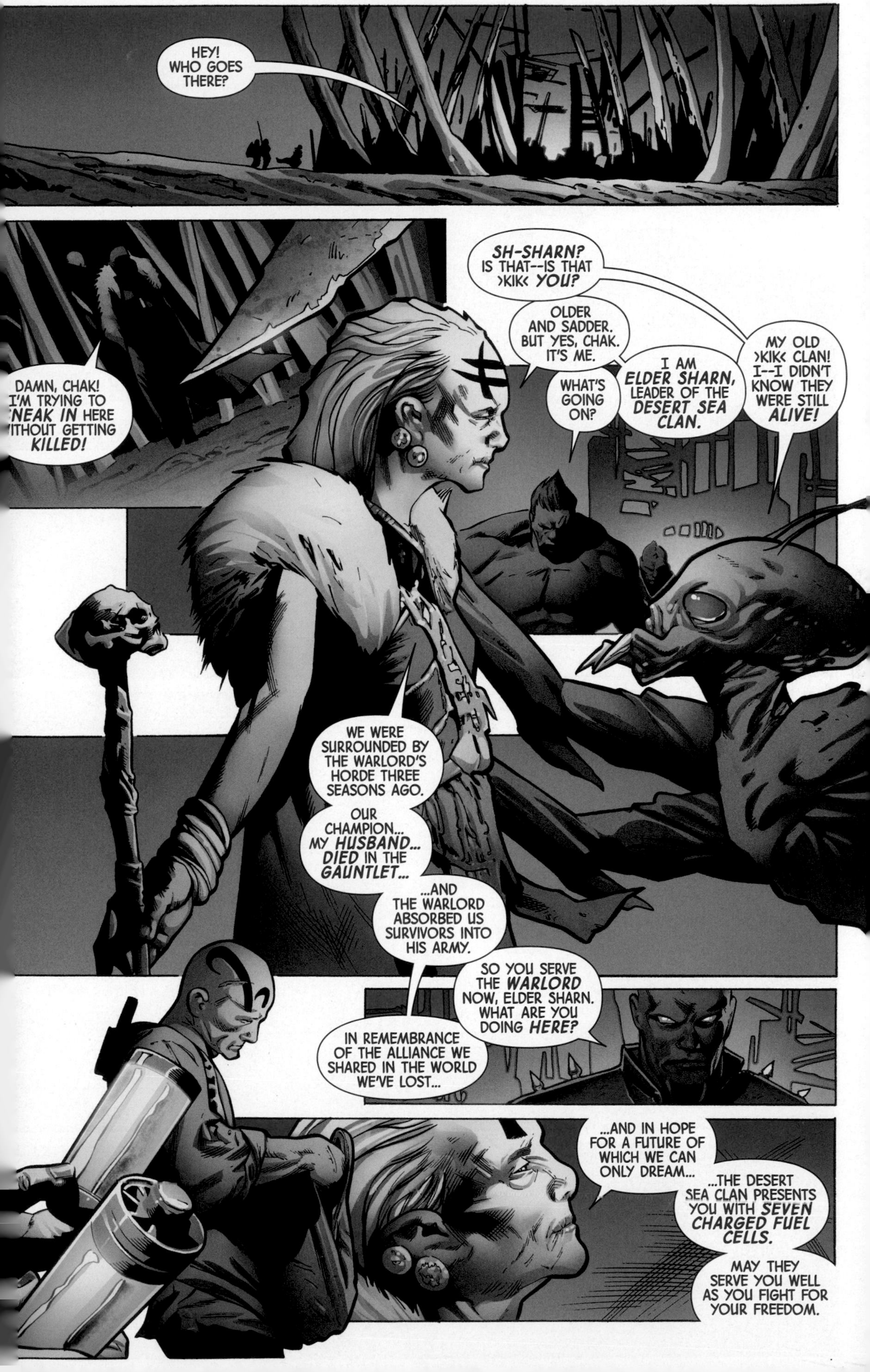

HEY! WHO GOES THERE?
DAMN, CHAK! I'M TRYING TO NEAK IN HERE ITHOUT GETTING KILLED!
SH-SHARN? IS THAT--IS THAT ›KIK‹ YOU?
OLDER AND SADDER. BUT YES, CHAK. IT'S ME.
WHAT'S GOING ON?
I AM ELDER SHARN, LEADER OF THE DESERT SEA CLAN.
MY OLD ›KIK‹ CLAN! I--I DIDN'T KNOW THEY WERE STILL ALIVE!
WE WERE SURROUNDED BY THE WARLORD'S HORDE THREE SEASONS AGO.
OUR CHAMPION... MY HUSBAND... DIED IN THE GAUNTLET...
...AND THE WARLORD ABSORBED US SURVIVORS INTO HIS ARMY.
SO YOU SERVE THE WARLORD NOW, ELDER SHARN. WHAT ARE YOU DOING HERE?
IN REMEMBRANCE OF THE ALLIANCE WE SHARED IN THE WORLD WE'VE LOST...
...AND IN HOPE FOR A FUTURE OF WHICH WE CAN ONLY DREAM...
...THE DESERT SEA CLAN PRESENTS YOU WITH SEVEN CHARGED FUEL CELLS.
MAY THEY SERVE YOU WELL AS YOU FIGHT FOR YOUR FREEDOM.

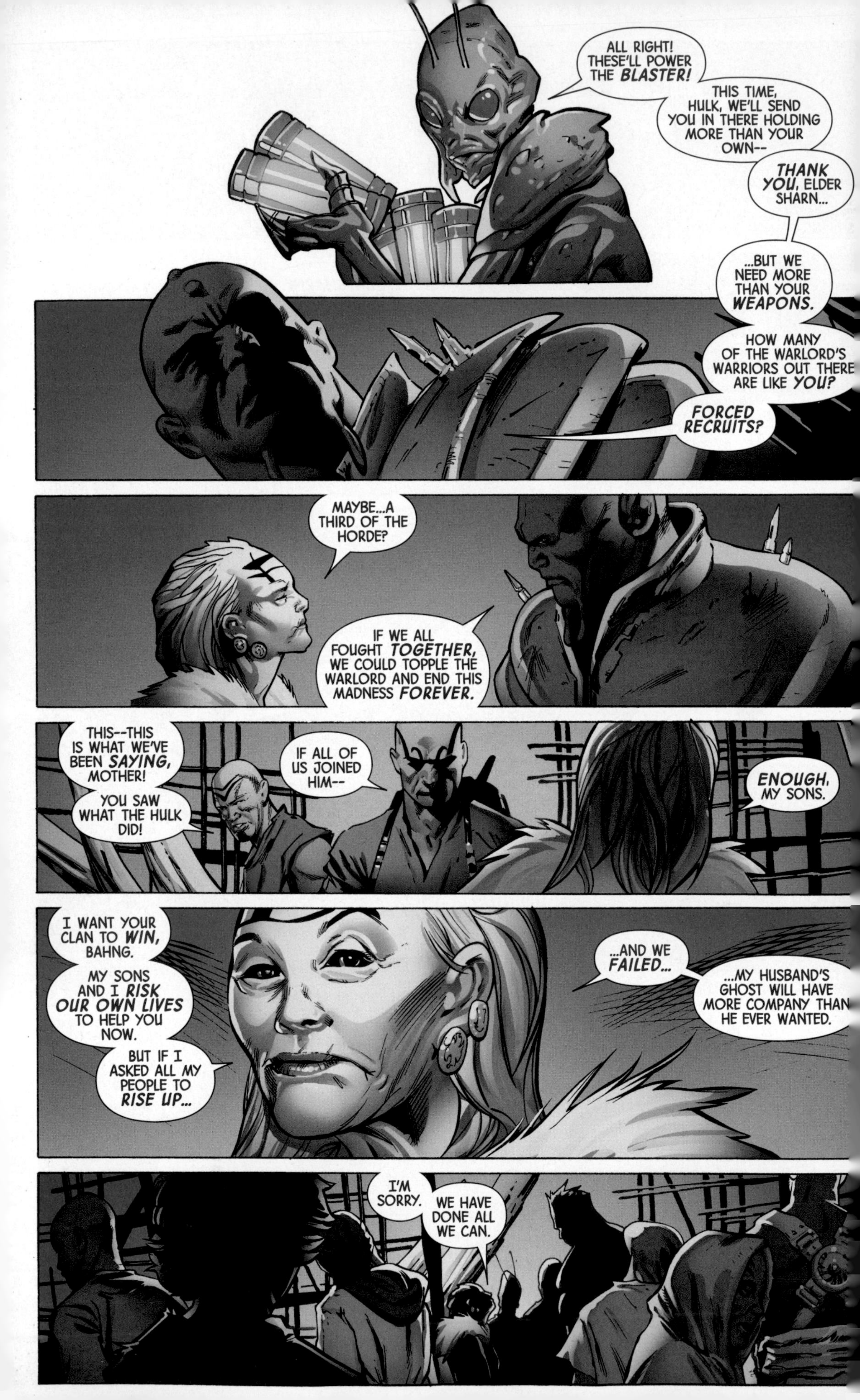
ALL RIGHT! THESE'LL POWER THE BLASTER!
THIS TIME, HULK, WE'LL SEND YOU IN THERE HOLDING MORE THAN YOUR OWN--
THANK YOU, ELDER SHARN...
...BUT WE NEED MORE THAN YOUR WEAPONS.
HOW MANY OF THE WARLORD'S WARRIORS OUT THERE ARE LIKE YOU?
FORCED RECRUITS?
MAYBE...A THIRD OF THE HORDE?
IF WE ALL FOUGHT TOGETHER, WE COULD TOPPLE THE WARLORD AND END THIS MADNESS FOREVER.
THIS--THIS IS WHAT WE'VE BEEN SAYING, MOTHER!
YOU SAW WHAT THE HULK DID!
IF ALL OF US JOINED HIM--
ENOUGH, MY SONS.
I WANT YOUR CLAN TO WIN, BAHNG.
MY SONS AND I RISK OUR OWN LIVES TO HELP YOU NOW.
BUT IF I ASKED ALL MY PEOPLE TO RISE UP...
...AND WE FAILED...
...MY HUSBAND'S GHOST WILL HAVE MORE COMPANY THAN HE EVER WANTED.
I'M SORRY.
WE HAVE DONE ALL WE CAN.

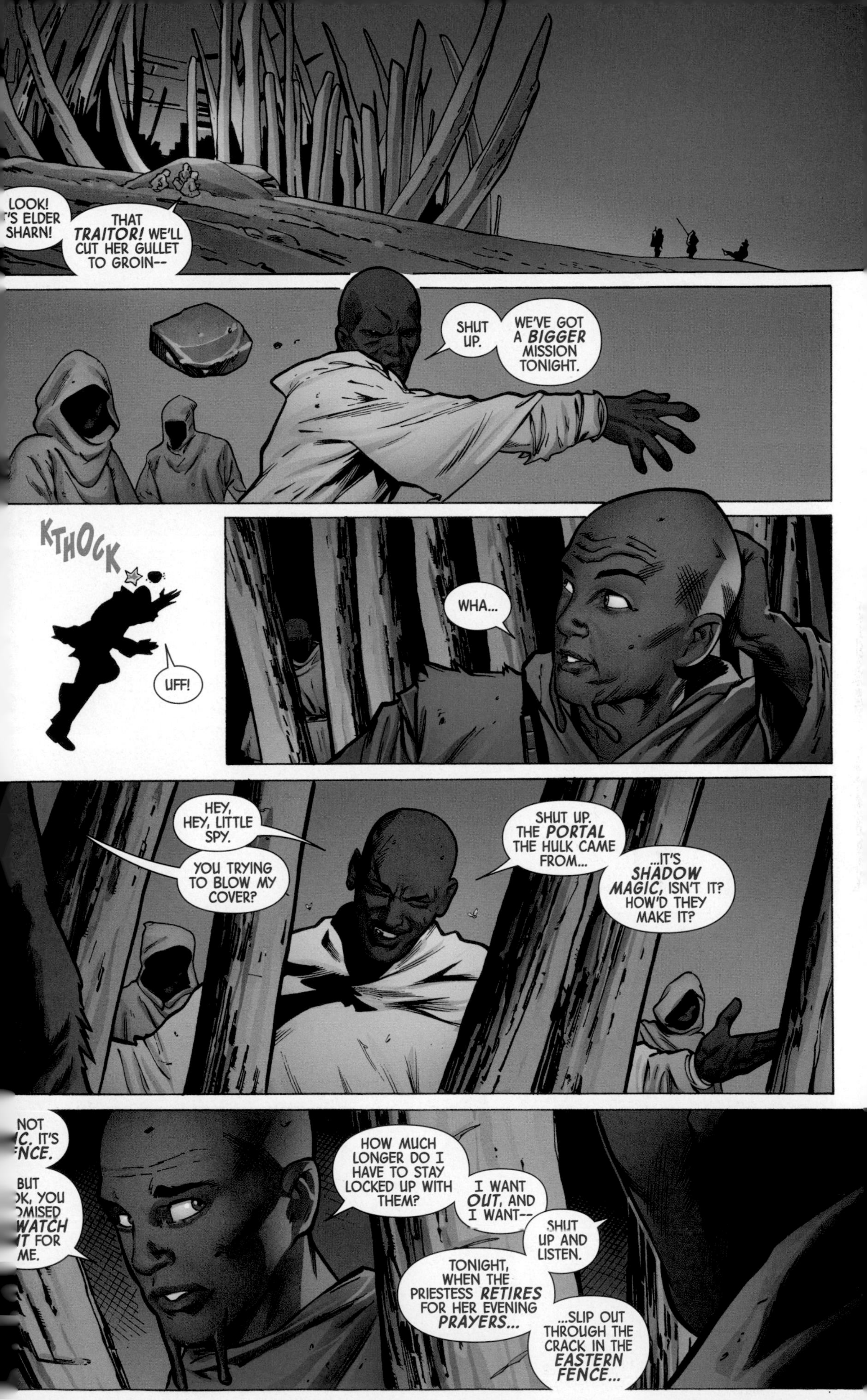
LOOK! 'T'S ELDER SHARN!
THAT TRAITOR! WE'LL CUT HER GULLET TO GROIN--
SHUT UP.
WE'VE GOT A BIGGER MISSION TONIGHT.
KTHOCK
UFF!
WHA...
HEY, HEY, LITTLE SPY.
YOU TRYING TO BLOW MY COVER?
SHUT UP. THE PORTAL THE HULK CAME FROM...
...IT'S SHADOW MAGIC, ISN'T IT? HOW'D THEY MAKE IT?
NOT
IC. IT'S
ENCE.
BUT
OK, YOU
OMISED
WATCH
IT FOR
ME.
HOW MUCH LONGER DO I HAVE TO STAY LOCKED UP WITH THEM?
I WANT OUT, AND I WANT--
SHUT UP AND LISTEN.
TONIGHT, WHEN THE PRIESTESS RETIRES FOR HER EVENING PRAYERS...
...SLIP OUT THROUGH THE CRACK IN THE EASTERN FENCE...

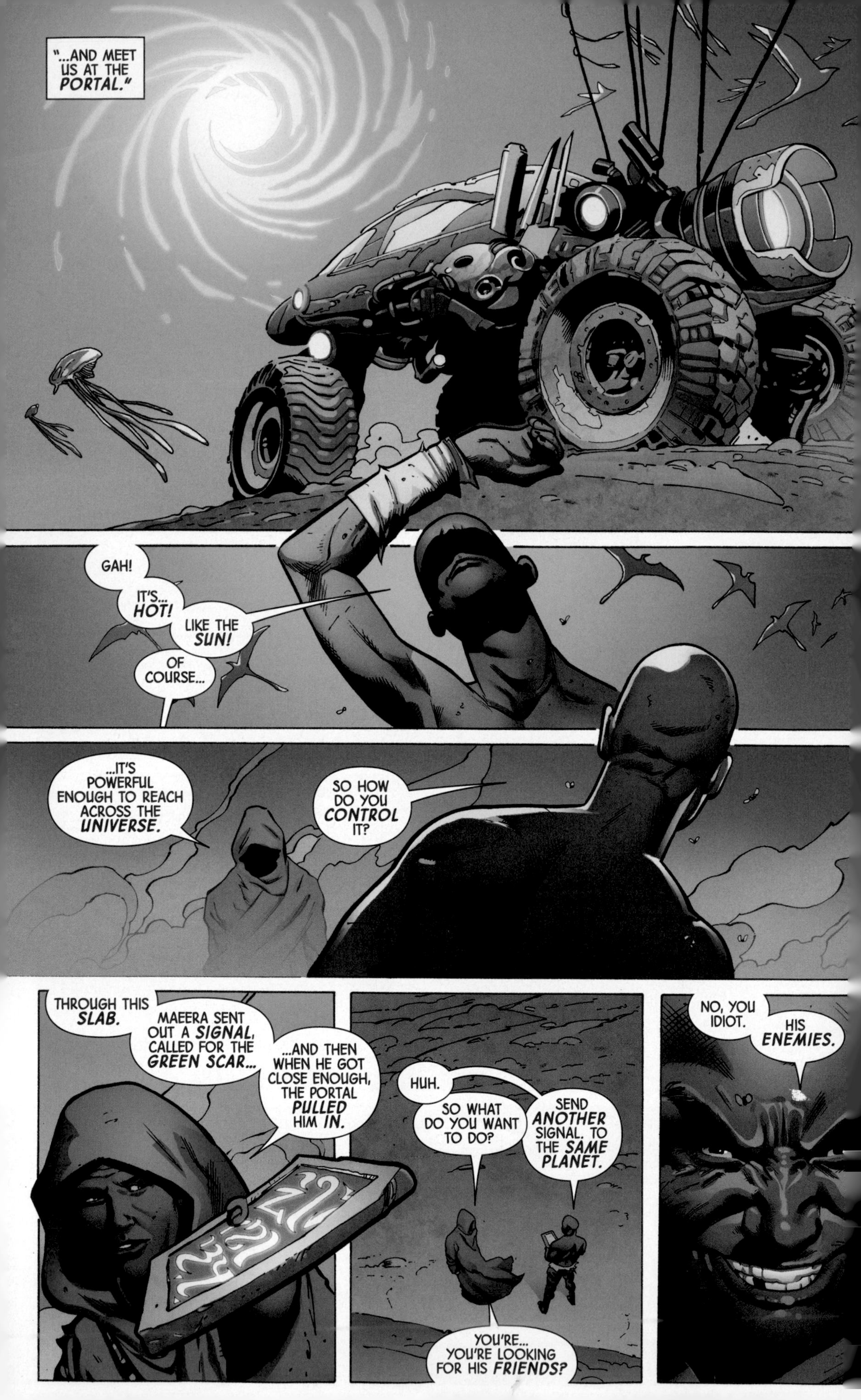

"...AND MEET US AT THE PORTAL."
GAH!
IT'S... HOT!
LIKE THE SUN!
OF COURSE...
...IT'S POWERFUL ENOUGH TO REACH ACROSS THE UNIVERSE.
SO HOW DO YOU CONTROL IT?
THROUGH THIS SLAB.
MAEERA SENT OUT A SIGNAL, CALLED FOR THE GREEN SCAR...
...AND THEN WHEN HE GOT CLOSE ENOUGH, THE PORTAL PULLED HIM IN.
HUH.
SO WHAT DO YOU WANT TO DO?
SEND ANOTHER SIGNAL. TO THE SAME PLANET.
YOU'RE... YOU'RE LOOKING FOR HIS FRIENDS?
NO, YOU IDIOT.
HIS ENEMIES.

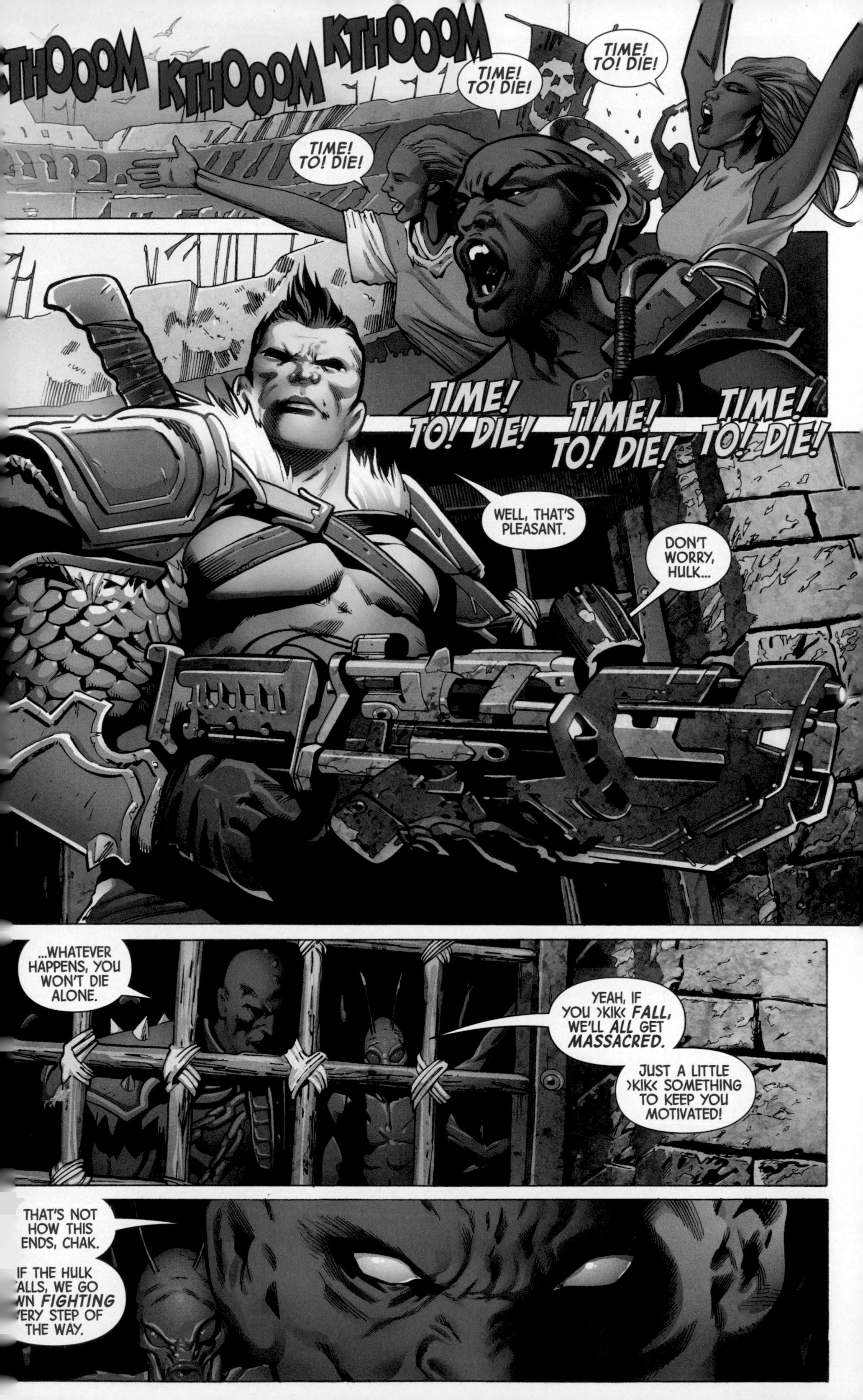
KTHOOOM KTHOOOM KTHOOOM
TIME! TO! DIE!
TIME! TO! DIE!
TIME! TO! DIE!
TIME! TO! DIE!
TIME! TO! DIE!
TIME! TO! DIE!
WELL, THAT'S PLEASANT.
DON'T WORRY, HULK...
...WHATEVER HAPPENS, YOU WON'T DIE ALONE.
YEAH, IF YOU ›KIK‹ FALL, WE'LL ALL GET MASSACRED.
JUST A LITTLE ›KIK‹ SOMETHING TO KEEP YOU MOTIVATED!
THAT'S NOT HOW THIS ENDS, CHAK.

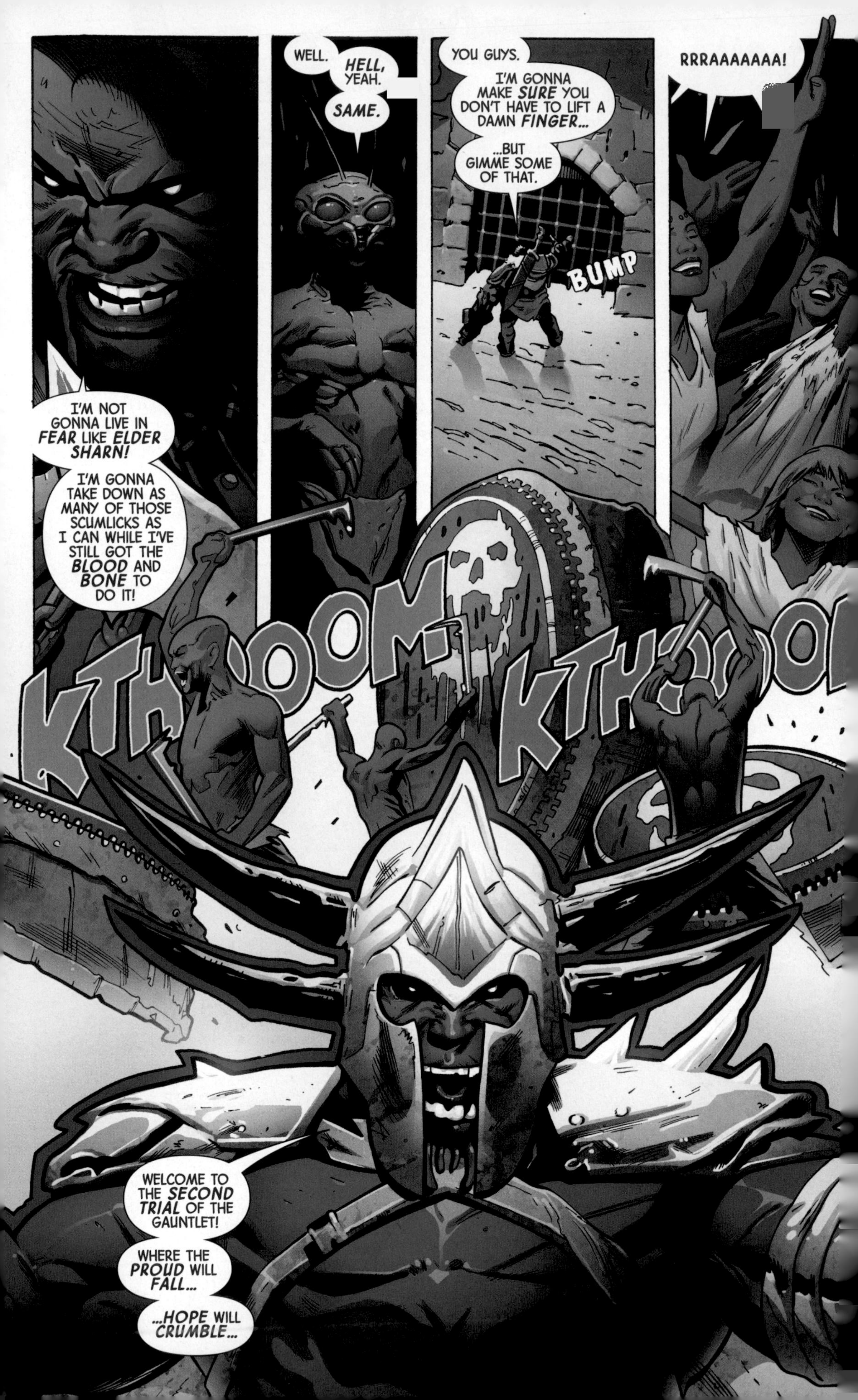
I'M NOT GONNA LIVE IN FEAR LIKE ELDER SHARN!
I'M GONNA TAKE DOWN AS MANY OF THOSE SCUMLICKS AS I CAN WHILE I'VE STILL GOT THE BLOOD AND BONE TO DO IT!
WELL.
HELL, YEAH.
SAME.
YOU GUYS.
I'M GONNA MAKE SURE YOU DON'T HAVE TO LIFT A DAMN FINGER...
...BUT GIMME SOME OF THAT.
BUMP
RRRAAAAAAA!
WELCOME TO THE SECOND TRIAL OF THE GAUNTLET!
WHERE THE PROUD WILL FALL...
...HOPE WILL CRUMBLE...

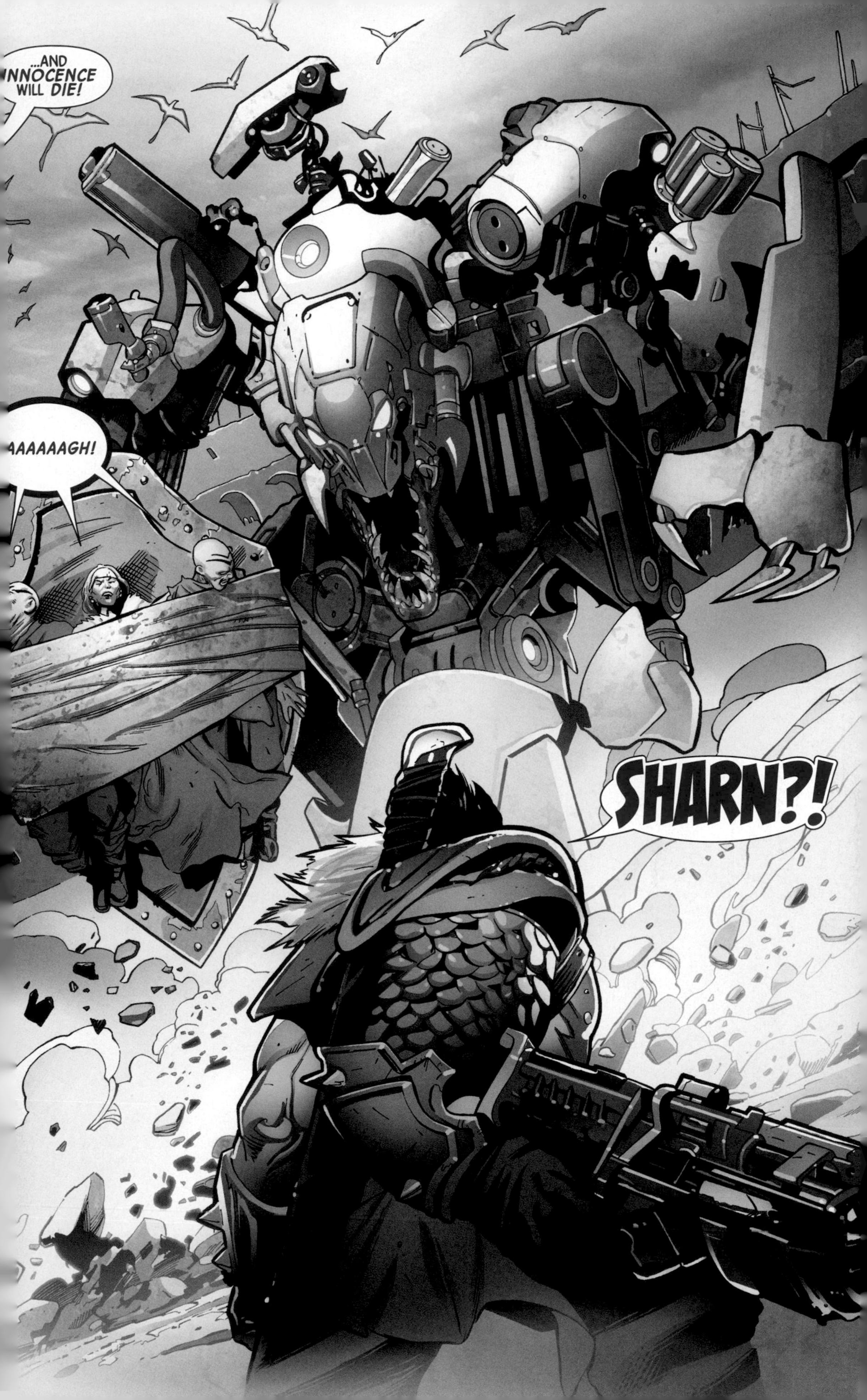
...AND INNOCENCE WILL DIE!
AAAAAAGH!
SHARN?!

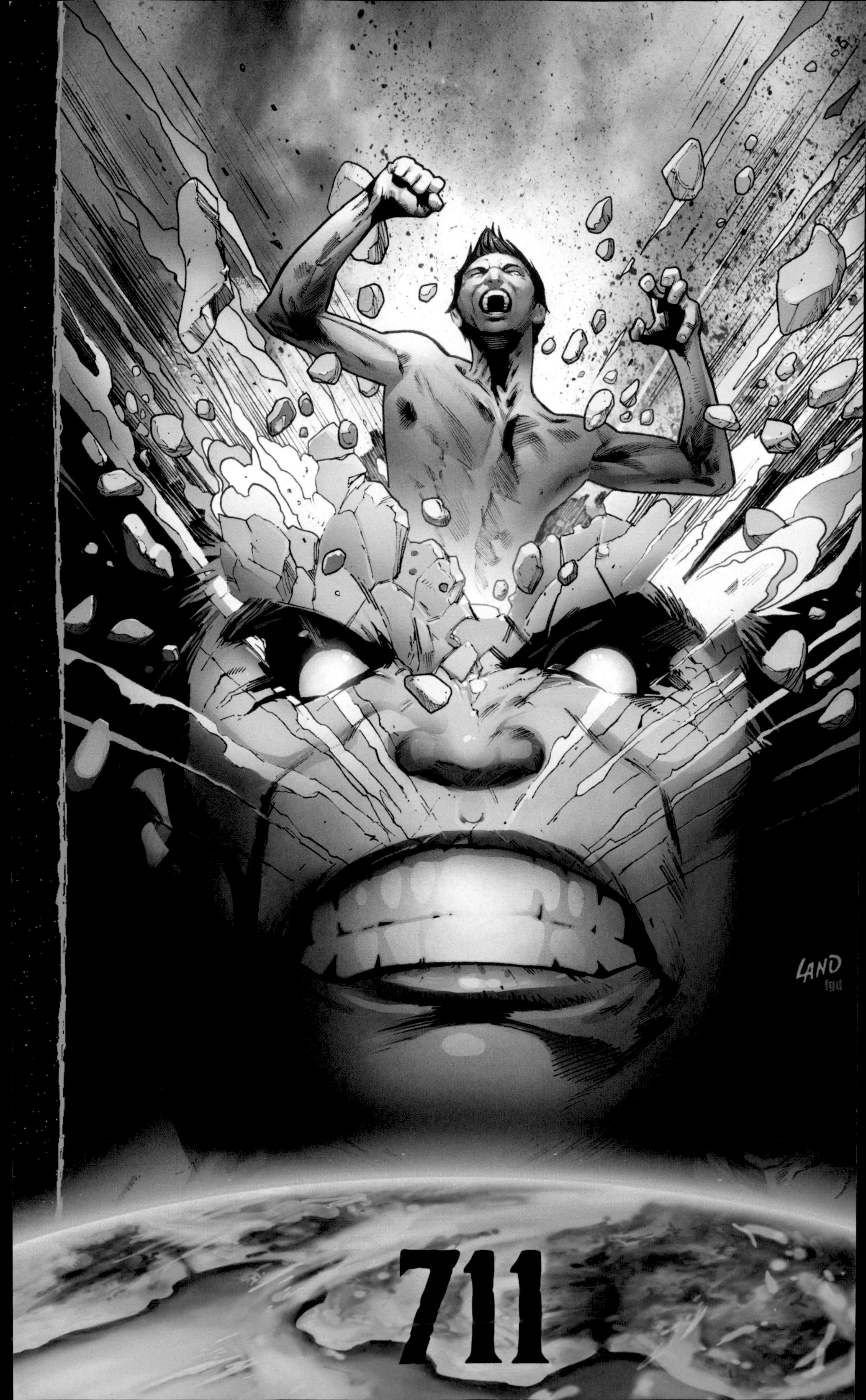
LAND
fgd
711

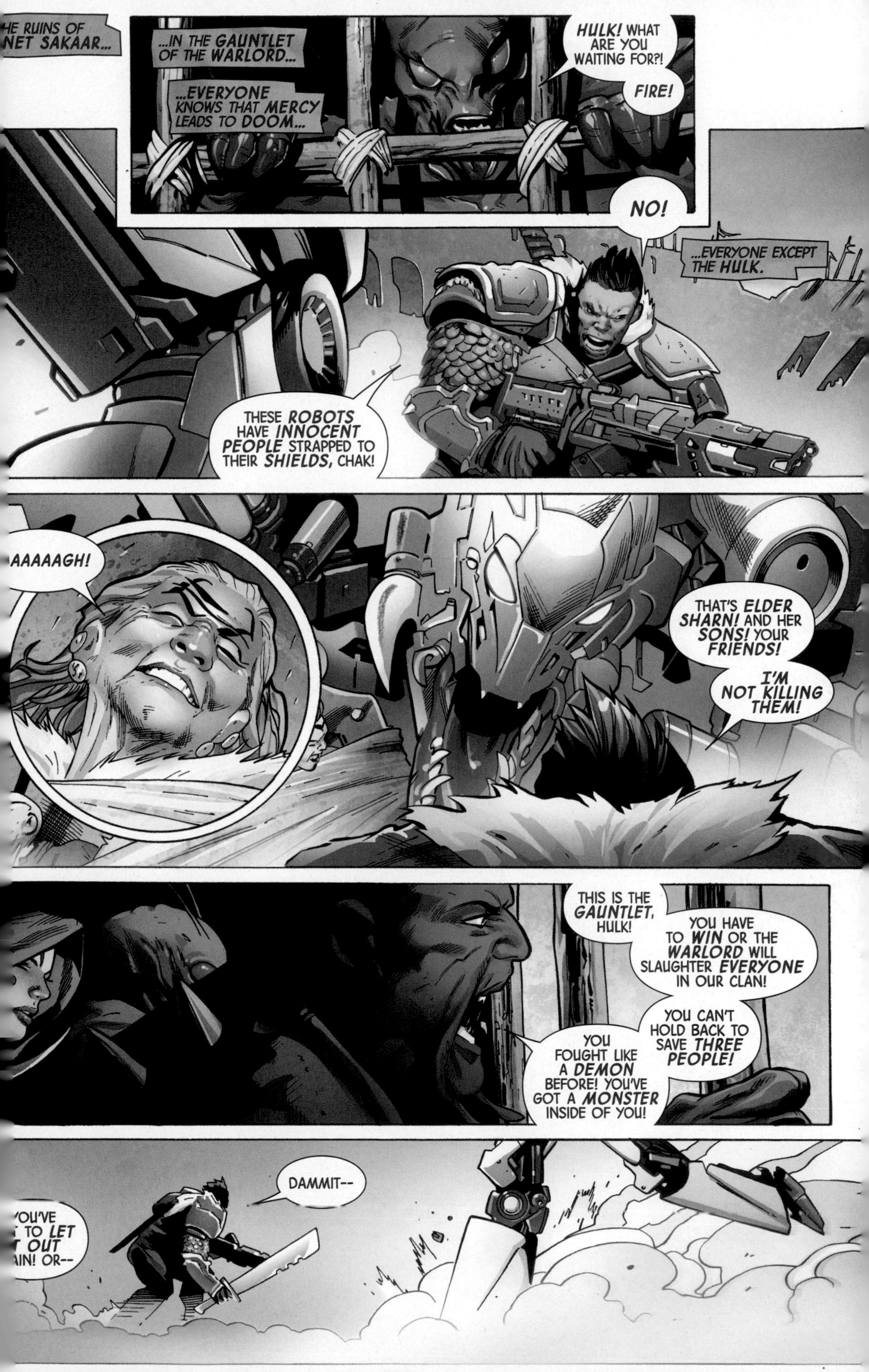
HE RUINS OF
NET SAKAAR...
...IN THE GAUNTLET OF THE WARLORD...
...EVERYONE KNOWS THAT MERCY LEADS TO DOOM...
HULK! WHAT ARE YOU WAITING FOR?!
FIRE!
NO!
...EVERYONE EXCEPT THE HULK.
THESE ROBOTS HAVE INNOCENT PEOPLE STRAPPED TO THEIR SHIELDS, CHAK!
AAAAAGH!
THAT'S ELDER SHARN! AND HER SONS! YOUR FRIENDS!
I'M NOT KILLING THEM!
THIS IS THE GAUNTLET, HULK!
YOU HAVE TO WIN OR THE WARLORD WILL SLAUGHTER EVERYONE IN OUR CLAN!
YOU CAN'T HOLD BACK TO SAVE THREE PEOPLE!
YOU FOUGHT LIKE A DEMON BEFORE! YOU'VE GOT A MONSTER INSIDE OF YOU!
DAMMIT--
YOU'VE
TO LET
OUT
AIN! OR--

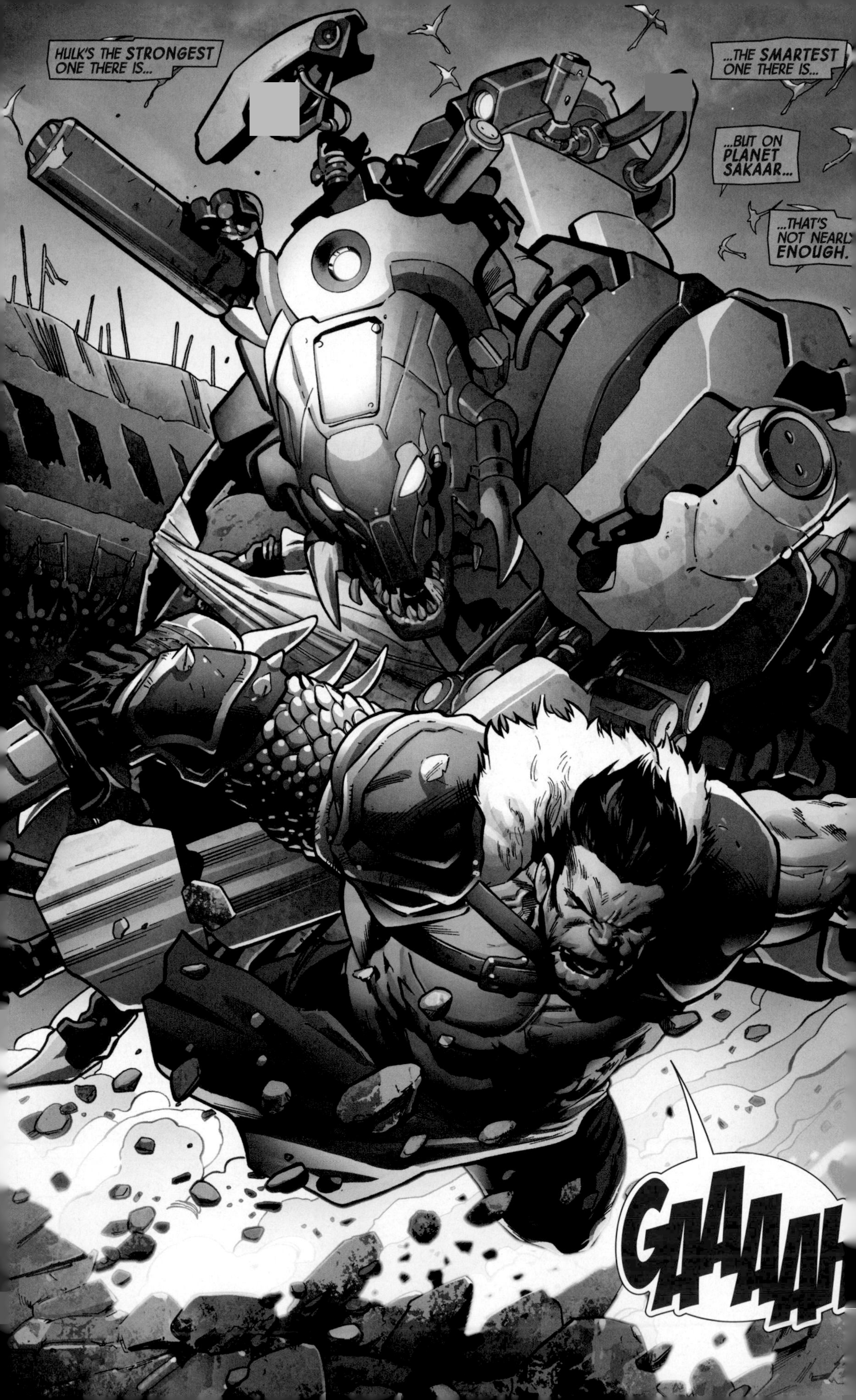
HULK'S THE STRONGEST ONE THERE IS...
...THE SMARTEST ONE THERE IS...
...BUT ON PLANET SAKAAR...
...THAT'S NOT NEARL ENOUGH.
GAAAAH

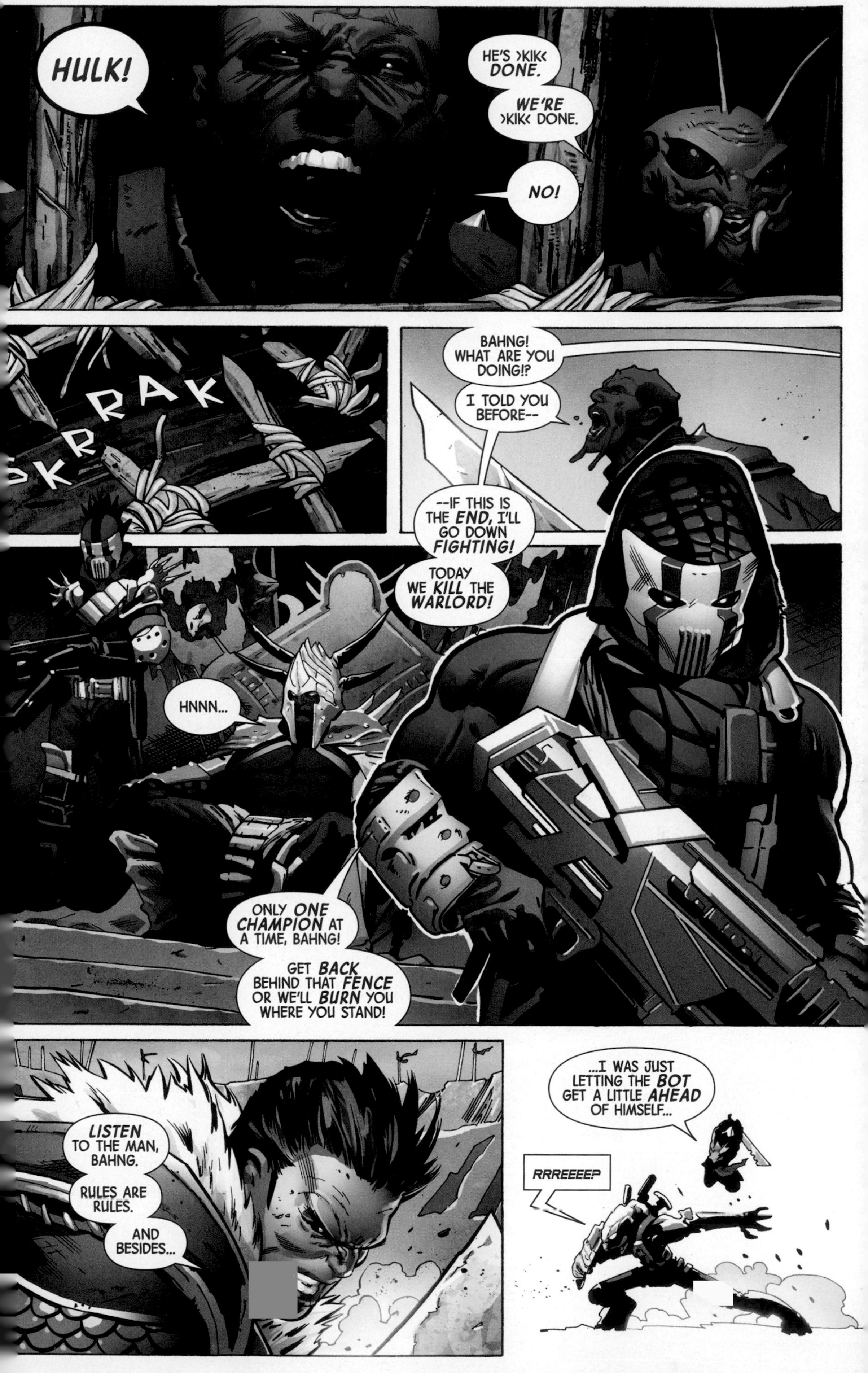
HULK!
HE'S ›KIK‹ DONE.
WE'RE ›KIK‹ DONE.
NO!
SKRRAK
BAHNG! WHAT ARE YOU DOING!?
I TOLD YOU BEFORE--
--IF THIS IS THE END, I'LL GO DOWN FIGHTING!
TODAY WE KILL THE WARLORD!
HNNN...
ONLY ONE CHAMPION AT A TIME, BAHNG!
GET BACK BEHIND THAT FENCE OR WE'LL BURN YOU WHERE YOU STAND!
LISTEN TO THE MAN, BAHNG.
RULES ARE RULES.
AND BESIDES...
...I WAS JUST LETTING THE BOT GET A LITTLE AHEAD OF HIMSELF...
RRREEEEP?

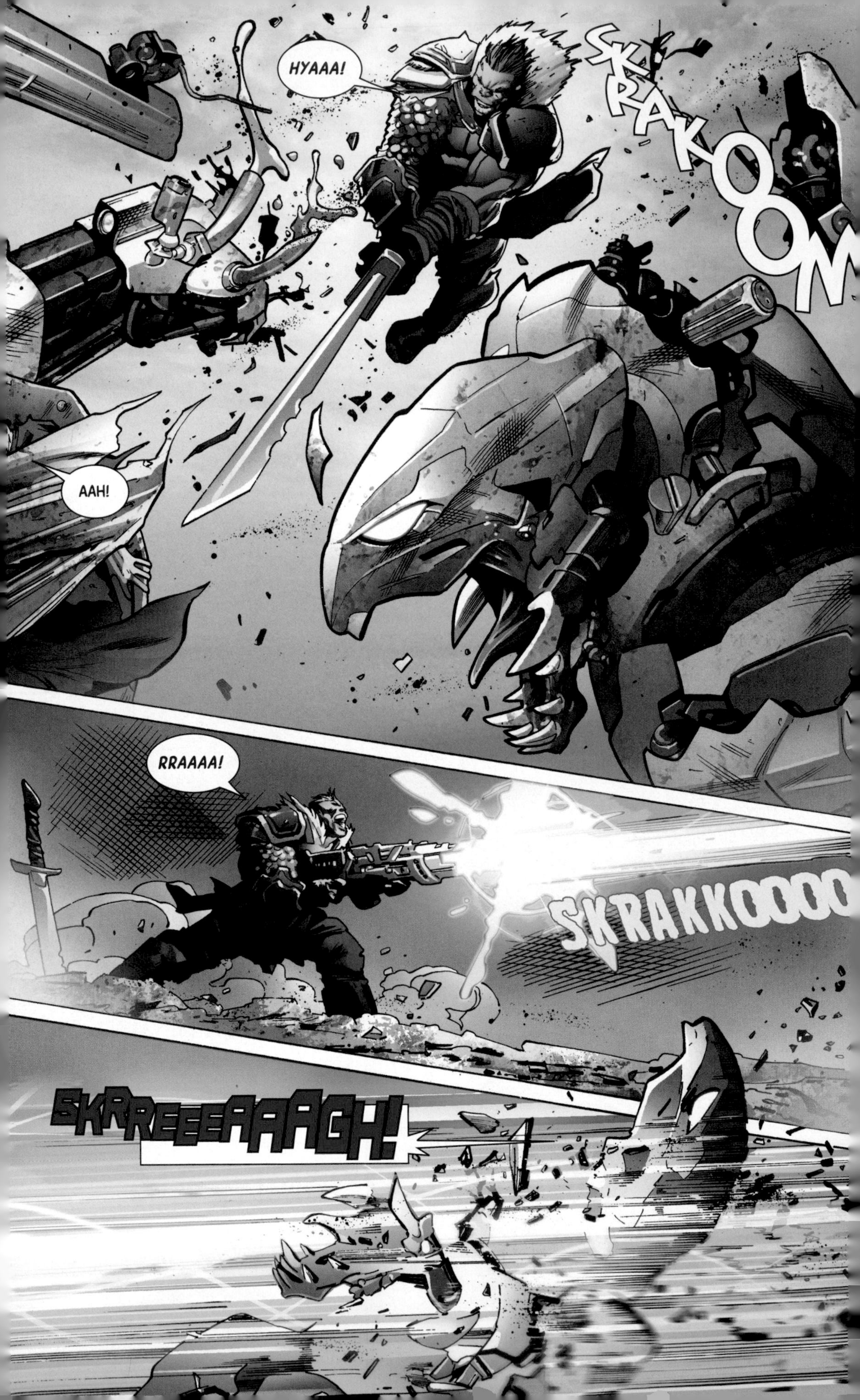
HYAAA!
SKRAKOOM
AAH!
RRAAAA!
SKRAKKOOOO
SKRREEEAAAGH!

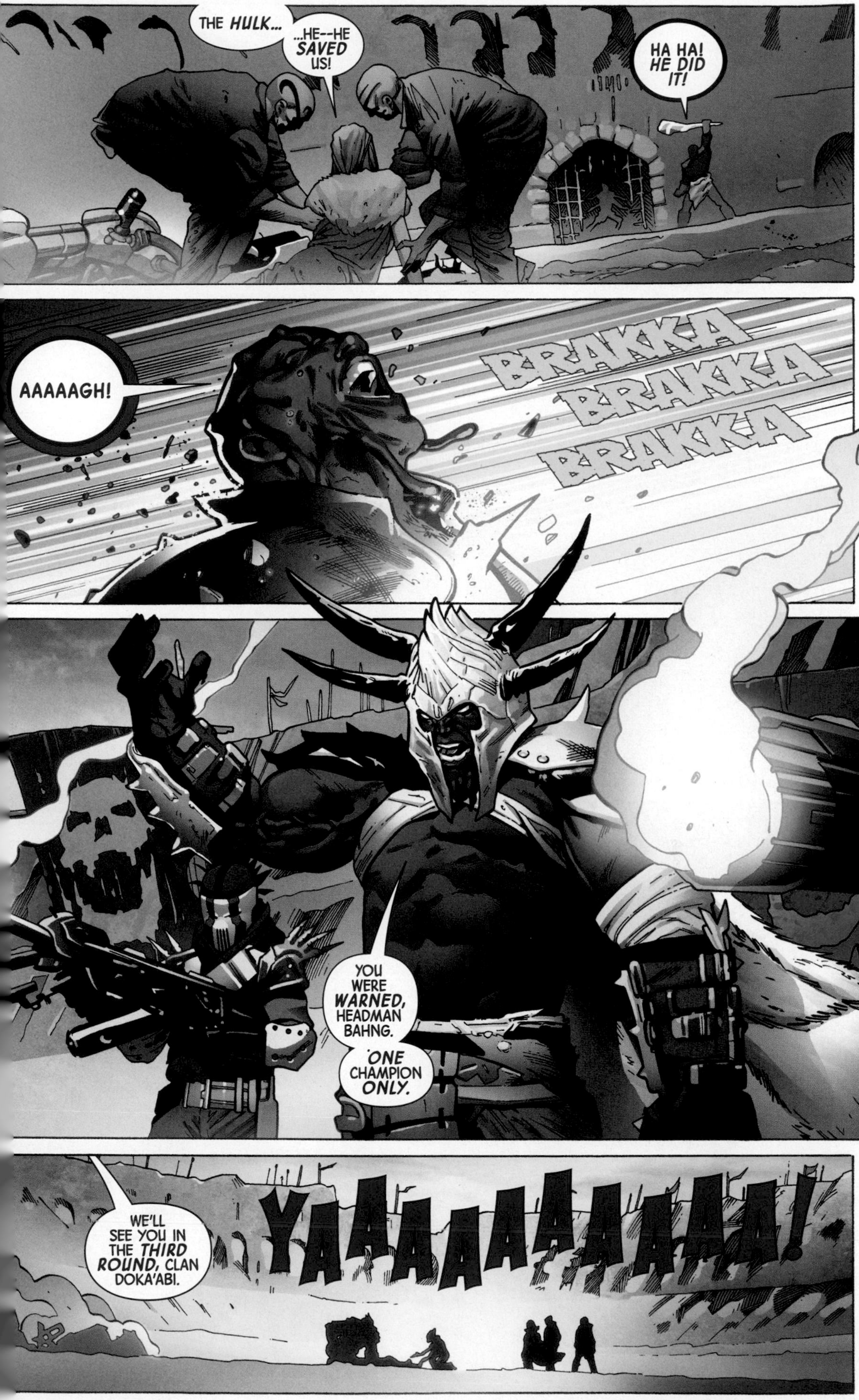
THE HULK...
...HE--HE SAVED US!
HA HA! HE DID IT!
AAAAAGH!
BRAKKA BRAKKA BRAKKA
YOU WERE WARNED, HEADMAN BAHNG.
ONE CHAMPION ONLY.
WE'LL SEE YOU IN THE THIRD ROUND, CLAN DOKA'ABI.
YAAAAAAAAAA!

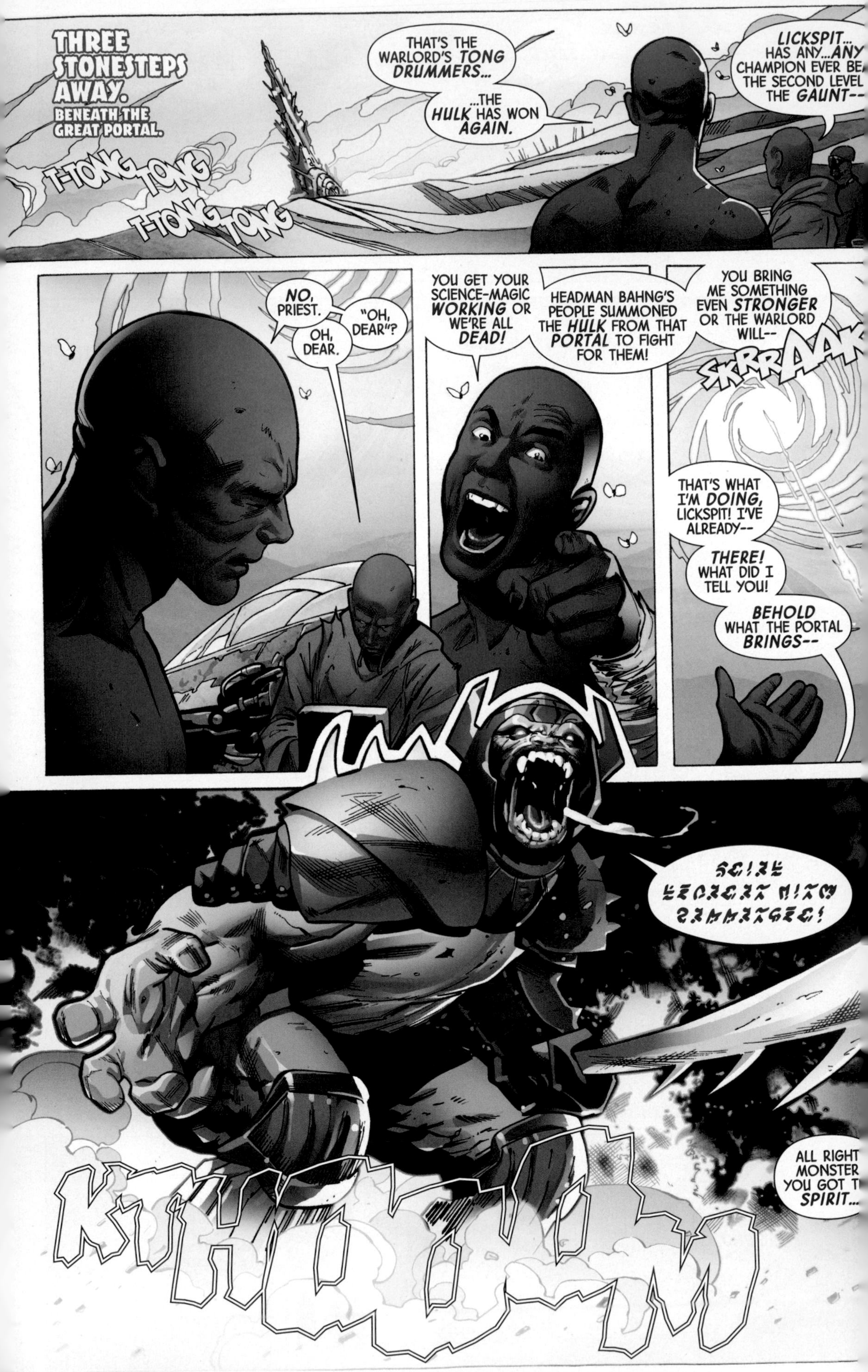
THREE STONESTEPS AWAY.
BENEATH THE GREAT PORTAL.
THAT'S THE WARLORD'S TONG DRUMMERS...
...THE HULK HAS WON AGAIN.
LICKSPIT... HAS ANY...ANY CHAMPION EVER BE THE SECOND LEVEL THE GAUNT--
T-TONG TONG T-TONG TONG
NO, PRIEST.
OH, DEAR.
"OH, DEAR"?
YOU GET YOUR SCIENCE-MAGIC WORKING OR WE'RE ALL DEAD!
HEADMAN BAHNG'S PEOPLE SUMMONED THE HULK FROM THAT PORTAL TO FIGHT FOR THEM!
YOU BRING ME SOMETHING EVEN STRONGER OR THE WARLORD WILL--
SKRRAAK
THAT'S WHAT I'M DOING, LICKSPIT! I'VE ALREADY--
THERE! WHAT DID I TELL YOU!
BEHOLD WHAT THE PORTAL BRINGS--
ALL RIGHT MONSTER YOU GOT T SPIRIT...
KTHOOOOM

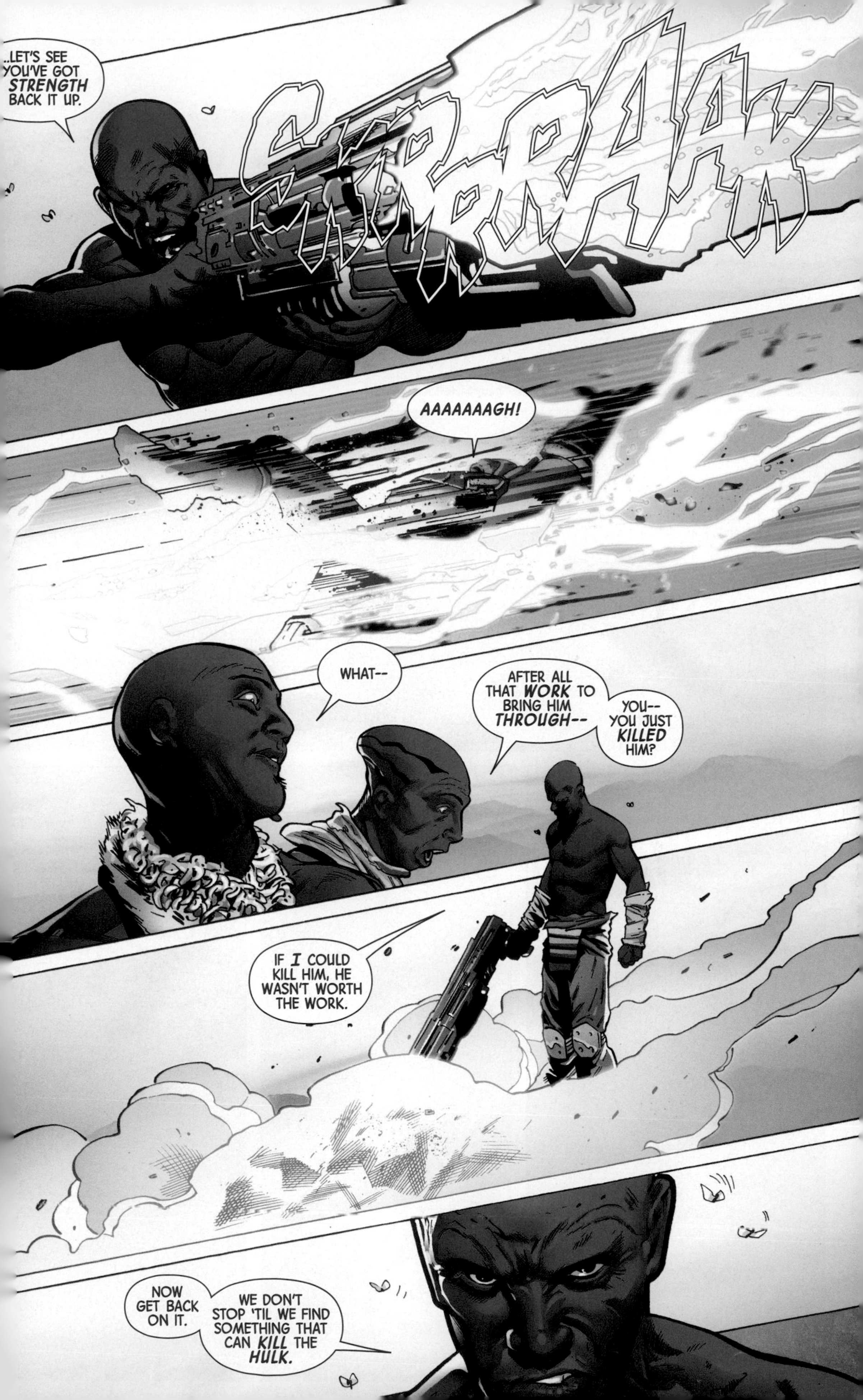
..LET'S SEE YOU'VE GOT STRENGTH BACK IT UP.
SKRRAAK
AAAAAAAGH!
WHAT--
AFTER ALL THAT WORK TO BRING HIM THROUGH--
YOU-- YOU JUST KILLED HIM?
IF I COULD KILL HIM, HE WASN'T WORTH THE WORK.
NOW GET BACK ON IT.
WE DON'T STOP 'TIL WE FIND SOMETHING THAT CAN KILL THE HULK.

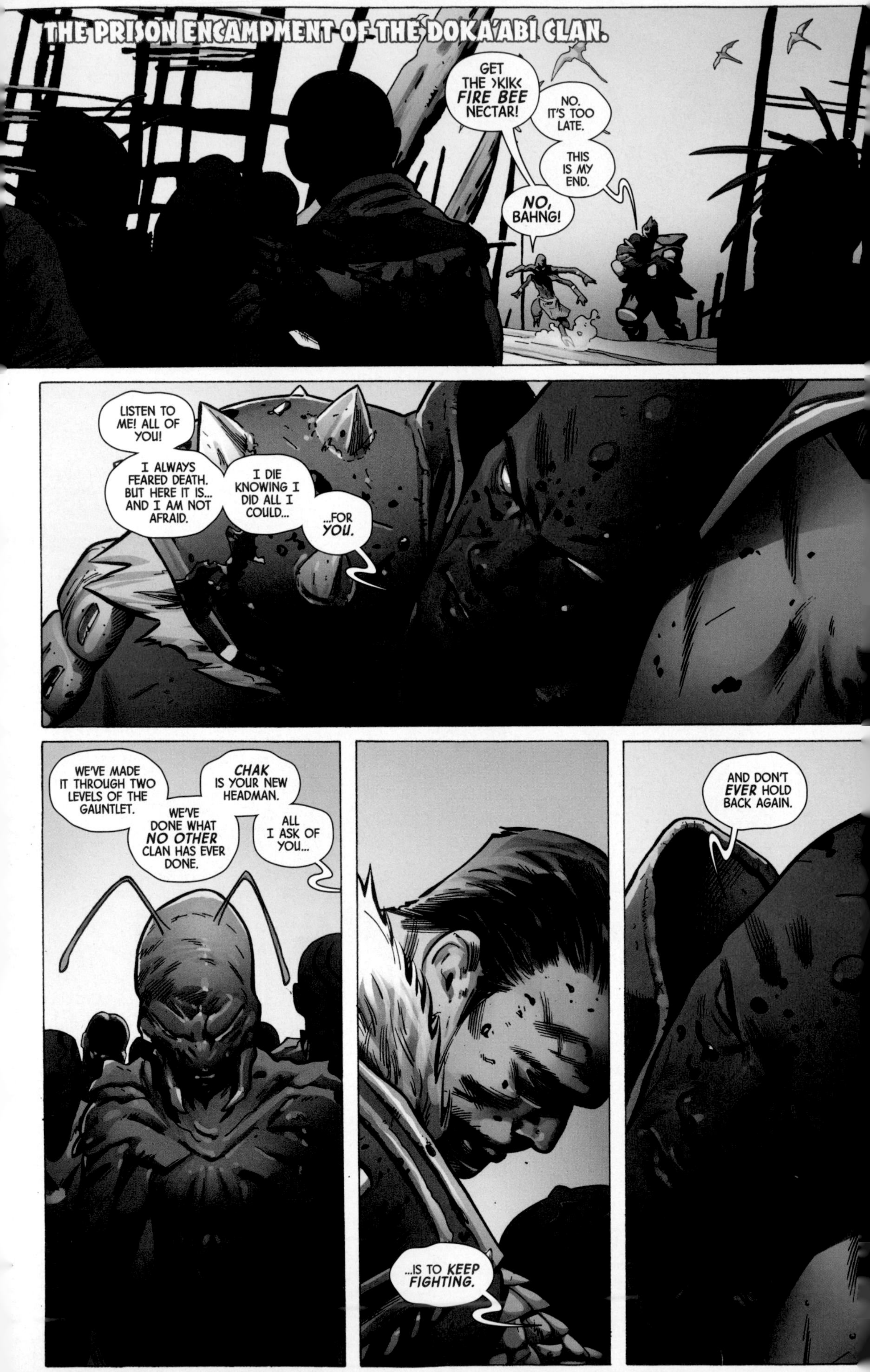
THE PRISON ENCAMPMENT OF THE DOKA'ABÍ CLAN.
GET THE >KIK< FIRE BEE NECTAR!
NO. IT'S TOO LATE.
THIS IS MY END.
NO, BAHNG!
LISTEN TO ME! ALL OF YOU!
I ALWAYS FEARED DEATH. BUT HERE IT IS... AND I AM NOT AFRAID.
I DIE KNOWING I DID ALL I COULD...
...FOR YOU.
WE'VE MADE IT THROUGH TWO LEVELS OF THE GAUNTLET.
WE'VE DONE WHAT NO OTHER CLAN HAS EVER DONE.
CHAK IS YOUR NEW HEADMAN.
ALL I ASK OF YOU...
...IS TO KEEP FIGHTING.
AND DON'T EVER HOLD BACK AGAIN.

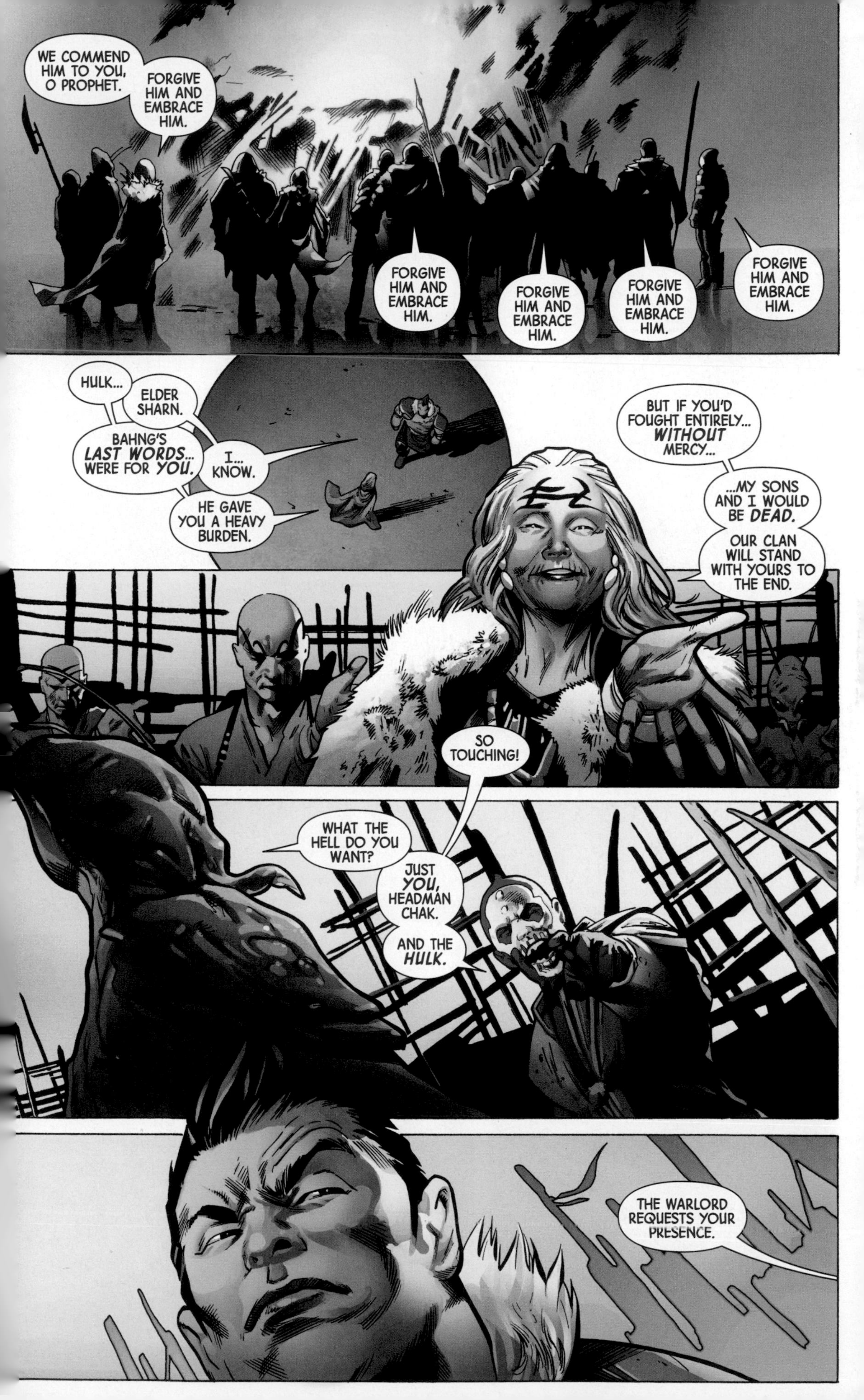
WE COMMEND HIM TO YOU, O PROPHET.
FORGIVE HIM AND EMBRACE HIM.
FORGIVE HIM AND EMBRACE HIM.
FORGIVE HIM AND EMBRACE HIM.
FORGIVE HIM AND EMBRACE HIM.
FORGIVE HIM AND EMBRACE HIM.
HULK...
ELDER SHARN.
BAHNG'S LAST WORDS... WERE FOR YOU.
I... KNOW.
HE GAVE YOU A HEAVY BURDEN.
BUT IF YOU'D FOUGHT ENTIRELY... WITHOUT MERCY...
...MY SONS AND I WOULD BE DEAD.
OUR CLAN WILL STAND WITH YOURS TO THE END.
SO TOUCHING!
WHAT THE HELL DO YOU WANT?
JUST YOU, HEADMAN CHAK.
AND THE HULK.
THE WARLORD REQUESTS YOUR PRESENCE.

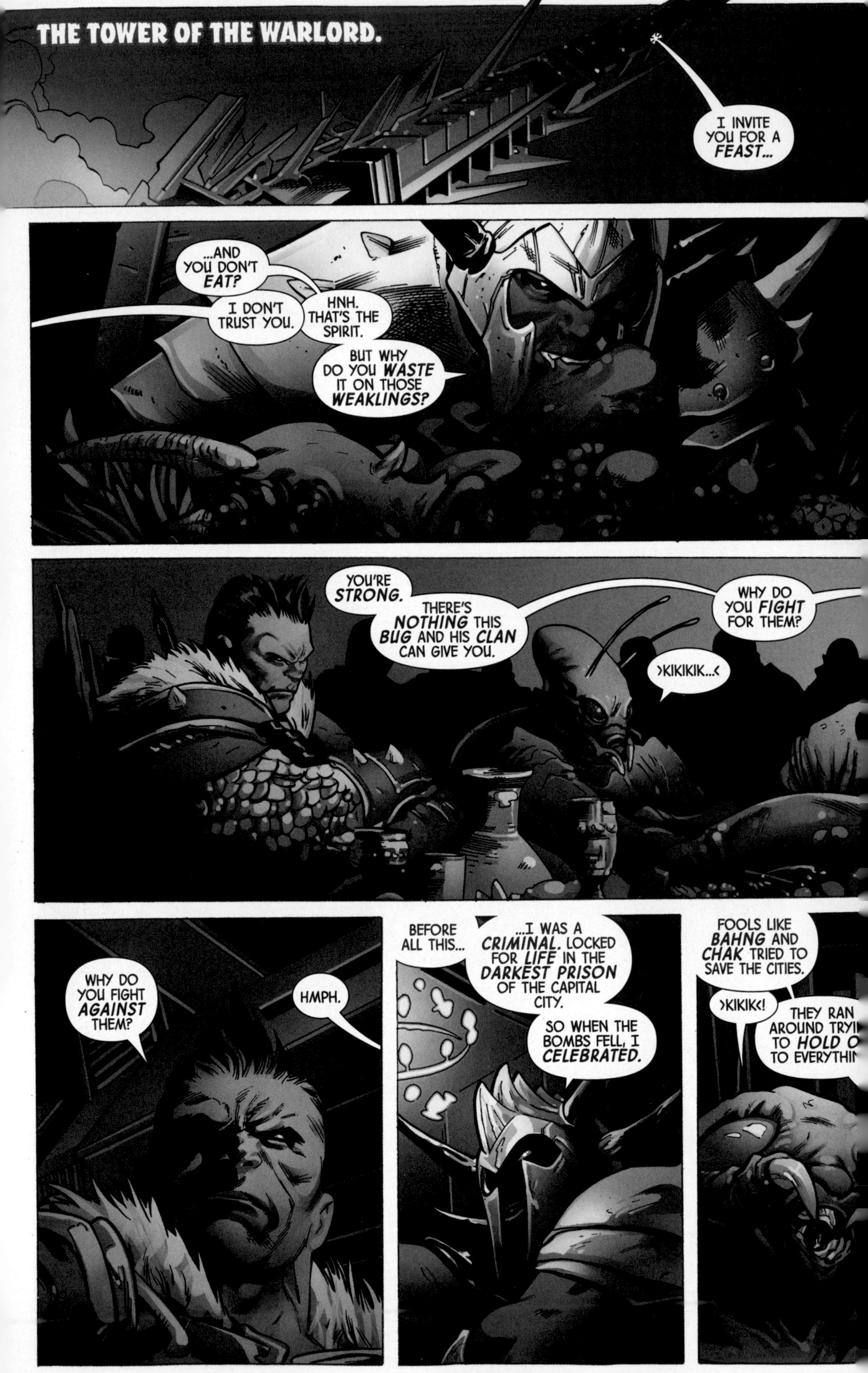
THE TOWER OF THE WARLORD.
I INVITE YOU FOR A FEAST...
...AND YOU DON'T EAT?
I DON'T TRUST YOU.
HNH. THAT'S THE SPIRIT.
BUT WHY DO YOU WASTE IT ON THOSE WEAKLINGS?
YOU'RE STRONG.
THERE'S NOTHING THIS BUG AND HIS CLAN CAN GIVE YOU.
WHY DO YOU FIGHT FOR THEM?
›KIKIKIK...‹
WHY DO YOU FIGHT AGAINST THEM?
HMPH.
BEFORE ALL THIS...
...I WAS A CRIMINAL. LOCKED FOR LIFE IN THE DARKEST PRISON OF THE CAPITAL CITY.
SO WHEN THE BOMBS FELL, I CELEBRATED.
FOOLS LIKE BAHNG AND CHAK TRIED TO SAVE THE CITIES.
›KIKIK‹!
THEY RAN AROUND TRYI TO HOLD O TO EVERYTHIN

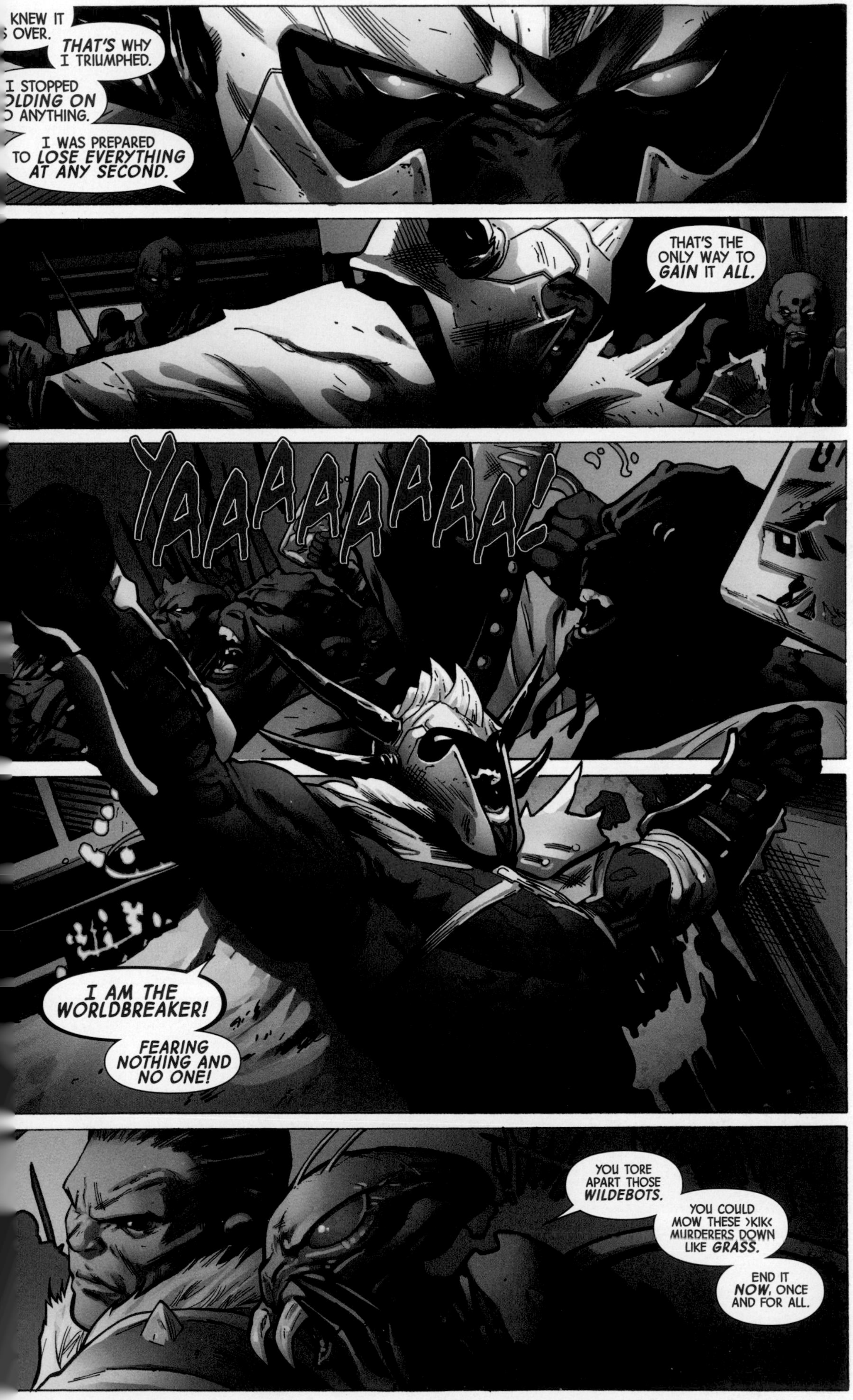

KNEW IT
S OVER.
THAT'S WHY I TRIUMPHED.
I STOPPED
OLDING ON
O ANYTHING.
I WAS PREPARED TO LOSE EVERYTHING AT ANY SECOND.
THAT'S THE ONLY WAY TO GAIN IT ALL.
YAAAAAAAA!
I AM THE WORLDBREAKER!
FEARING NOTHING AND NO ONE!
YOU TORE APART THOSE WILDEBOTS.
YOU COULD MOW THESE >KIK< MURDERERS DOWN LIKE GRASS.
END IT NOW, ONCE AND FOR ALL.

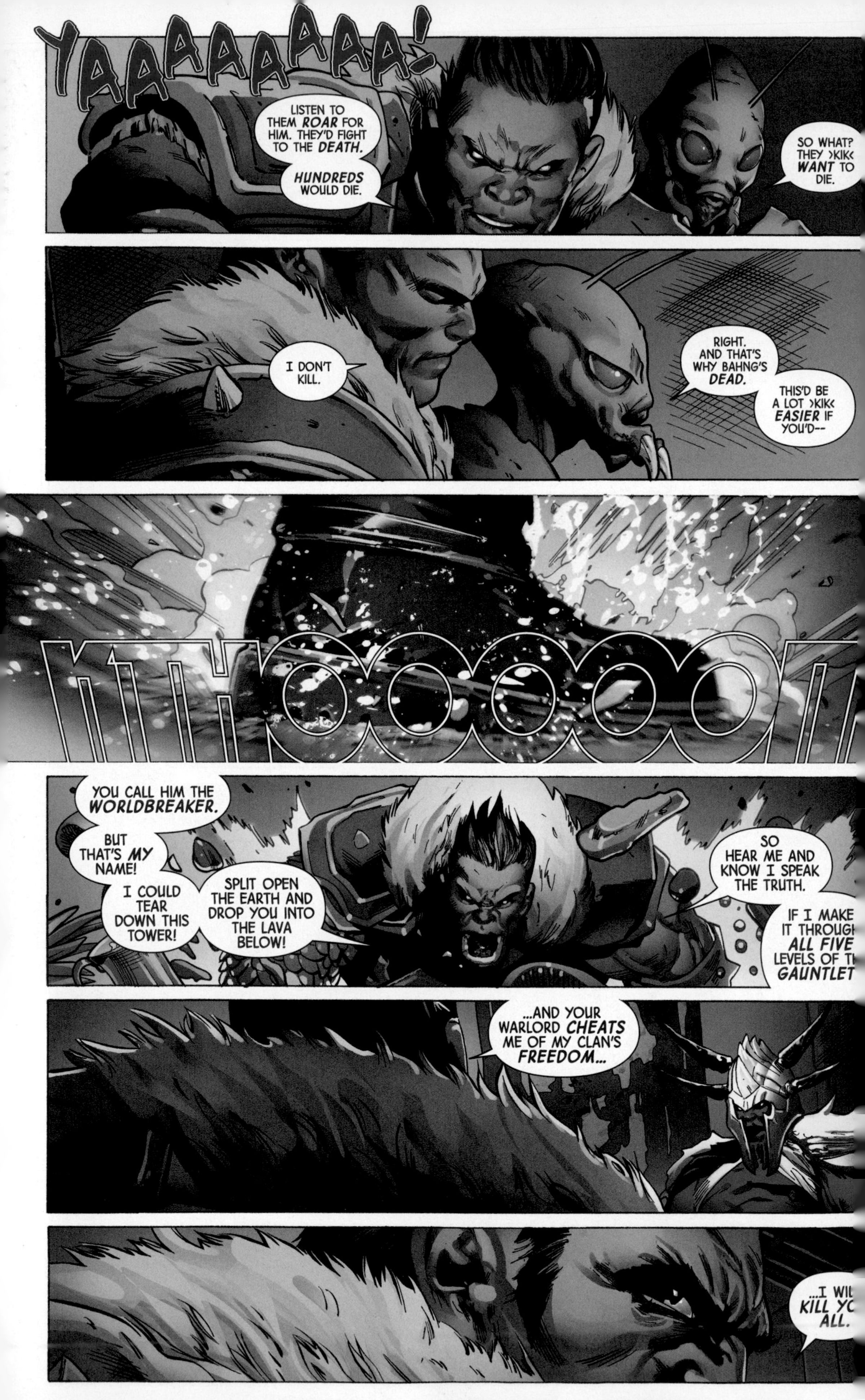
YAAAAAAAA!
LISTEN TO THEM ROAR FOR HIM. THEY'D FIGHT TO THE DEATH.
HUNDREDS WOULD DIE.
SO WHAT? THEY ›KIK‹ WANT TO DIE.
I DON'T KILL.
RIGHT. AND THAT'S WHY BAHNG'S DEAD.
THIS'D BE A LOT ›KIK‹ EASIER IF YOU'D--
YOU CALL HIM THE WORLDBREAKER.
BUT THAT'S MY NAME!
I COULD TEAR DOWN THIS TOWER!
SPLIT OPEN THE EARTH AND DROP YOU INTO THE LAVA BELOW!
SO HEAR ME AND KNOW I SPEAK THE TRUTH.
IF I MAKE IT THROUGH ALL FIVE LEVELS OF T GAUNTLET
...AND YOUR WARLORD CHEATS ME OF MY CLAN'S FREEDOM...
...I WIL KILL YO ALL.

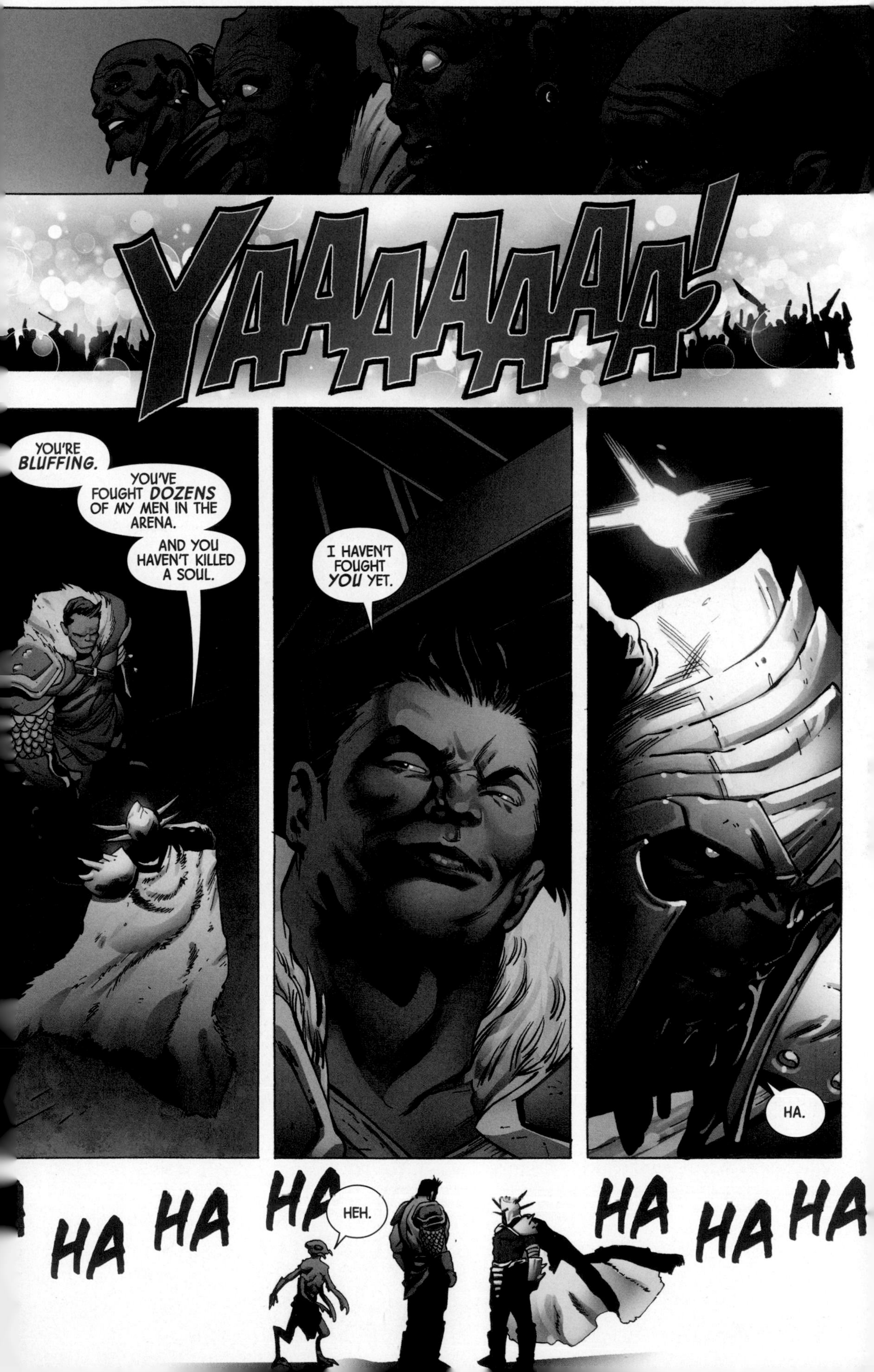
YAAAAAAA!
YOU'RE BLUFFING.
YOU'VE FOUGHT DOZENS OF MY MEN IN THE ARENA.
AND YOU HAVEN'T KILLED A SOUL.
I HAVEN'T FOUGHT YOU YET.
HA.
HA HA HA
HEH.
HA HA HA HA

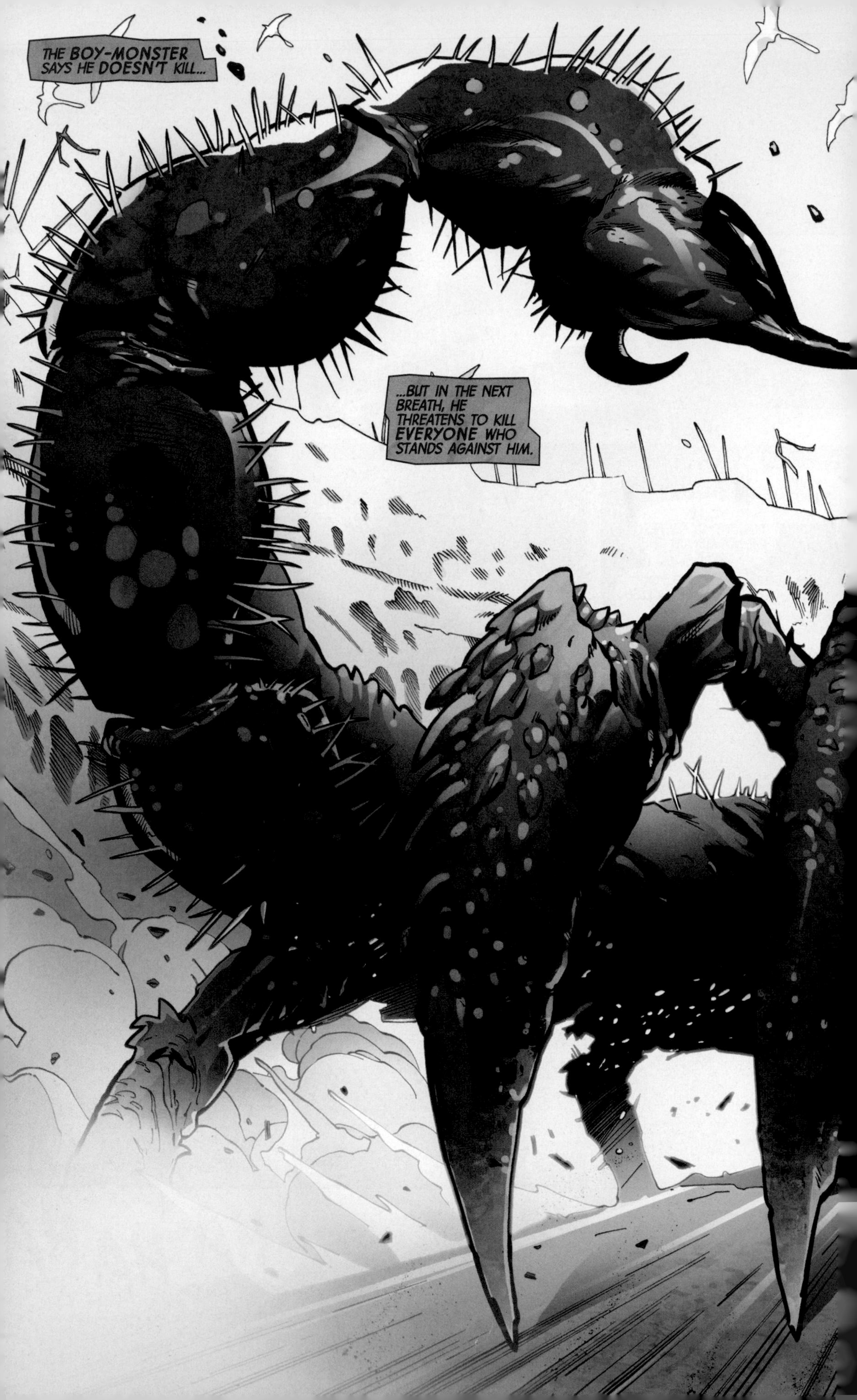
THE BOY-MONSTER SAYS HE DOESN'T KILL...
...BUT IN THE NEXT BREATH, HE THREATENS TO KILL EVERYONE WHO STANDS AGAINST HIM.

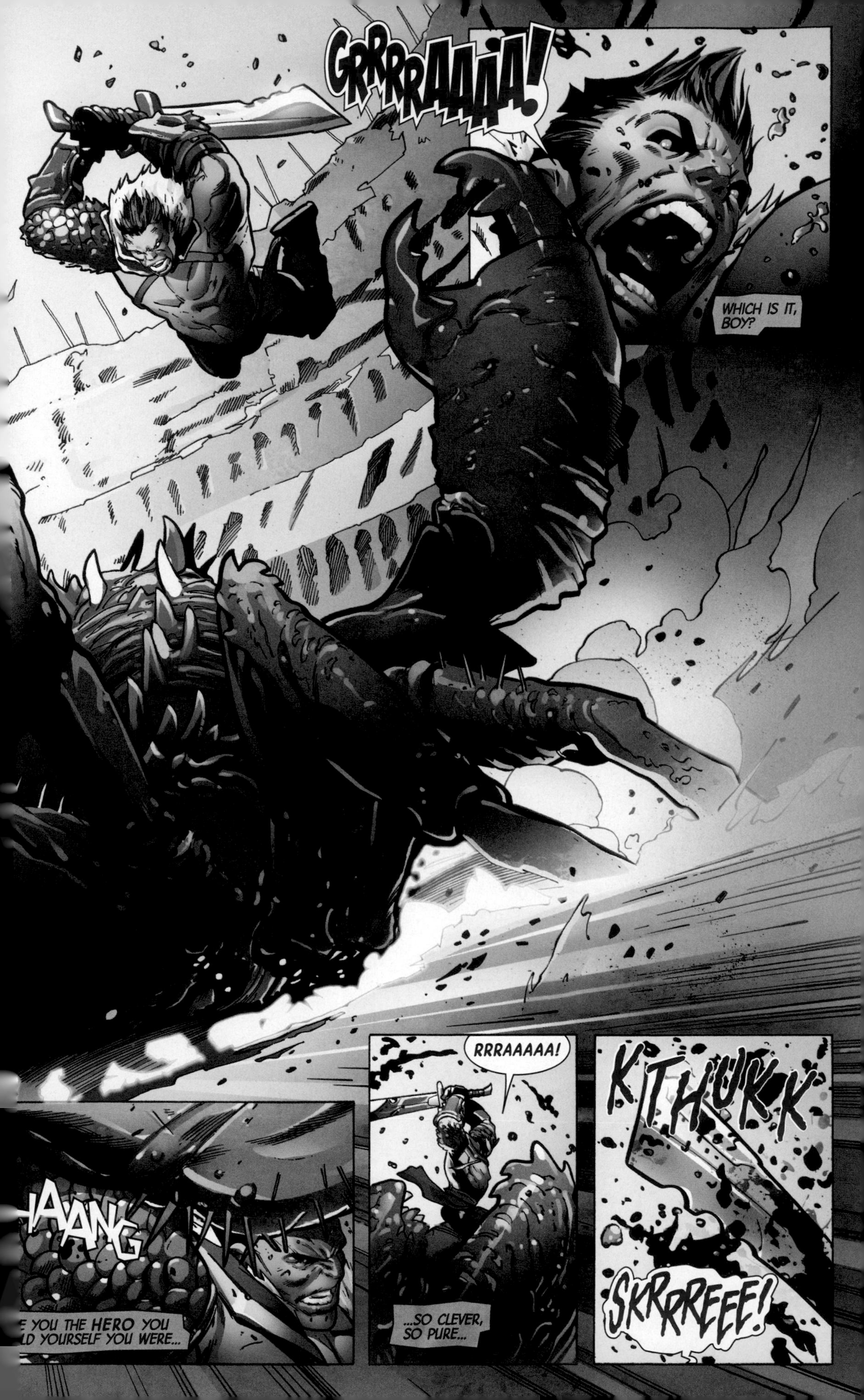
GRRRAAAAA!
WHICH IS IT, BOY?
HAANG
E YOU THE HERO YOU
LD YOURSELF YOU WERE...
RRRAAAAA!
...SO CLEVER, SO PURE...
KTHUKK
SKRRREEE!

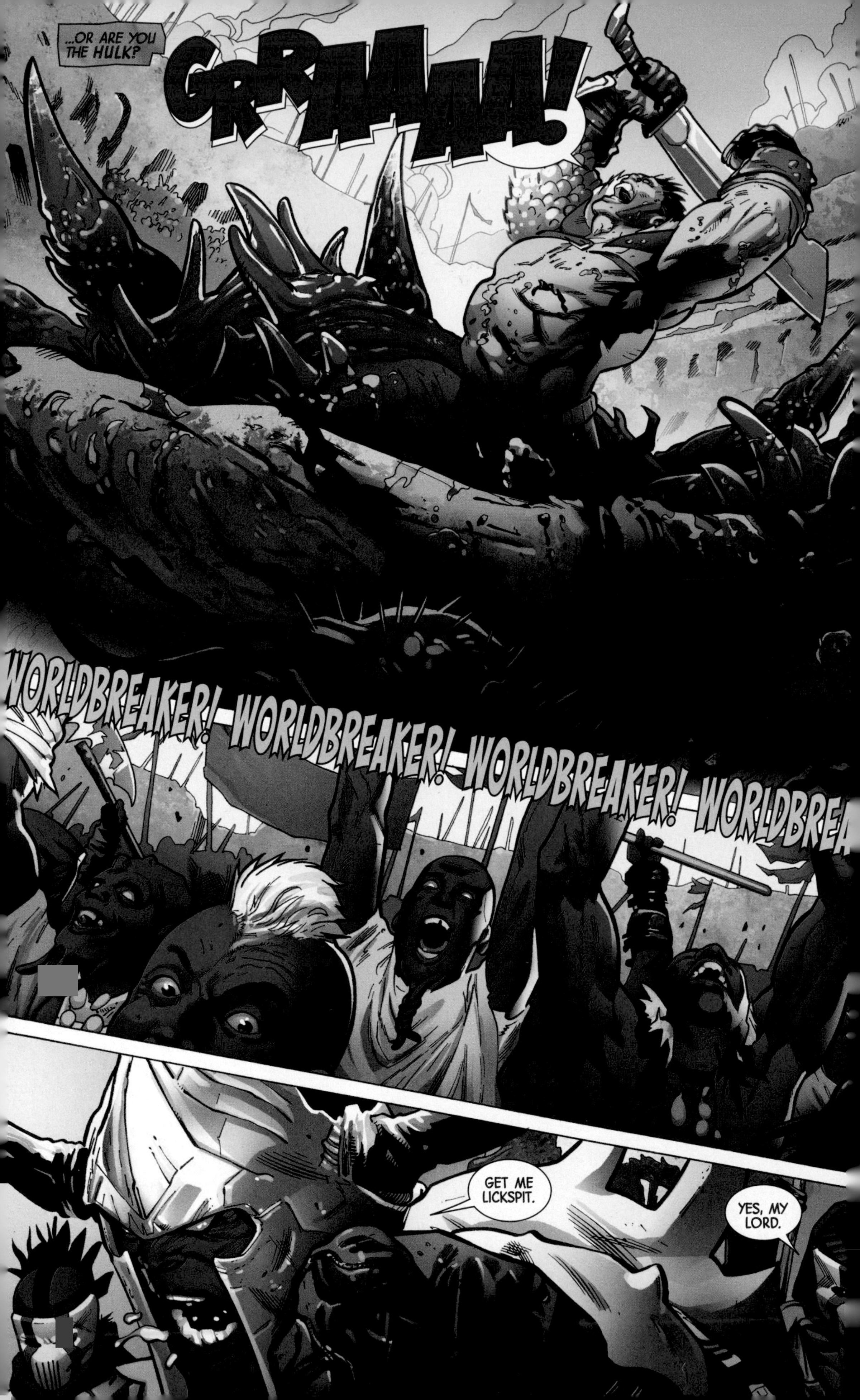
...OR ARE YOU THE HULK?
GRRAAAAA!
WORLDBREAKER! WORLDBREAKER! WORLDBREAKER! WORLDBREA
GET ME LICKSPIT.
YES, MY LORD.

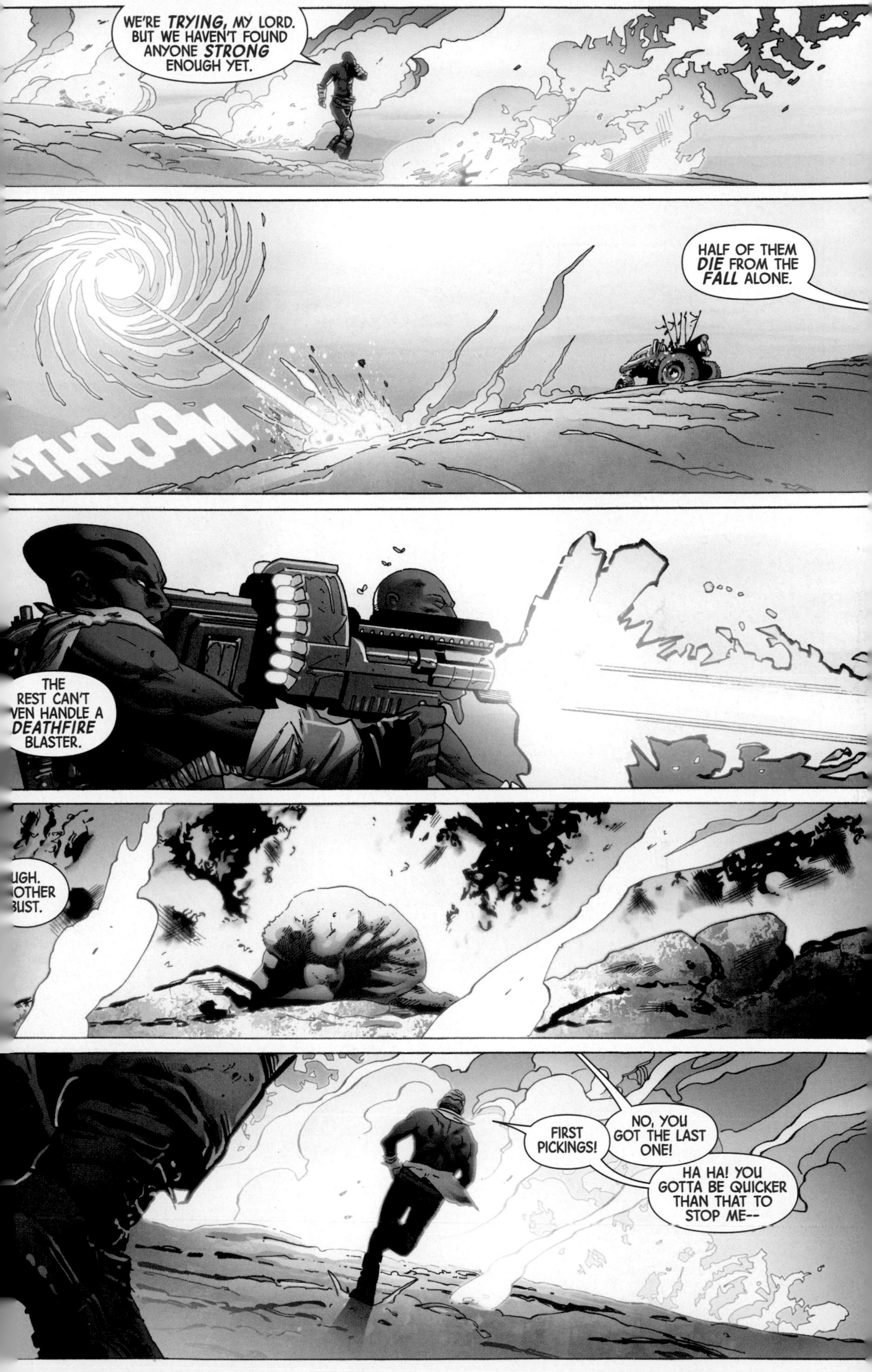
WE'RE TRYING, MY LORD. BUT WE HAVEN'T FOUND ANYONE STRONG ENOUGH YET.
HALF OF THEM DIE FROM THE FALL ALONE.
THOOOM
THE REST CAN'T VEN HANDLE A DEATHFIRE BLASTER.
UGH. OTHER BUST.
FIRST PICKINGS!
NO, YOU GOT THE LAST ONE!
HA HA! YOU GOTTA BE QUICKER THAN THAT TO STOP ME--

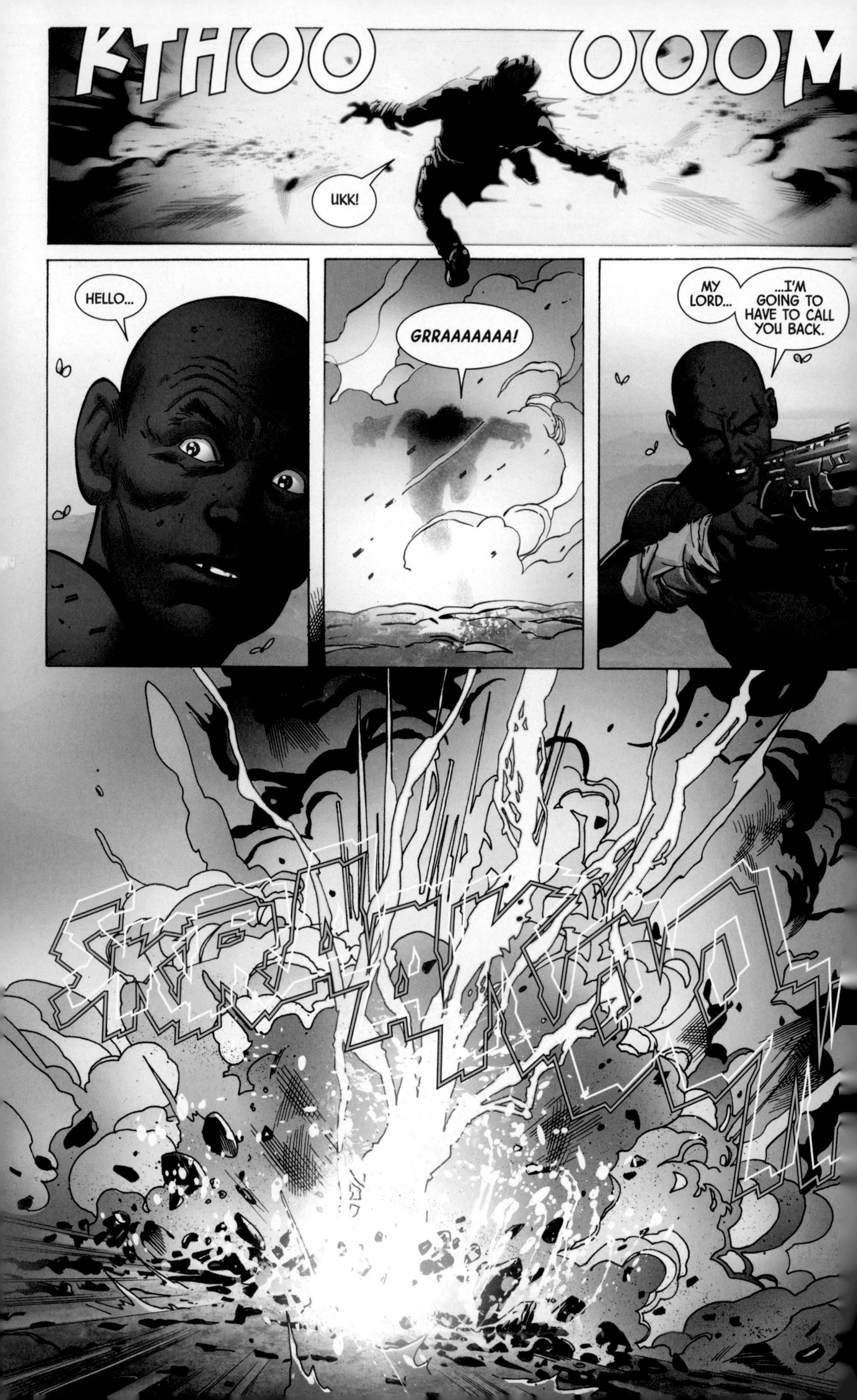
KTHOOOOOM
UKK!
HELLO...
GRRAAAAAAA!
MY LORD...
...I'M GOING TO HAVE TO CALL YOU BACK.

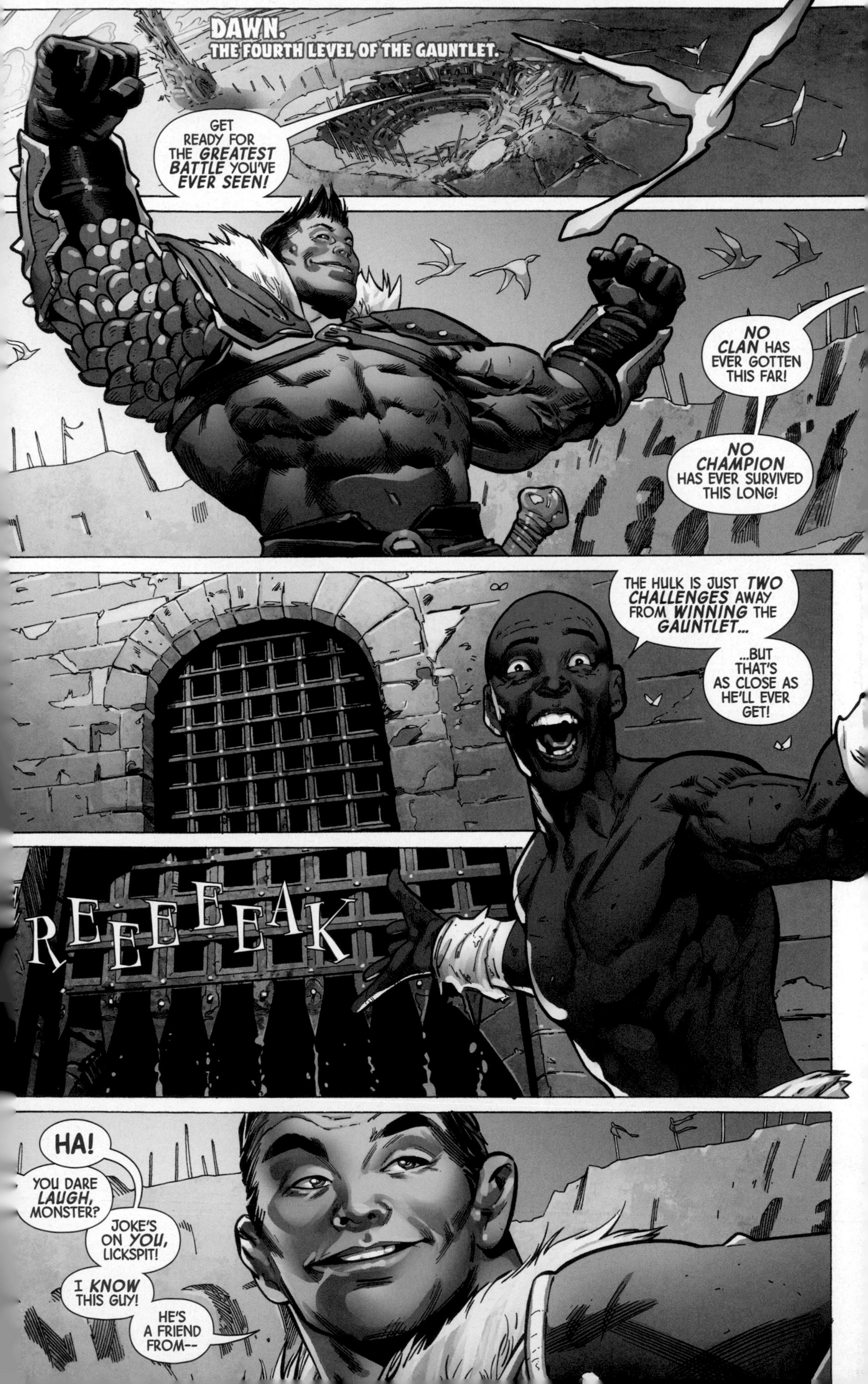
DAWN.
THE FOURTH LEVEL OF THE GAUNTLET.
GET READY FOR THE GREATEST BATTLE YOU'VE EVER SEEN!
NO CLAN HAS EVER GOTTEN THIS FAR!
NO CHAMPION HAS EVER SURVIVED THIS LONG!
THE HULK IS JUST TWO CHALLENGES AWAY FROM WINNING THE GAUNTLET...
...BUT THAT'S AS CLOSE AS HE'LL EVER GET!
REEEEAK
HA!
YOU DARE LAUGH, MONSTER?
JOKE'S ON YOU, LICKSPIT!
I KNOW THIS GUY!
HE'S A FRIEND FROM--

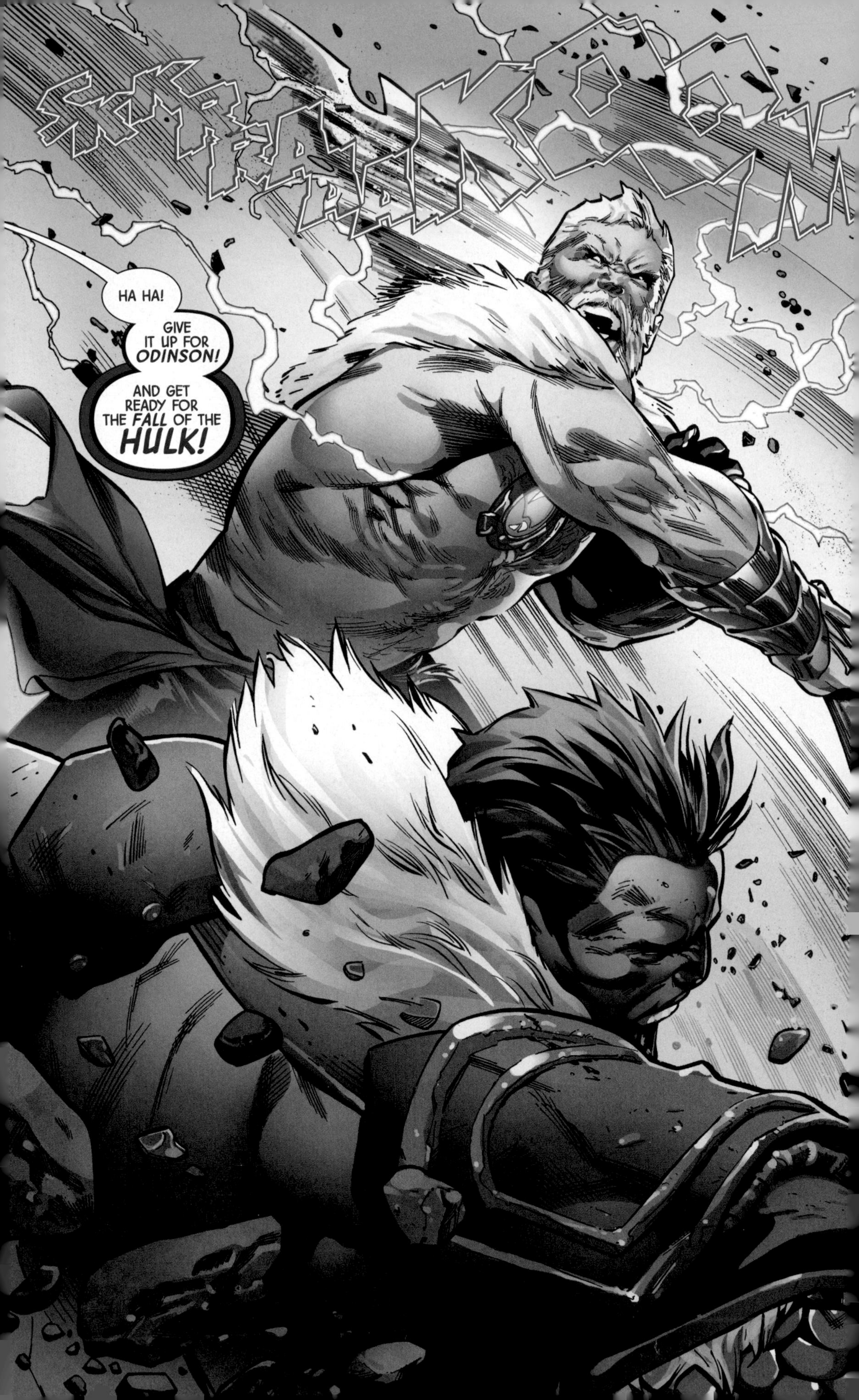
HA HA!
GIVE IT UP FOR ODINSON!
AND GET READY FOR THE FALL OF THE HULK!

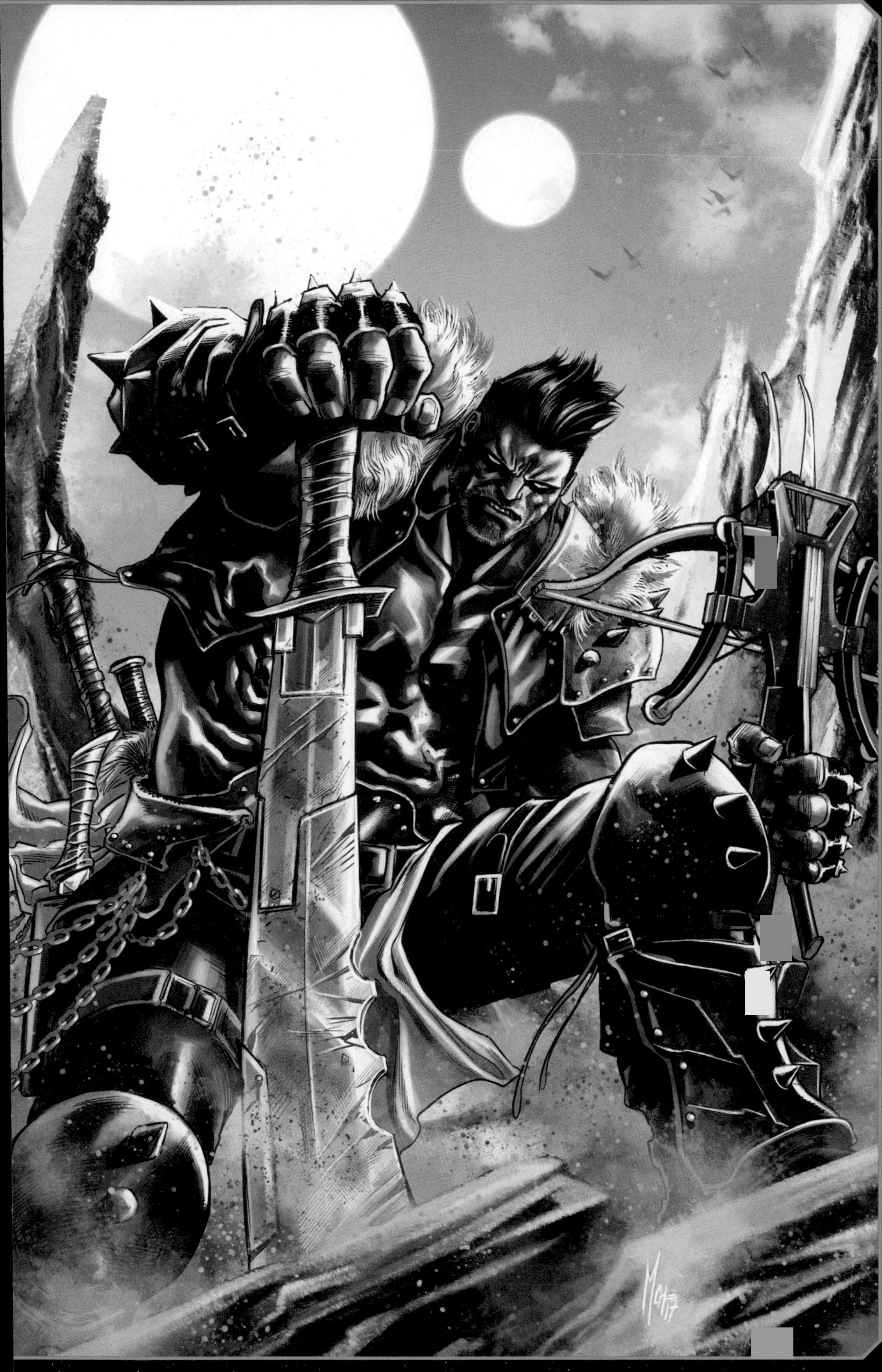

MARCO CHECCHETTO
#711 VARIANT

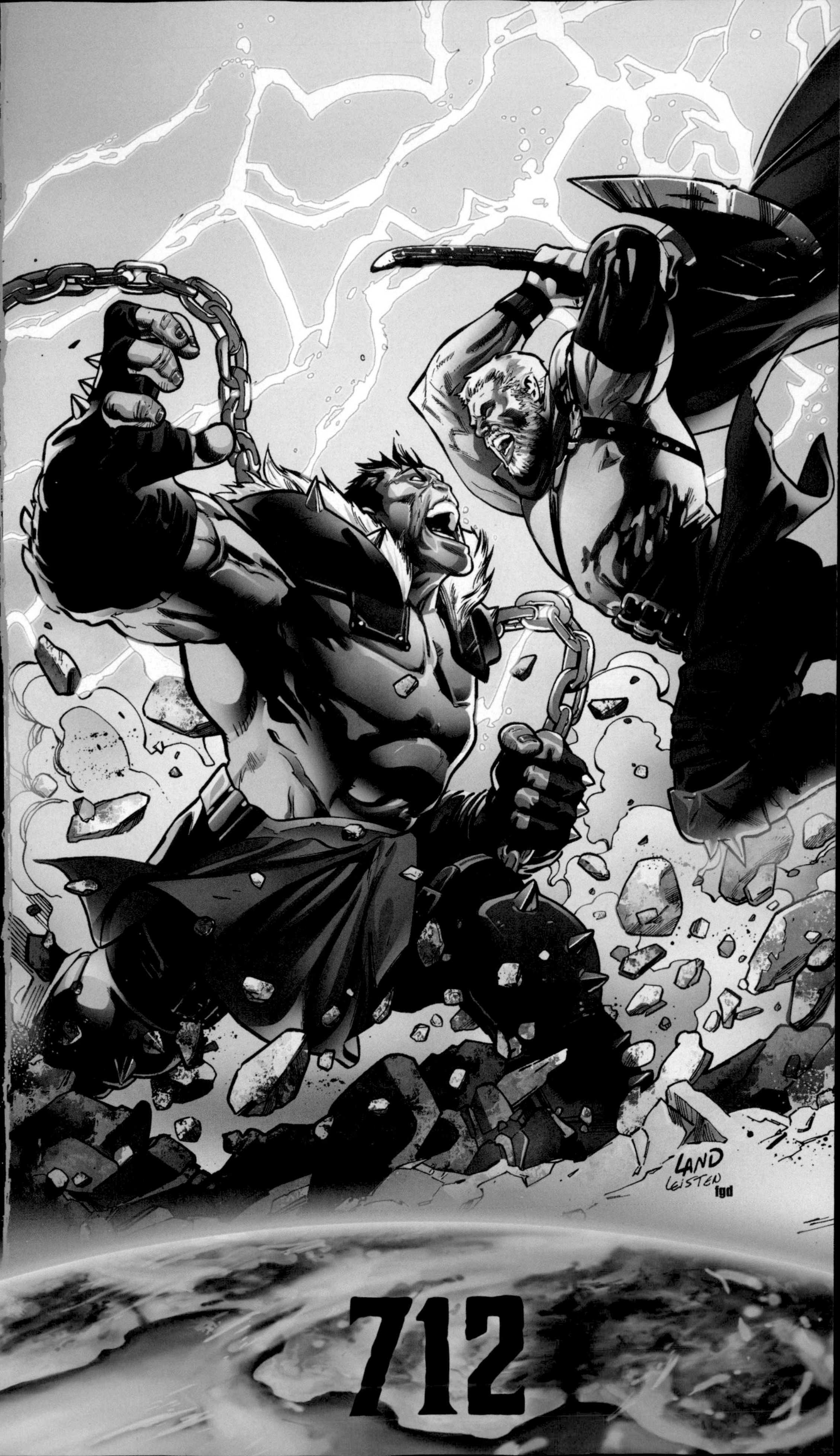
LAND
LEISTEN
fgd
712

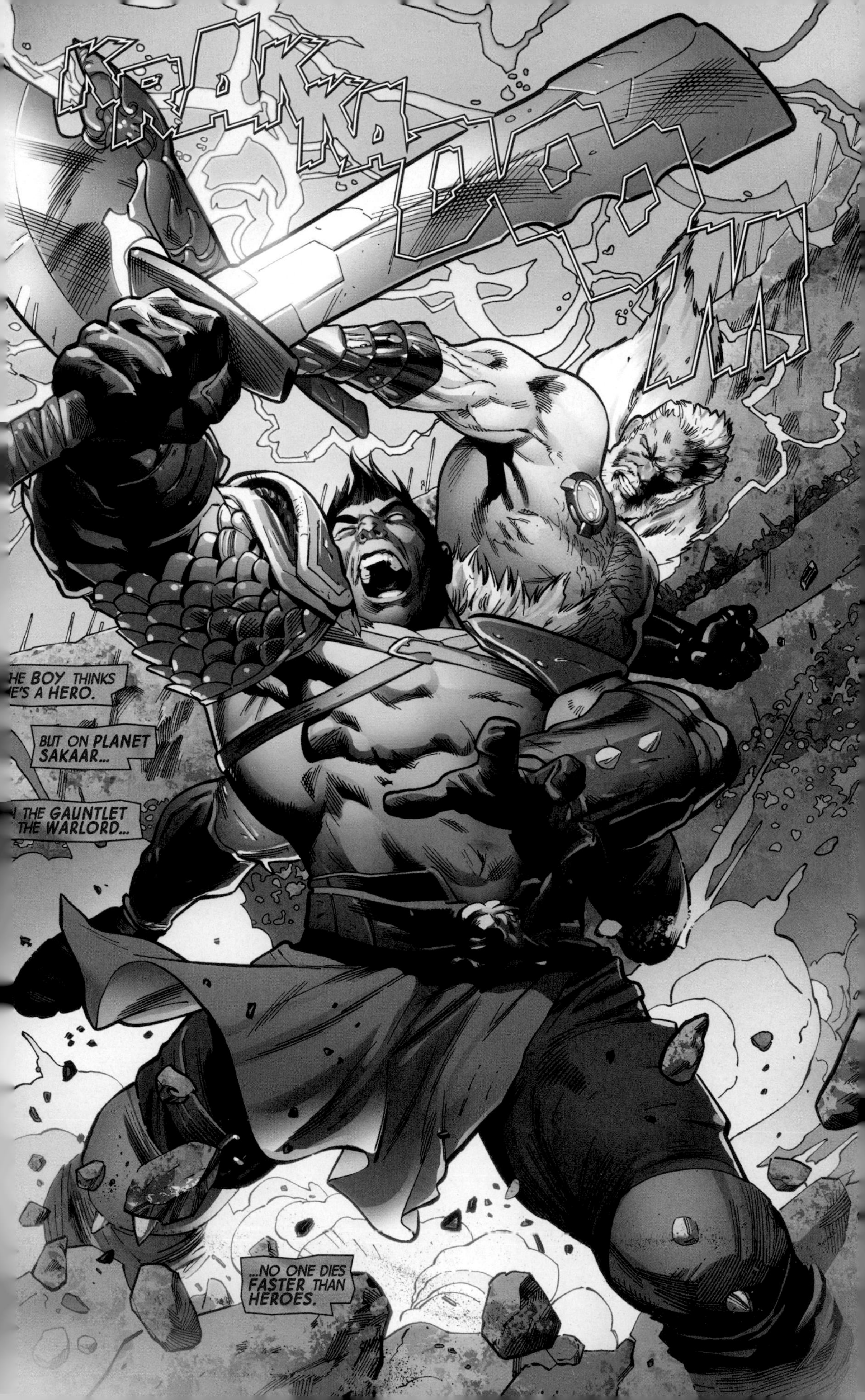
HE BOY THINKS
E'S A HERO.
BUT ON PLANET SAKAAR...
N THE GAUNTLET
THE WARLORD...
...NO ONE DIES FASTER THAN HEROES.

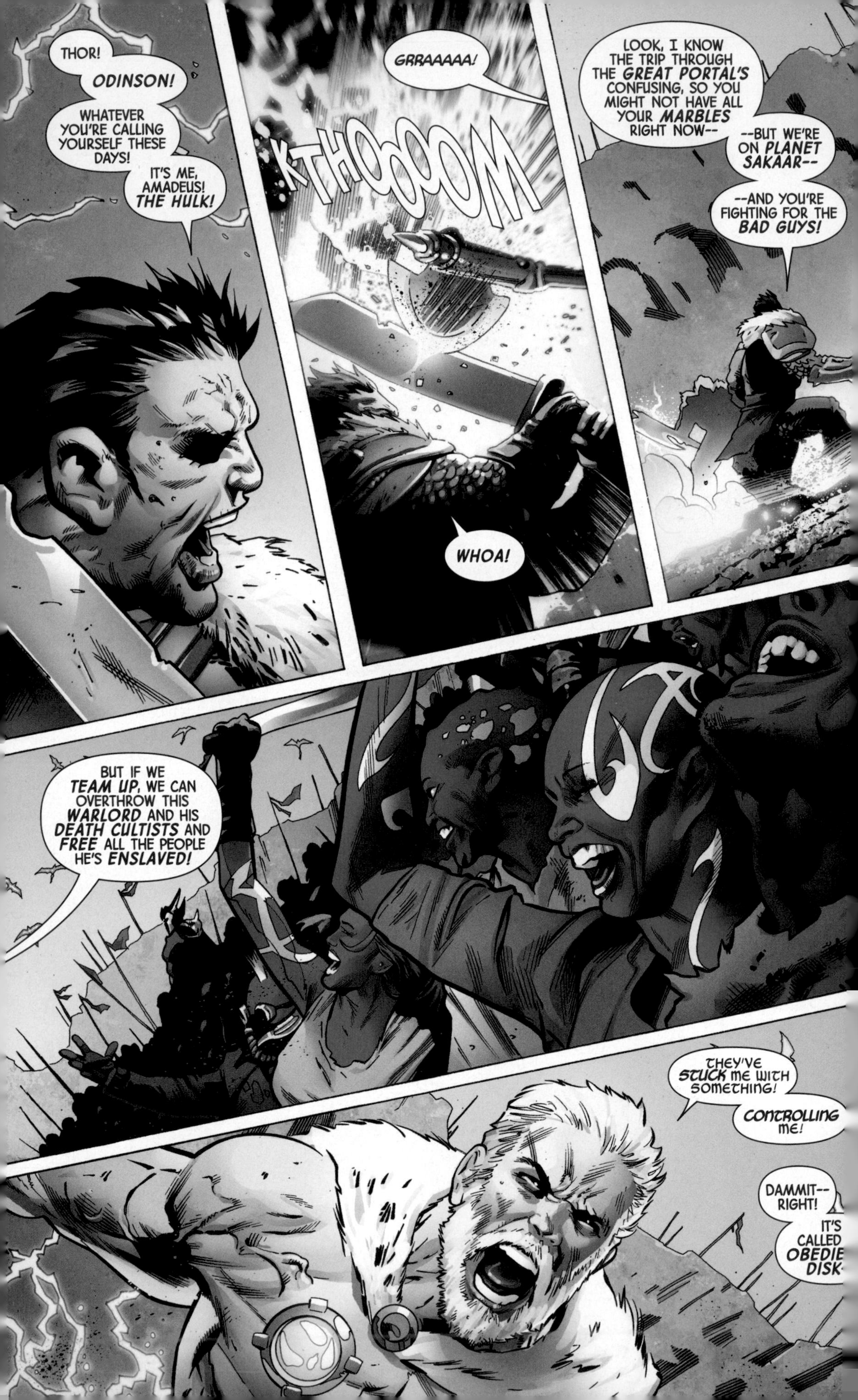
THOR!
ODINSON!
WHATEVER YOU'RE CALLING YOURSELF THESE DAYS!
IT'S ME, AMADEUS! THE HULK!
GRRAAAAA!
KTHOOOOM
WHOA!
LOOK, I KNOW THE TRIP THROUGH THE GREAT PORTAL'S CONFUSING, SO YOU MIGHT NOT HAVE ALL YOUR MARBLES RIGHT NOW--
--BUT WE'RE ON PLANET SAKAAR--
--AND YOU'RE FIGHTING FOR THE BAD GUYS!
BUT IF WE TEAM UP, WE CAN OVERTHROW THIS WARLORD AND HIS DEATH CULTISTS AND FREE ALL THE PEOPLE HE'S ENSLAVED!
THEY'VE STUCK ME WITH SOMETHING!
CONTROLLING ME!
DAMMIT-- RIGHT!
IT'S CALLED OBEDIE DISK

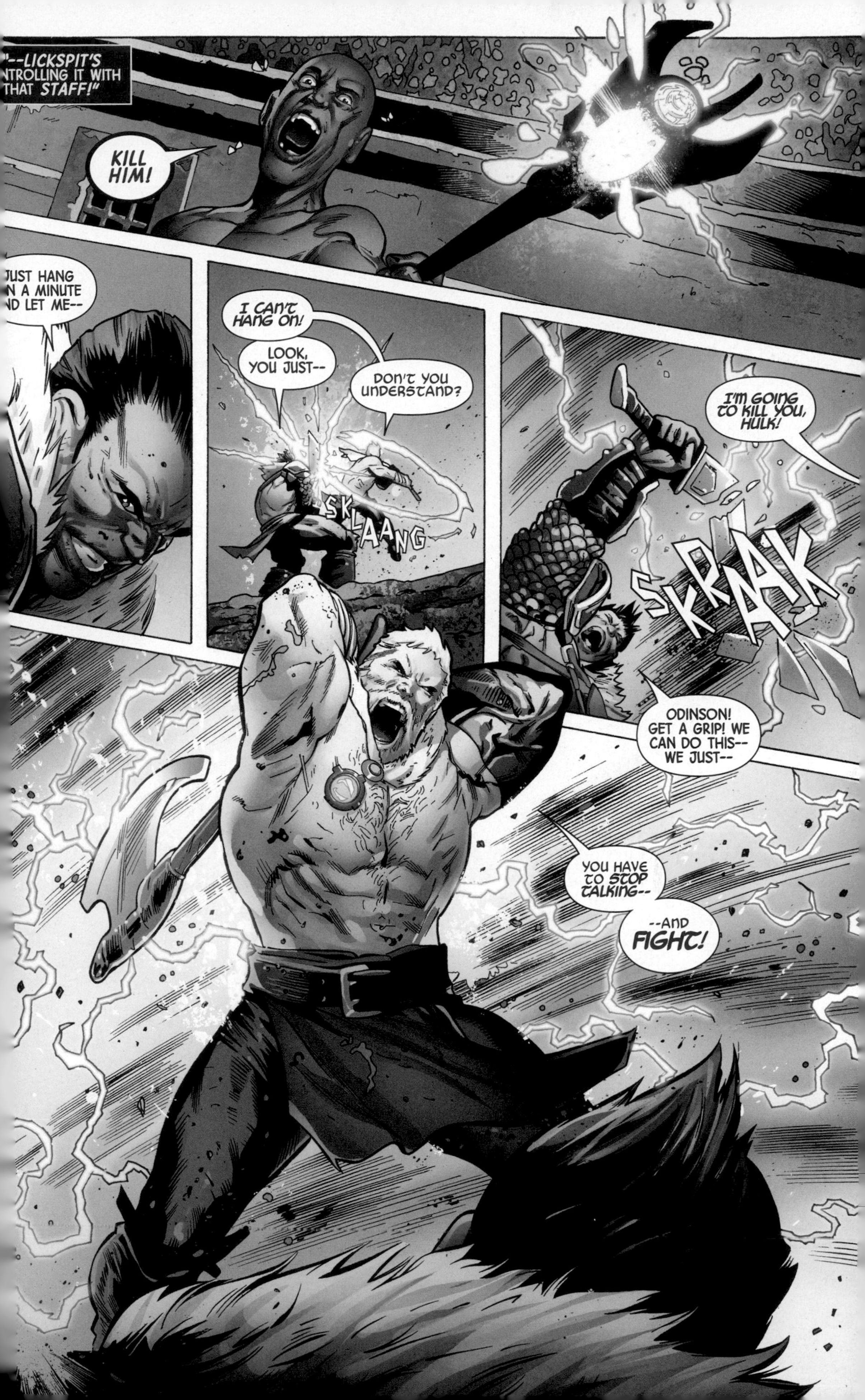
"--LICKSPIT'S
NTROLLING IT WITH
THAT STAFF!"
KILL HIM!
JUST HANG
N A MINUTE
ND LET ME--
I CAN'T HANG ON!
LOOK, YOU JUST--
DON'T YOU UNDERSTAND?
SKLAANG
I'M GOING TO KILL YOU, HULK!
SKRAAK
ODINSON! GET A GRIP! WE CAN DO THIS-- WE JUST--
YOU HAVE TO STOP TALKING--
--AND FIGHT!

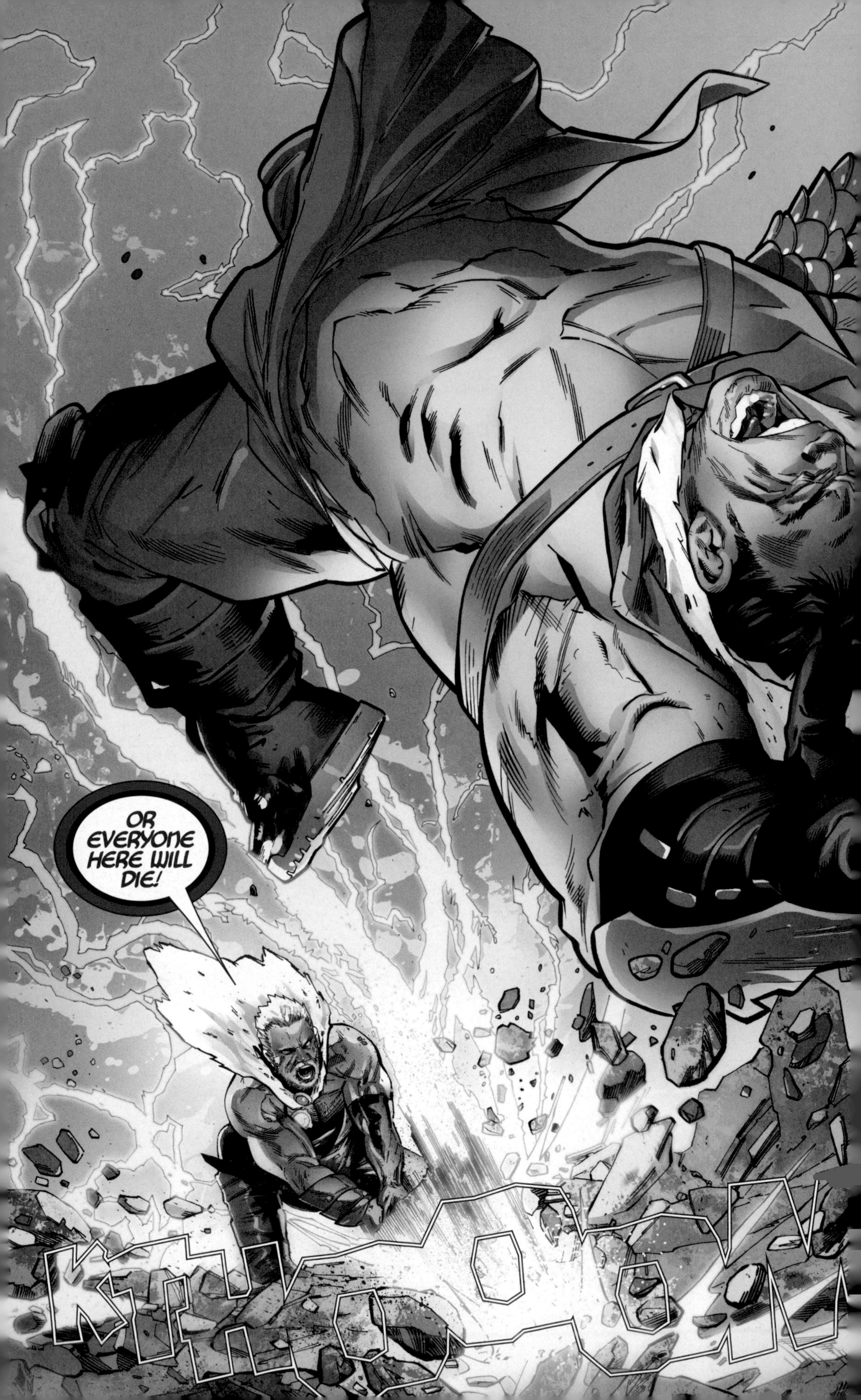
OR EVERYONE HERE WILL DIE!

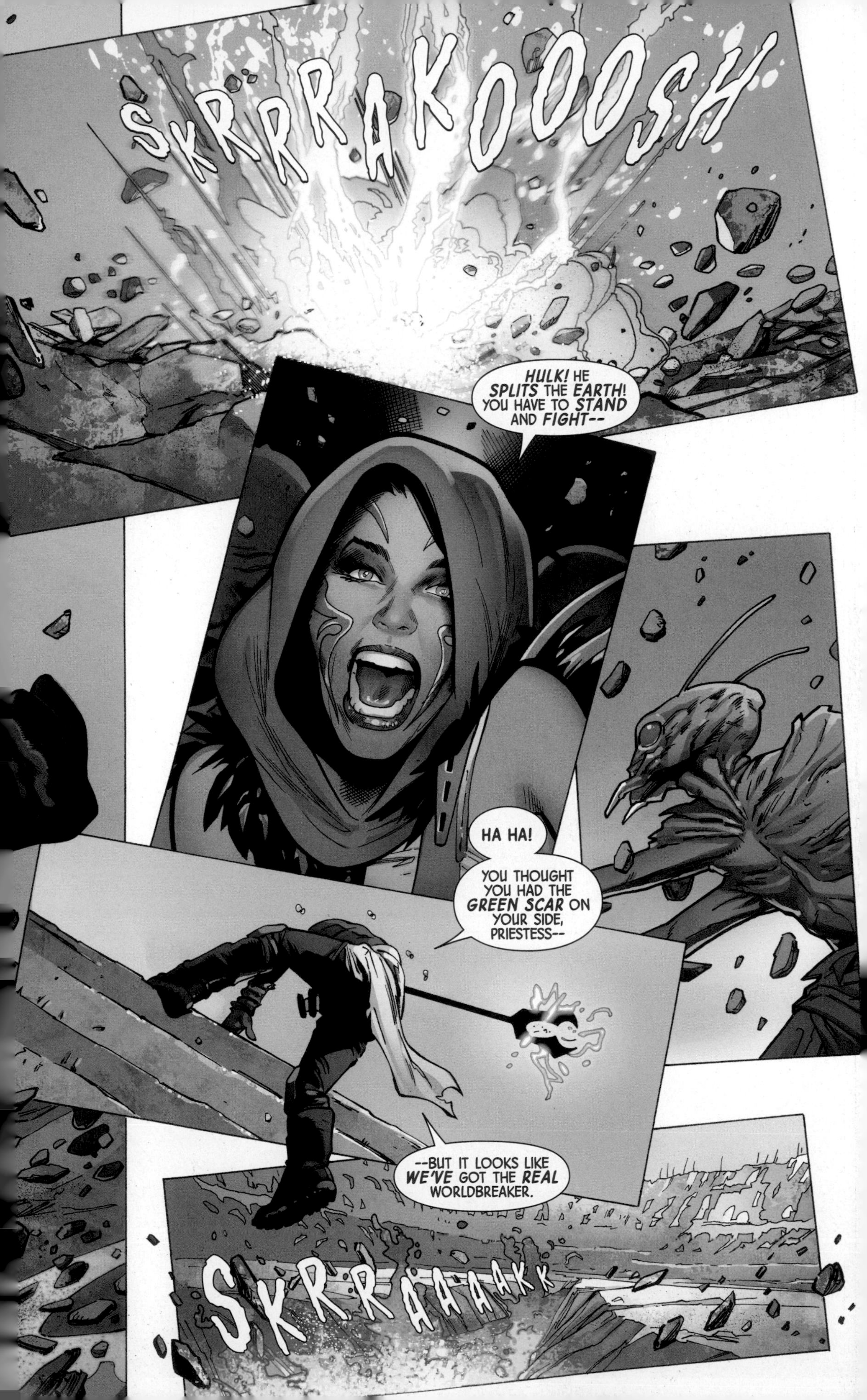
SKRRRAKOOOSH
HULK! HE SPLITS THE EARTH! YOU HAVE TO STAND AND FIGHT--
HA HA!
YOU THOUGHT YOU HAD THE GREEN SCAR ON YOUR SIDE, PRIESTESS--
--BUT IT LOOKS LIKE WE'VE GOT THE REAL WORLDBREAKER.
SKRRAAAAKK

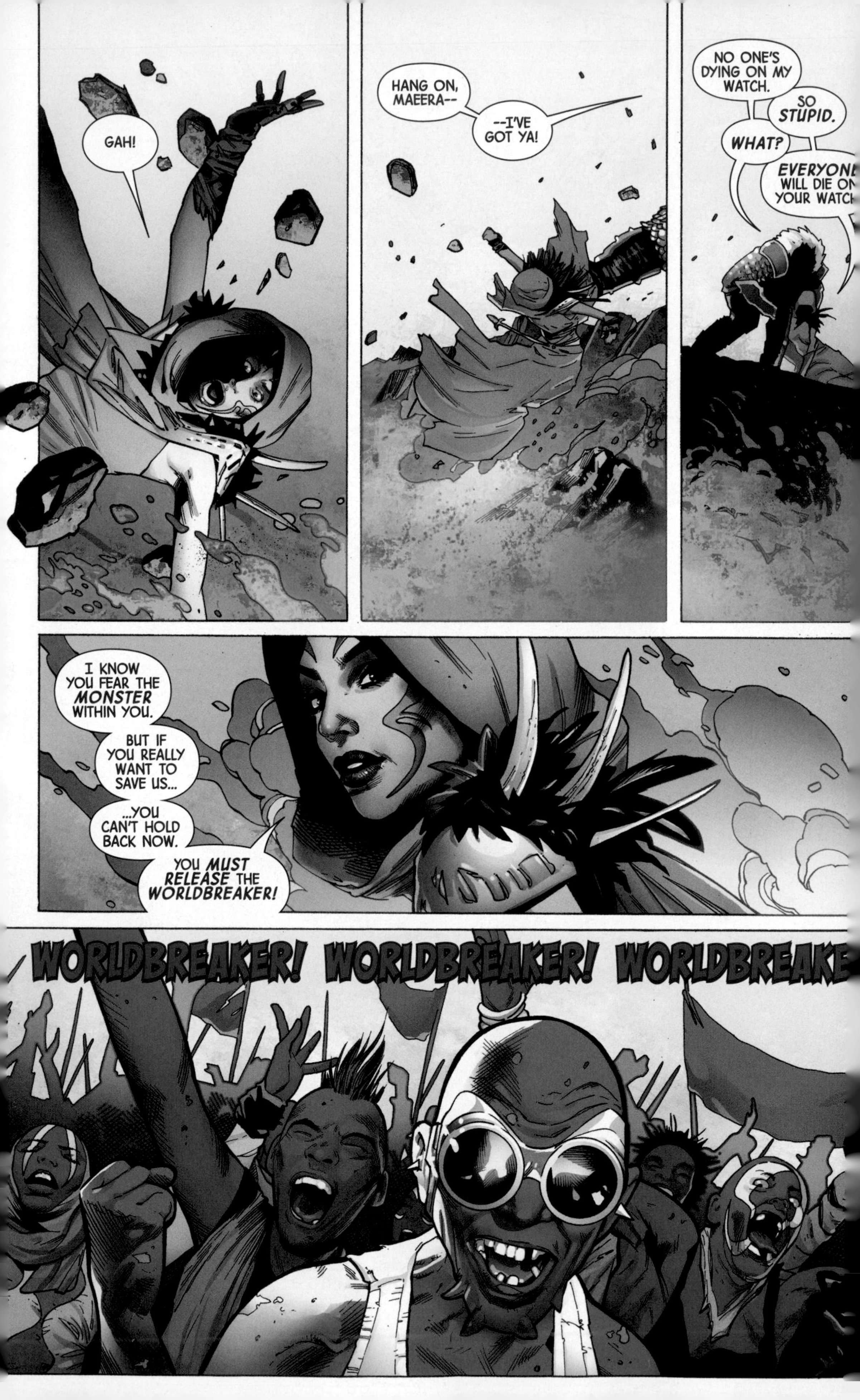
GAH!
HANG ON, MAEERA--
--I'VE GOT YA!
NO ONE'S DYING ON MY WATCH.
SO STUPID.
WHAT?
EVERYONE WILL DIE ON YOUR WATCH
I KNOW YOU FEAR THE MONSTER WITHIN YOU.
BUT IF YOU REALLY WANT TO SAVE US...
...YOU CAN'T HOLD BACK NOW.
YOU MUST RELEASE THE WORLDBREAKER!
WORLDBREAKER! WORLDBREAKER! WORLDBREAKE

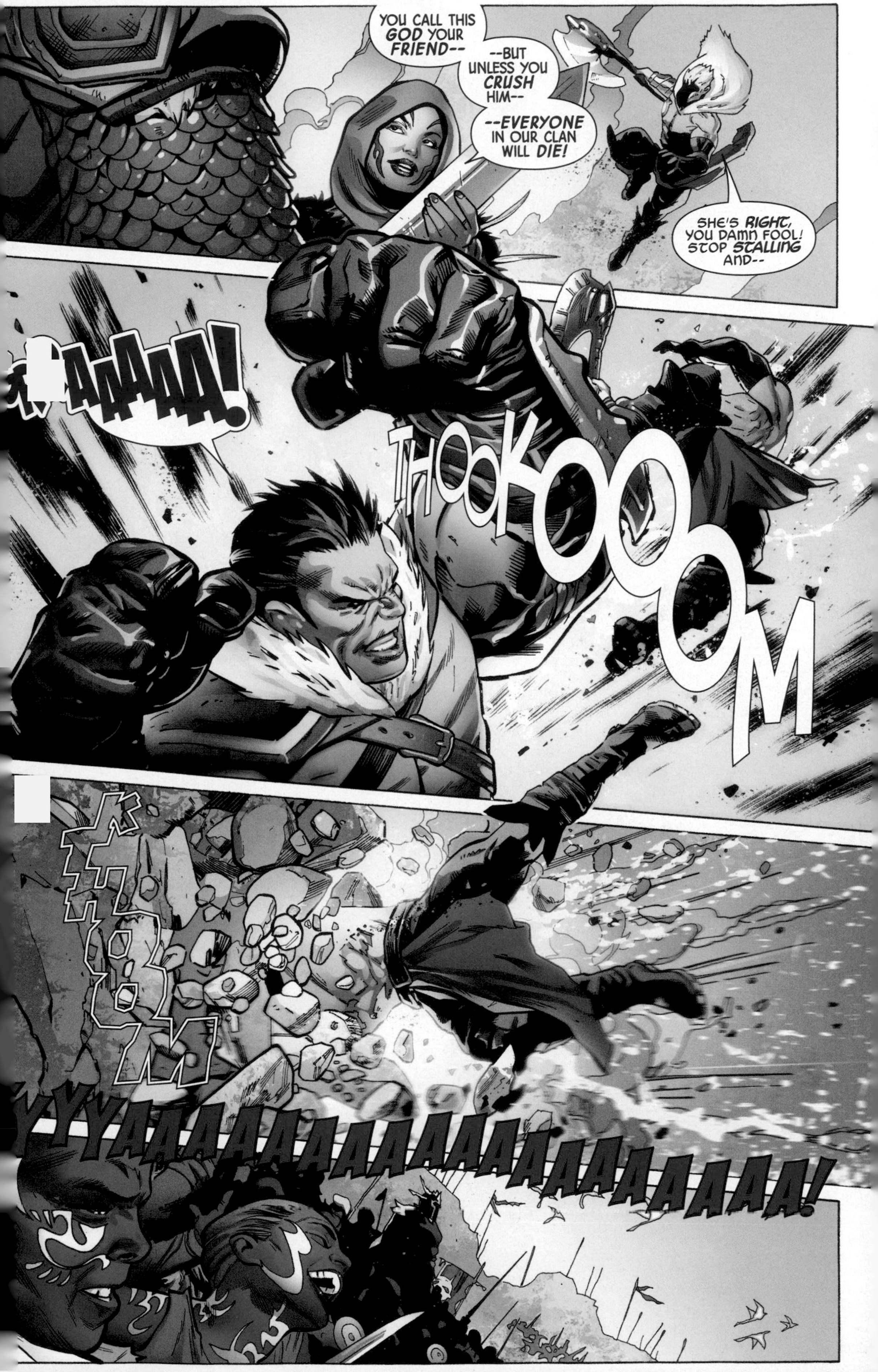
YOU CALL THIS GOD YOUR FRIEND--
--BUT UNLESS YOU CRUSH HIM--
--EVERYONE IN OUR CLAN WILL DIE!
SHE'S RIGHT, YOU DAMN FOOL! STOP STALLING AND--
AAAAAA!
THOOKOOOOOM
YYAAAAAAAAAAAAAAAAAAA!

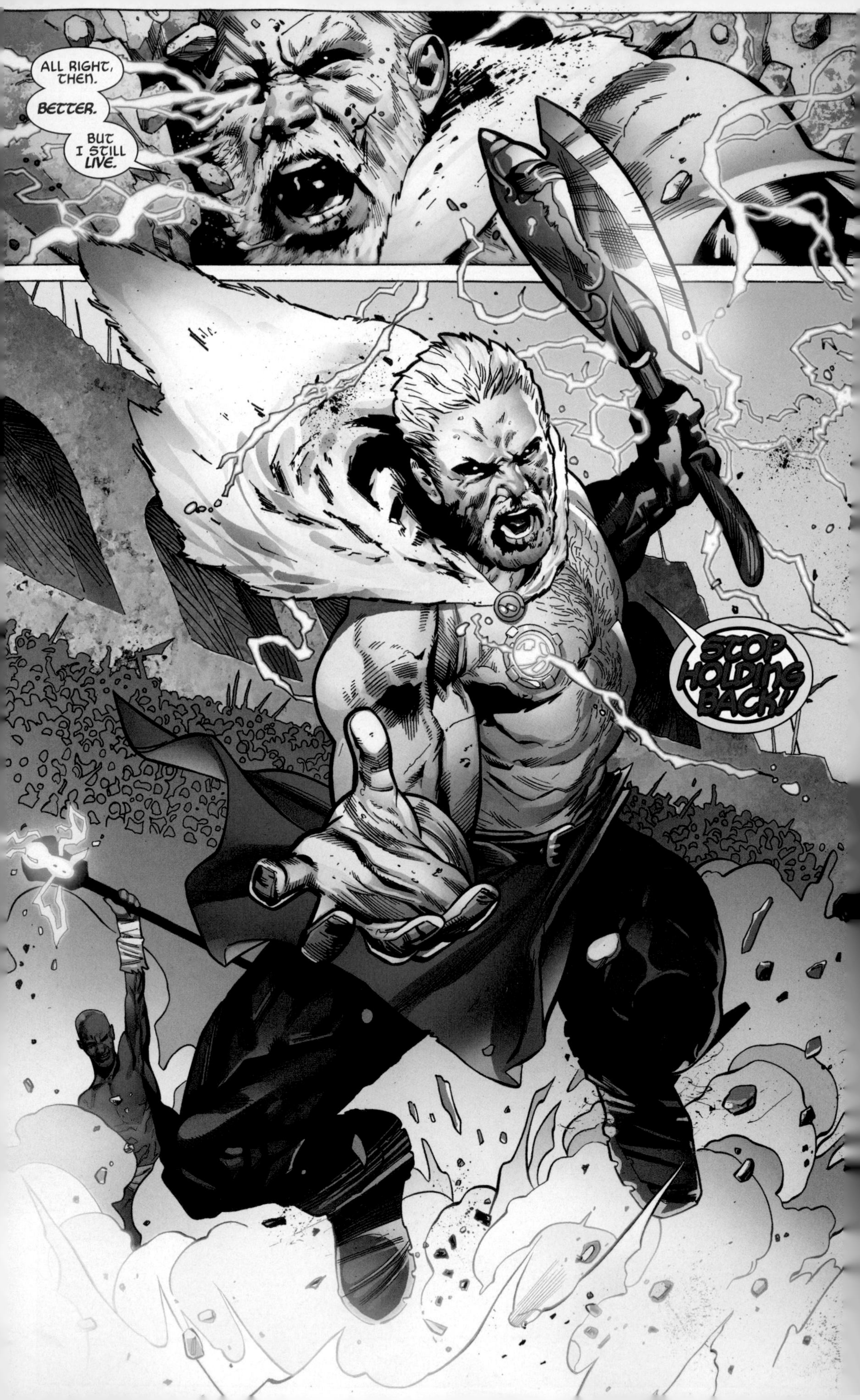
ALL RIGHT, THEN.
BETTER.
BUT I STILL LIVE.
STOP HOLDING BACK!

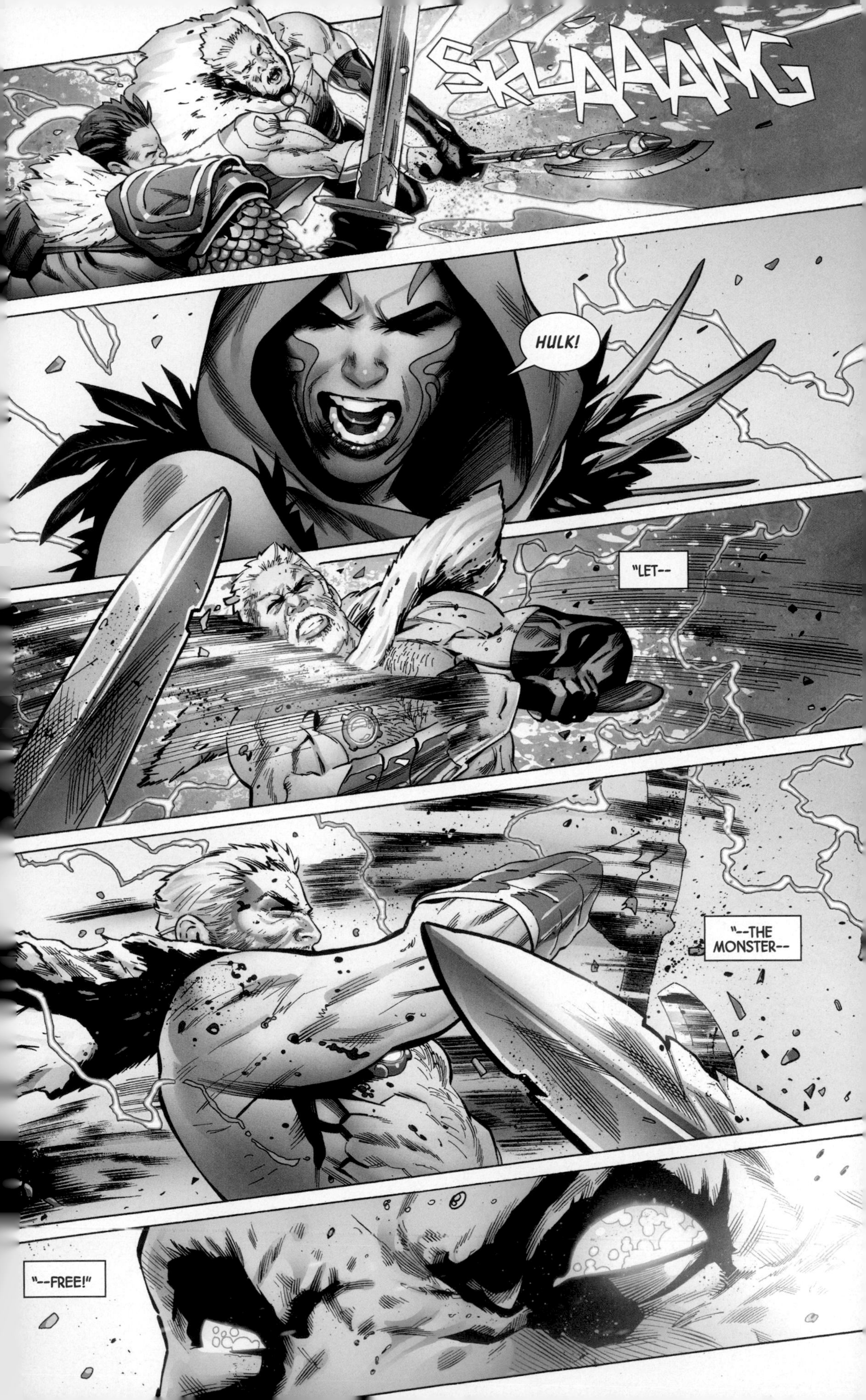
SKLAAANG
HULK!
"LET--
"--THE MONSTER--
"--FREE!"

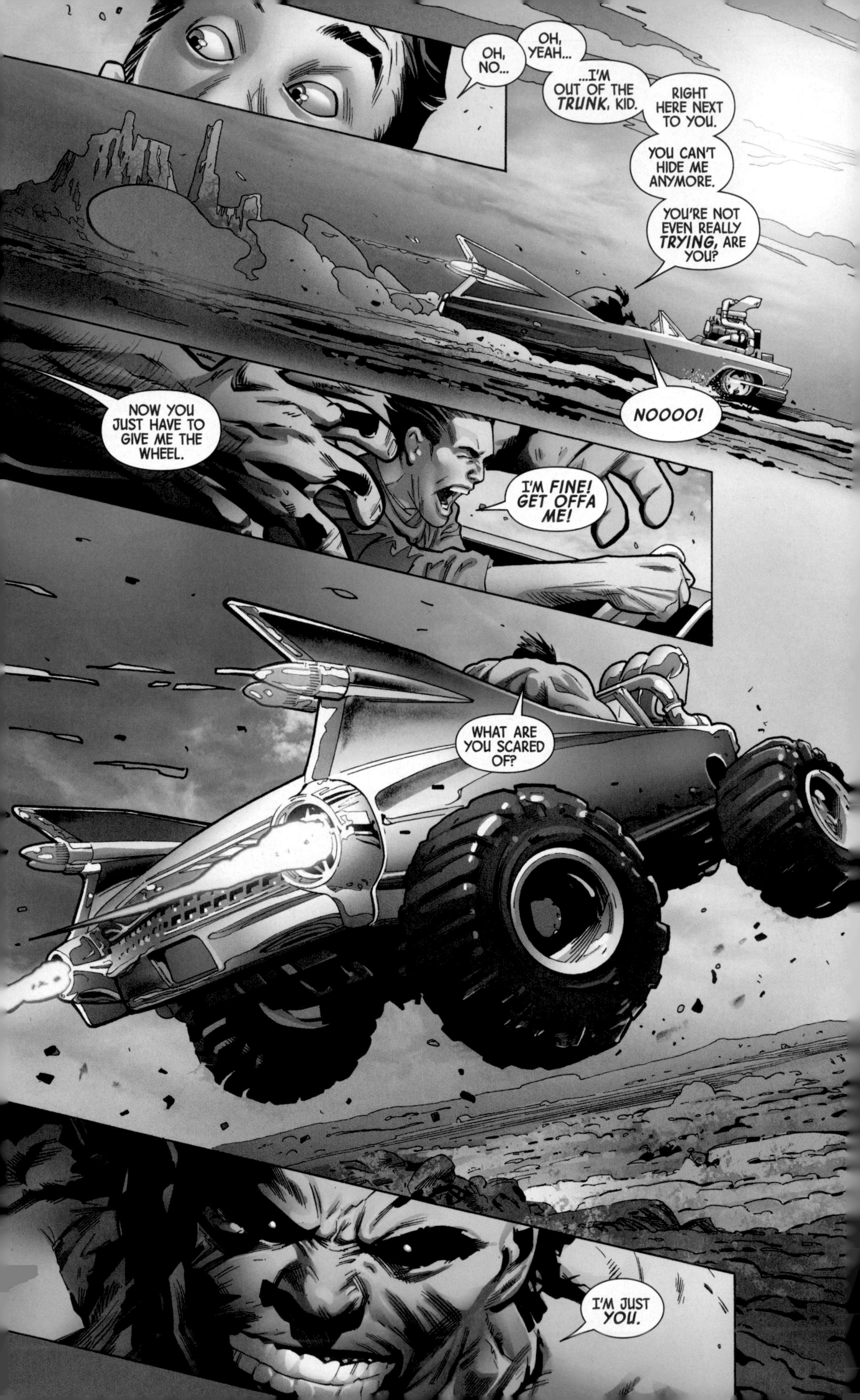

OH, NO...
OH, YEAH...
...I'M OUT OF THE TRUNK, KID.
RIGHT HERE NEXT TO YOU.
YOU CAN'T HIDE ME ANYMORE.
YOU'RE NOT EVEN REALLY TRYING, ARE YOU?
NOOOO!
NOW YOU JUST HAVE TO GIVE ME THE WHEEL.
I'M FINE! GET OFFA ME!
WHAT ARE YOU SCARED OF?
I'M JUST YOU.

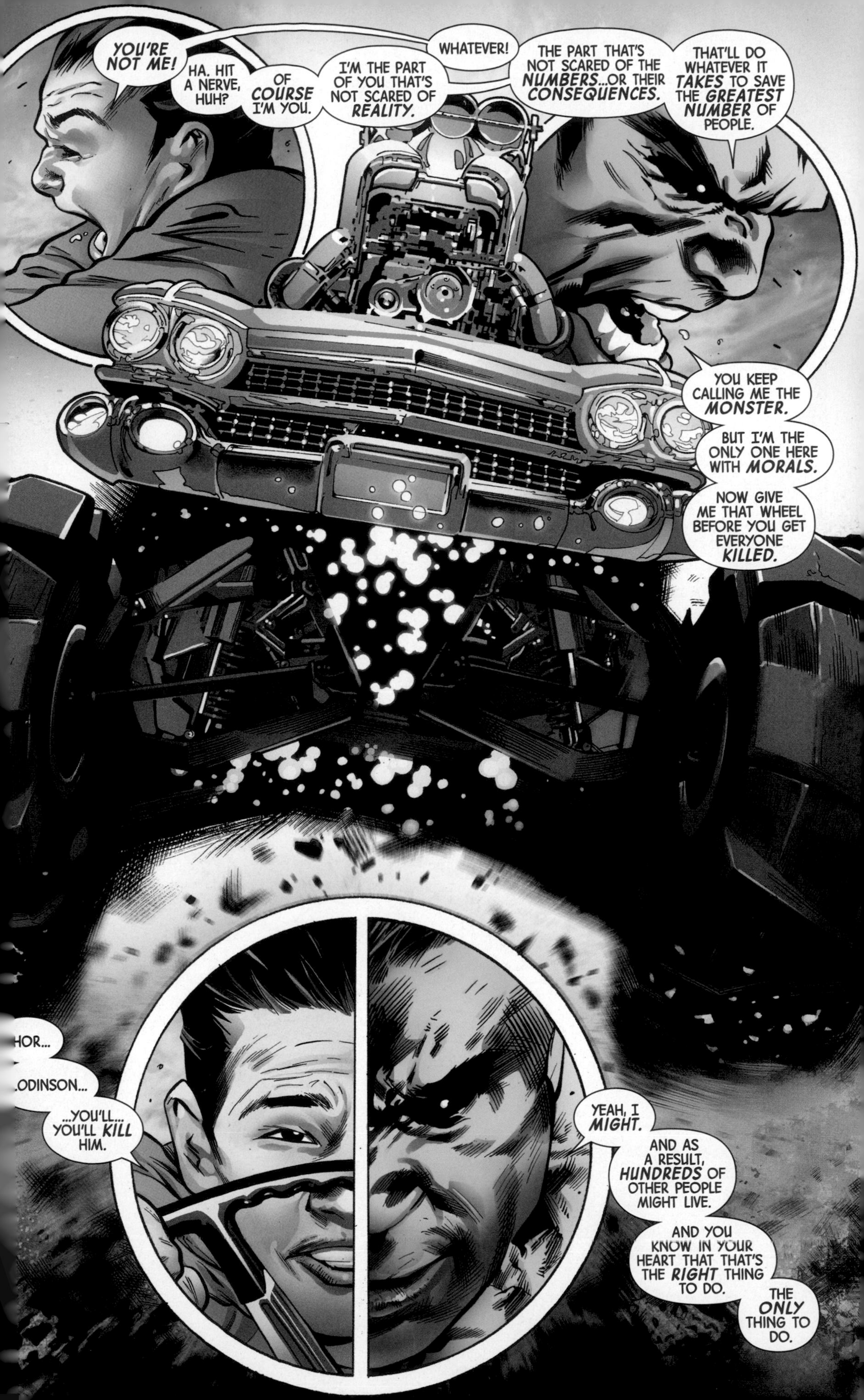
YOU'RE NOT ME!
HA. HIT A NERVE, HUH?
OF COURSE I'M YOU.
I'M THE PART OF YOU THAT'S NOT SCARED OF REALITY.
WHATEVER!
THE PART THAT'S NOT SCARED OF THE NUMBERS...OR THEIR CONSEQUENCES.
THAT'LL DO WHATEVER IT TAKES TO SAVE THE GREATEST NUMBER OF PEOPLE.
YOU KEEP CALLING ME THE MONSTER.
BUT I'M THE ONLY ONE HERE WITH MORALS.
NOW GIVE ME THAT WHEEL BEFORE YOU GET EVERYONE KILLED.
HOR...
ODINSON...
...YOU'LL... YOU'LL KILL HIM.
YEAH, I MIGHT.
AND AS A RESULT, HUNDREDS OF OTHER PEOPLE MIGHT LIVE.
AND YOU KNOW IN YOUR HEART THAT THAT'S THE RIGHT THING TO DO.
THE ONLY THING TO DO.

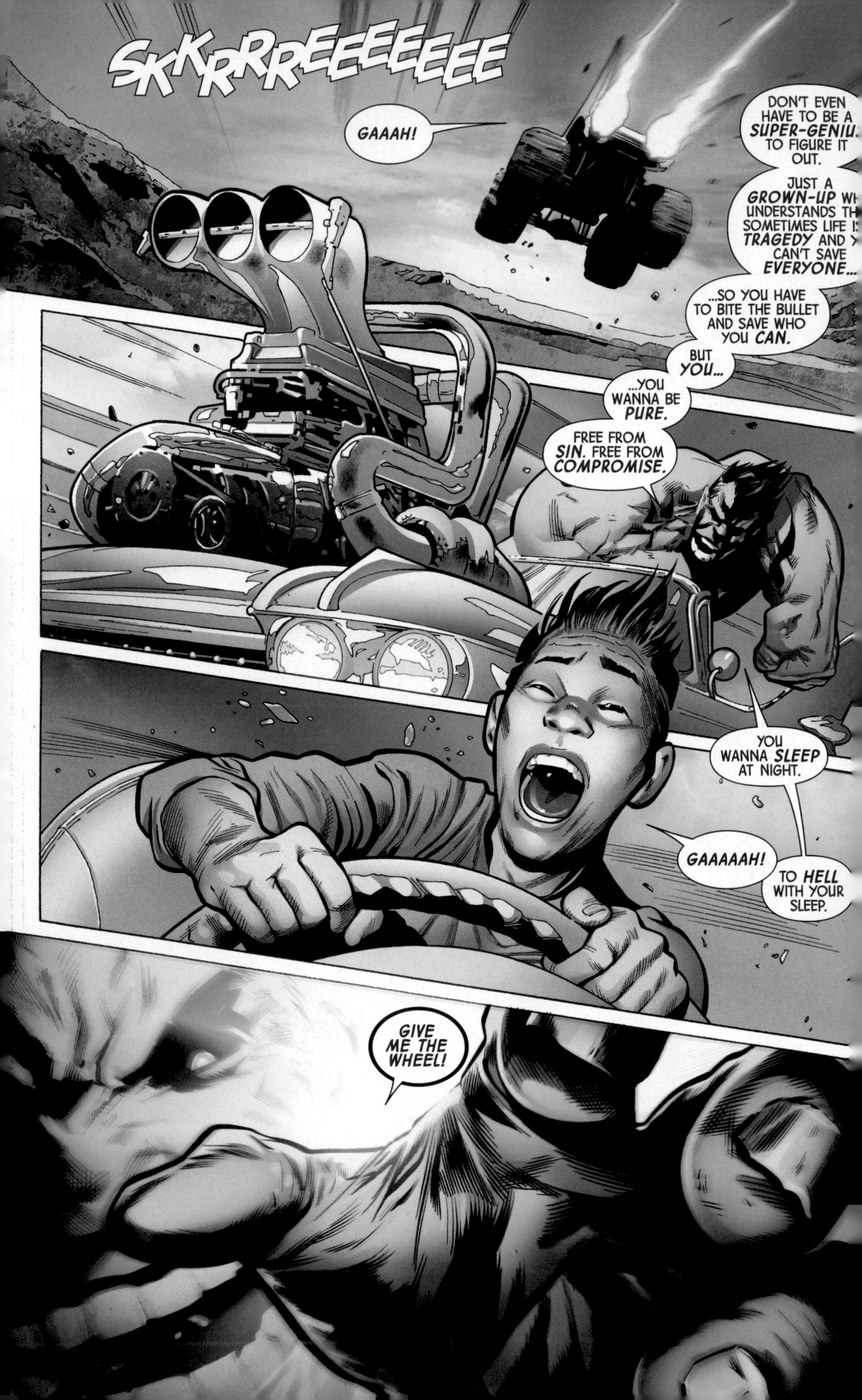
SKKRRREEEEEEEE
GAAAH!
DON'T EVEN HAVE TO BE A SUPER-GENIU
TO FIGURE IT OUT.
JUST A GROWN-UP W
UNDERSTANDS TH
SOMETIMES LIFE I
TRAGEDY AND Y
CAN'T SAVE EVERYONE...
...SO YOU HAVE TO BITE THE BULLET AND SAVE WHO YOU CAN.
BUT YOU...
...YOU WANNA BE PURE.
FREE FROM SIN. FREE FROM COMPROMISE.
YOU WANNA SLEEP AT NIGHT.
GAAAAAH!
TO HELL WITH YOUR SLEEP.
GIVE ME THE WHEEL!

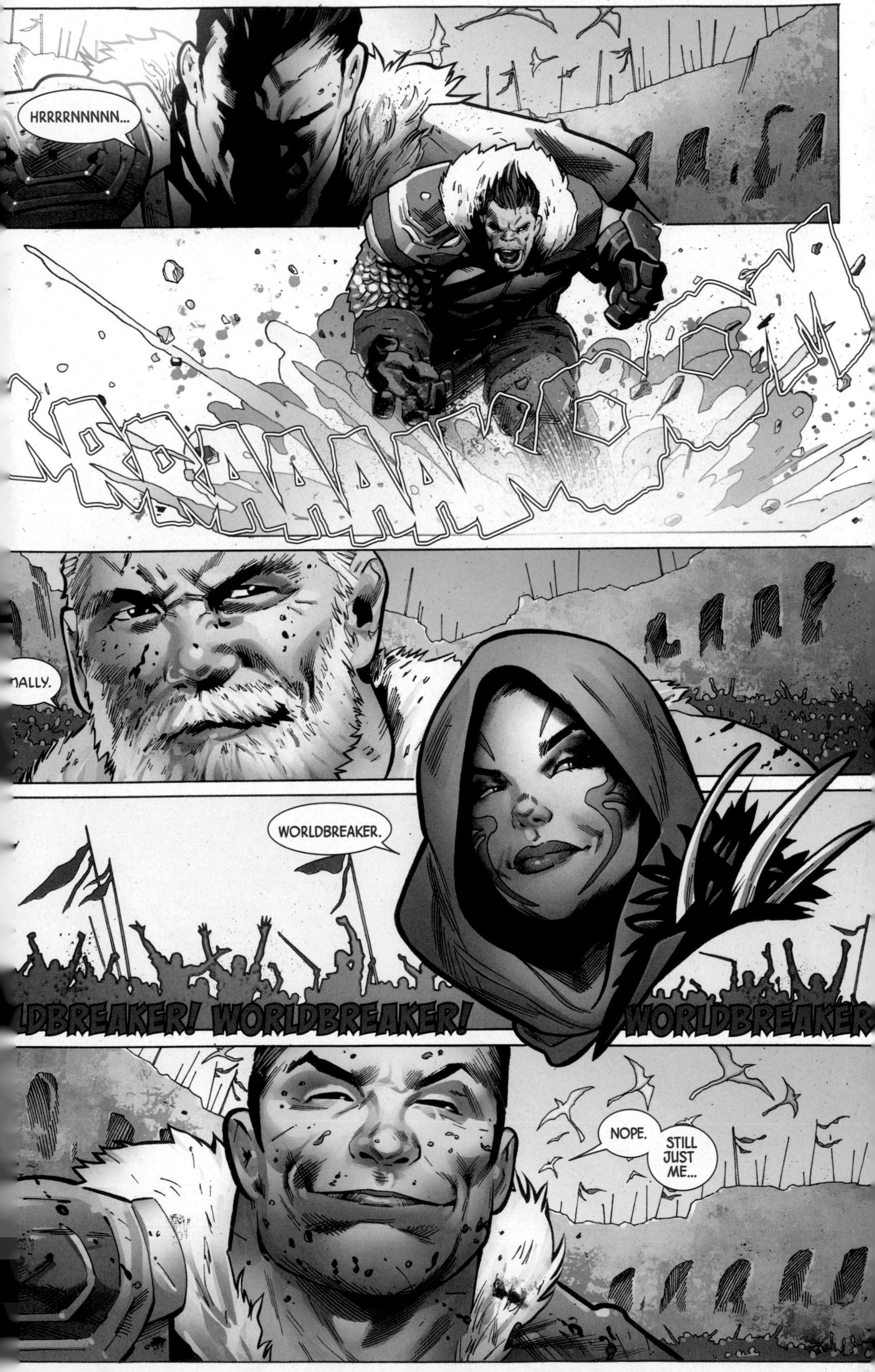
HRRRRNNNNN...
NALLY.
WORLDBREAKER.
LDBREAKER! WORLDBREAKER! WORLDBREAKER
NOPE.
STILL JUST ME...

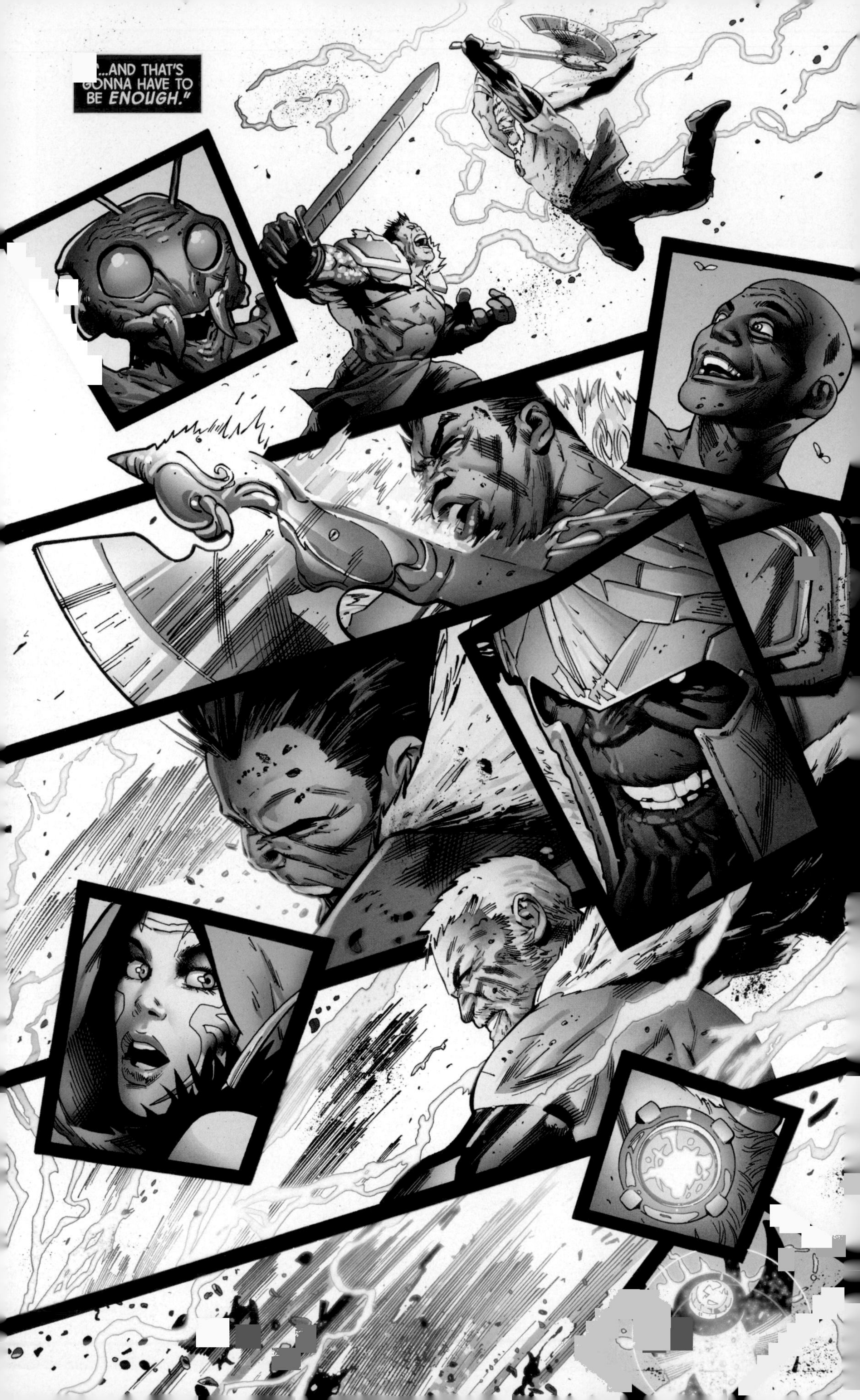
...AND THAT'S GONNA HAVE TO BE ENOUGH."

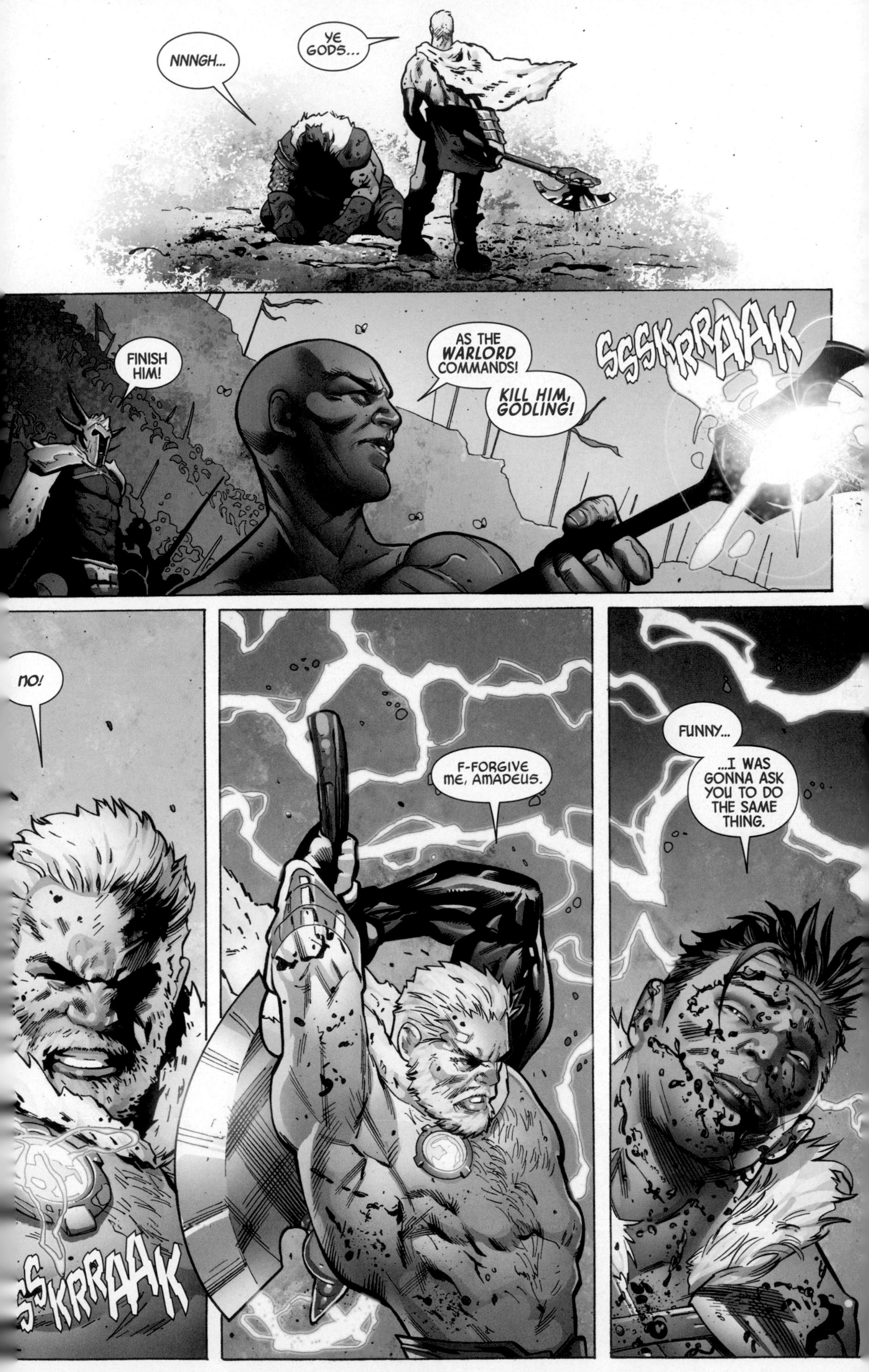
NNNGH...
YE GODS...
FINISH HIM!
AS THE WARLORD COMMANDS!
KILL HIM, GODLING!
SSSKRRAAK
no!
SSKRRAAK
F-FORGIVE ME, AMADEUS.
FUNNY...
...I WAS GONNA ASK YOU TO DO THE SAME THING.

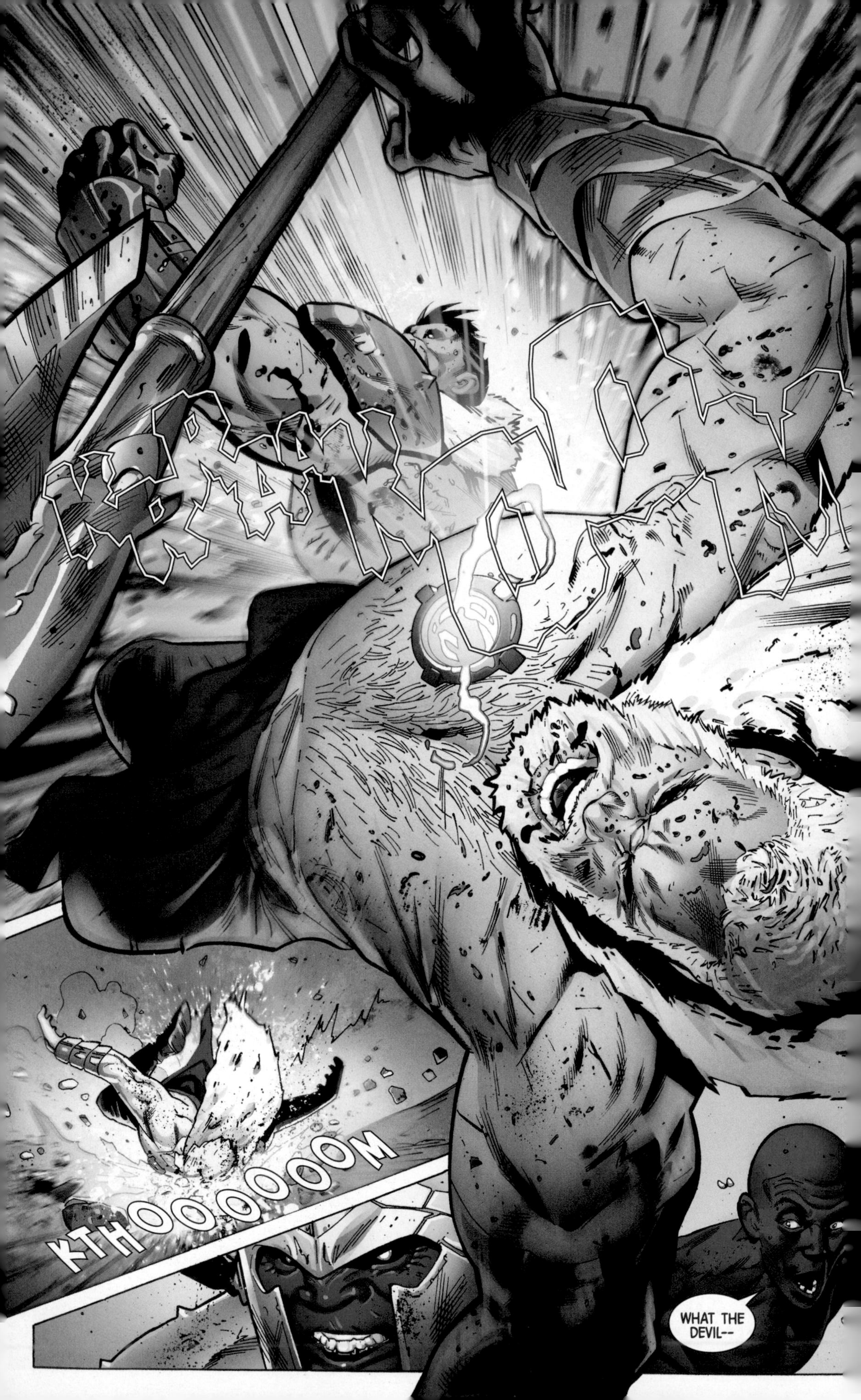
KTHOOOOOOM
WHAT THE DEVIL--

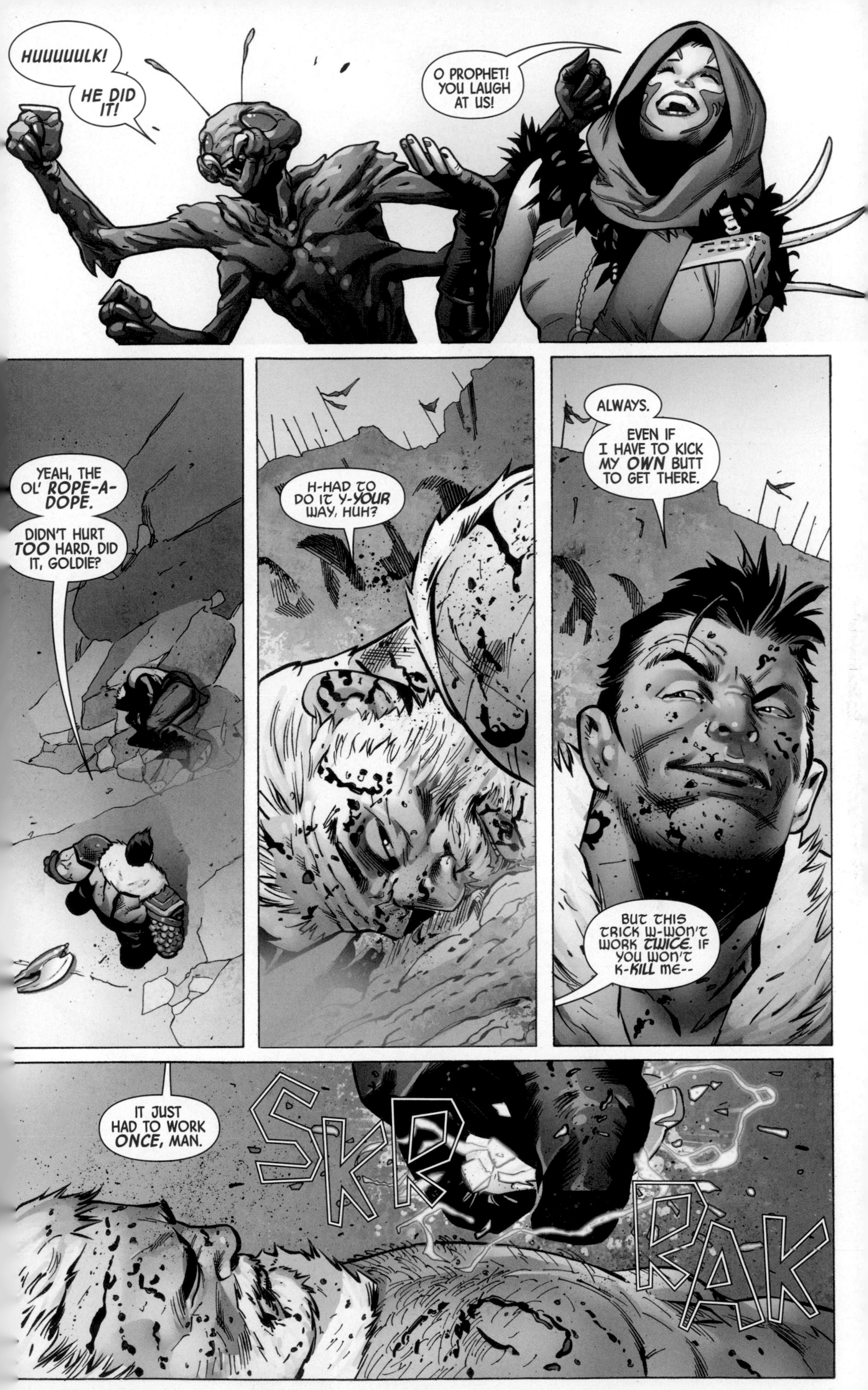
HUUUUULK!
HE DID IT!
O PROPHET! YOU LAUGH AT US!
YEAH, THE OL' ROPE-A-DOPE.
DIDN'T HURT TOO HARD, DID IT, GOLDIE?
H-HAD TO DO IT Y-YOUR WAY, HUH?
ALWAYS.
EVEN IF I HAVE TO KICK MY OWN BUTT TO GET THERE.
BUT THIS TRICK W-WON'T WORK TWICE. IF YOU WON'T K-KILL ME--
IT JUST HAD TO WORK ONCE, MAN.
SKRRAK

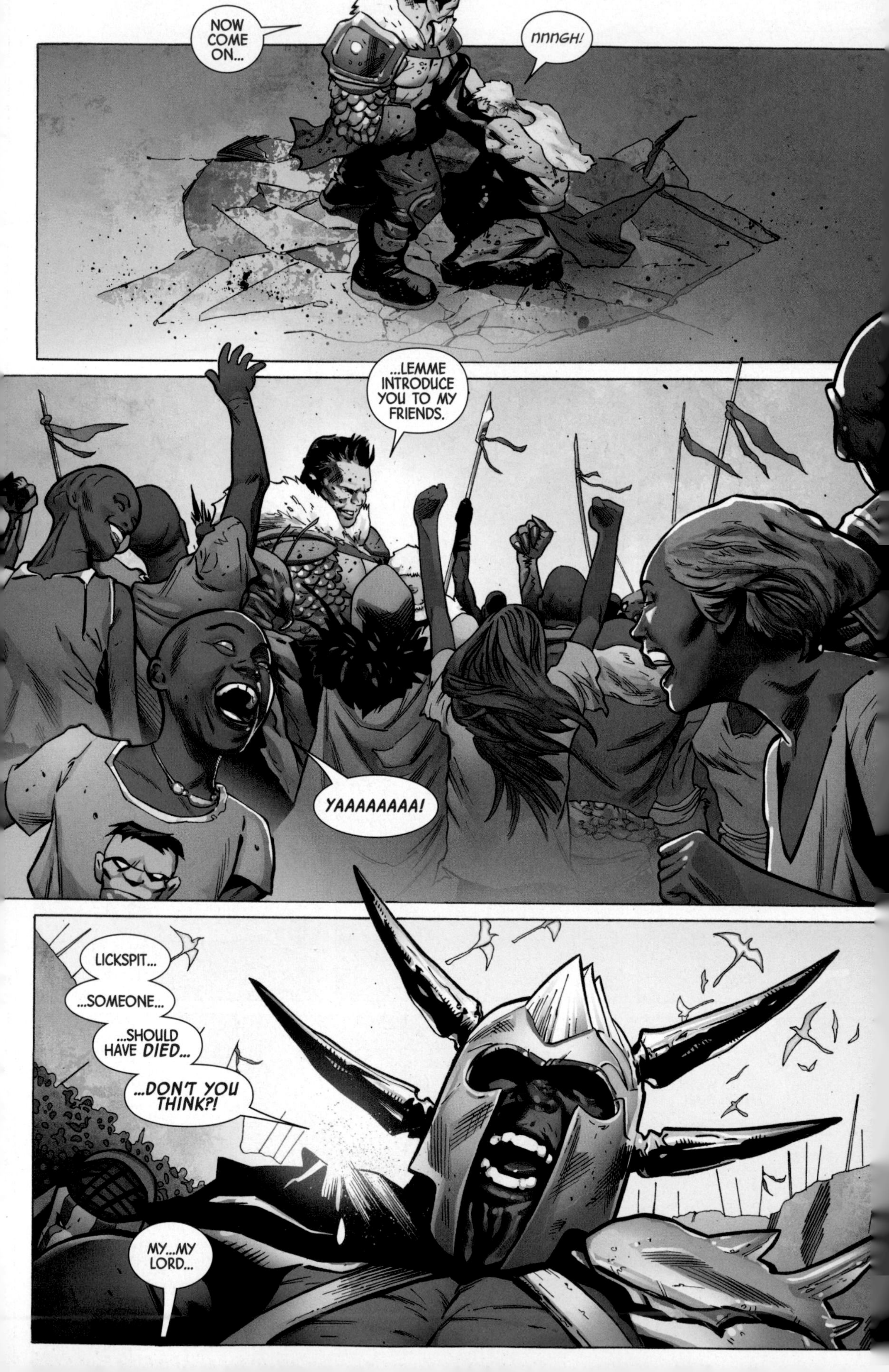
NOW COME ON...
nnnGH!
...LEMME INTRODUCE YOU TO MY FRIENDS.
YAAAAAAAA!
LICKSPIT...
...SOMEONE...
...SHOULD HAVE DIED...
...DON'T YOU THINK?!
MY...MY LORD...

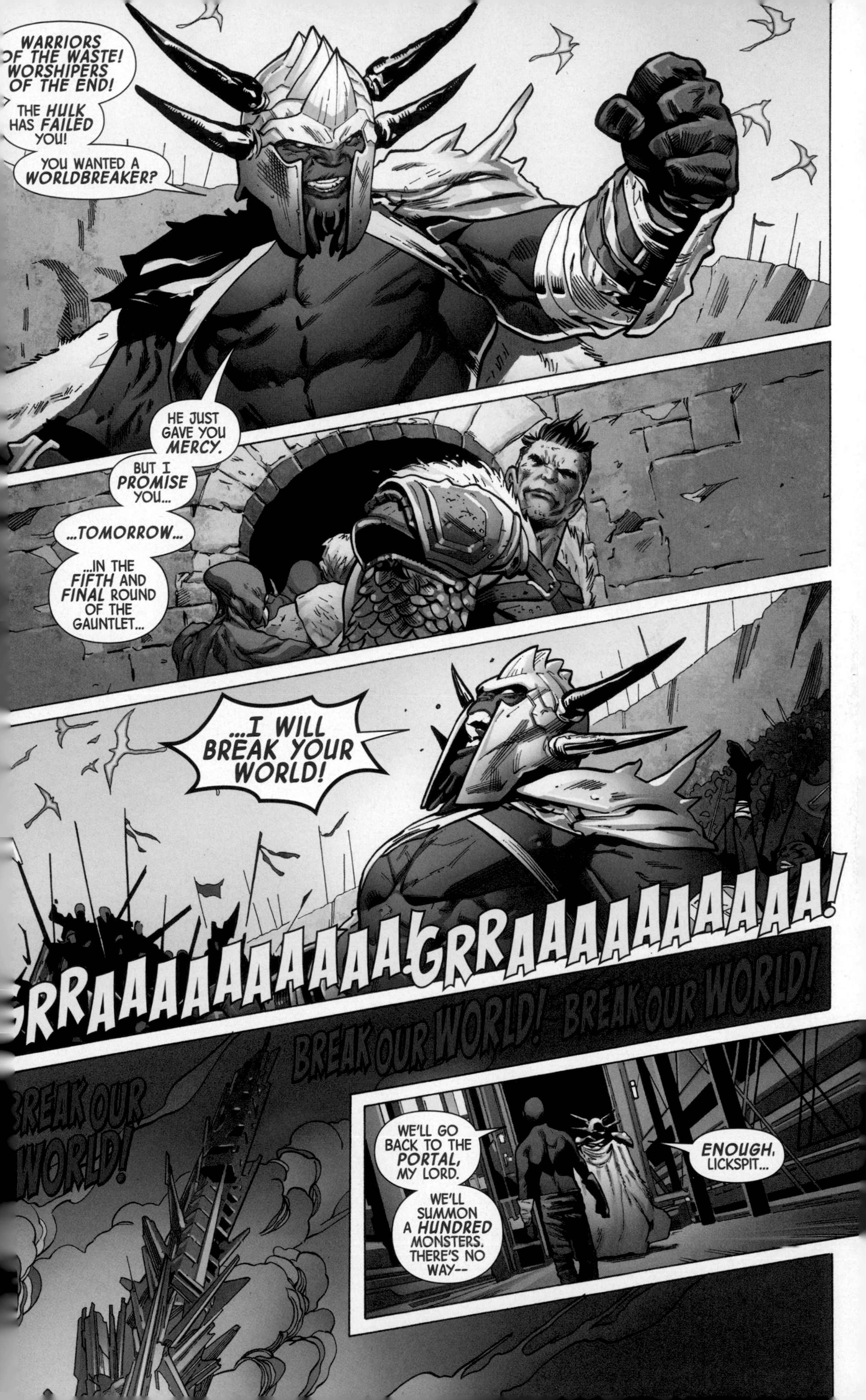
WARRIORS OF THE WASTE! WORSHIPERS OF THE END!
THE HULK HAS FAILED YOU!
YOU WANTED A WORLDBREAKER?
HE JUST GAVE YOU MERCY.
BUT I PROMISE YOU...
...TOMORROW...
...IN THE FIFTH AND FINAL ROUND OF THE GAUNTLET...
...I WILL BREAK YOUR WORLD!
GRRAAAAAAAAAAA!
GRRAAAAAAAAAAA!
BREAK OUR WORLD!
BREAK OUR WORLD!
BREAK OUR WORLD!
WE'LL GO BACK TO THE PORTAL, MY LORD.
WE'LL SUMMON A HUNDRED MONSTERS. THERE'S NO WAY--
ENOUGH, LICKSPIT...

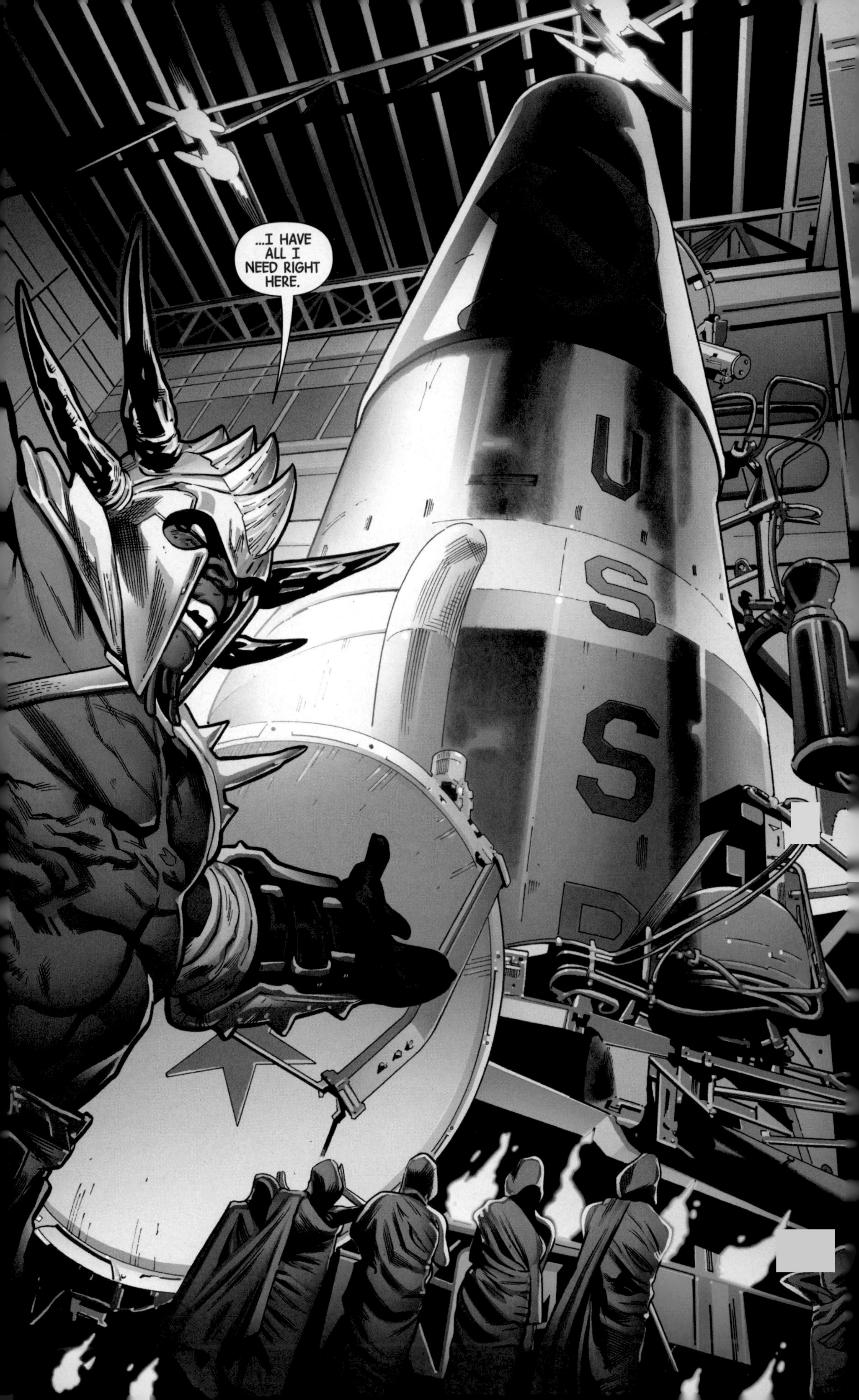
...I HAVE ALL I NEED RIGHT HERE.

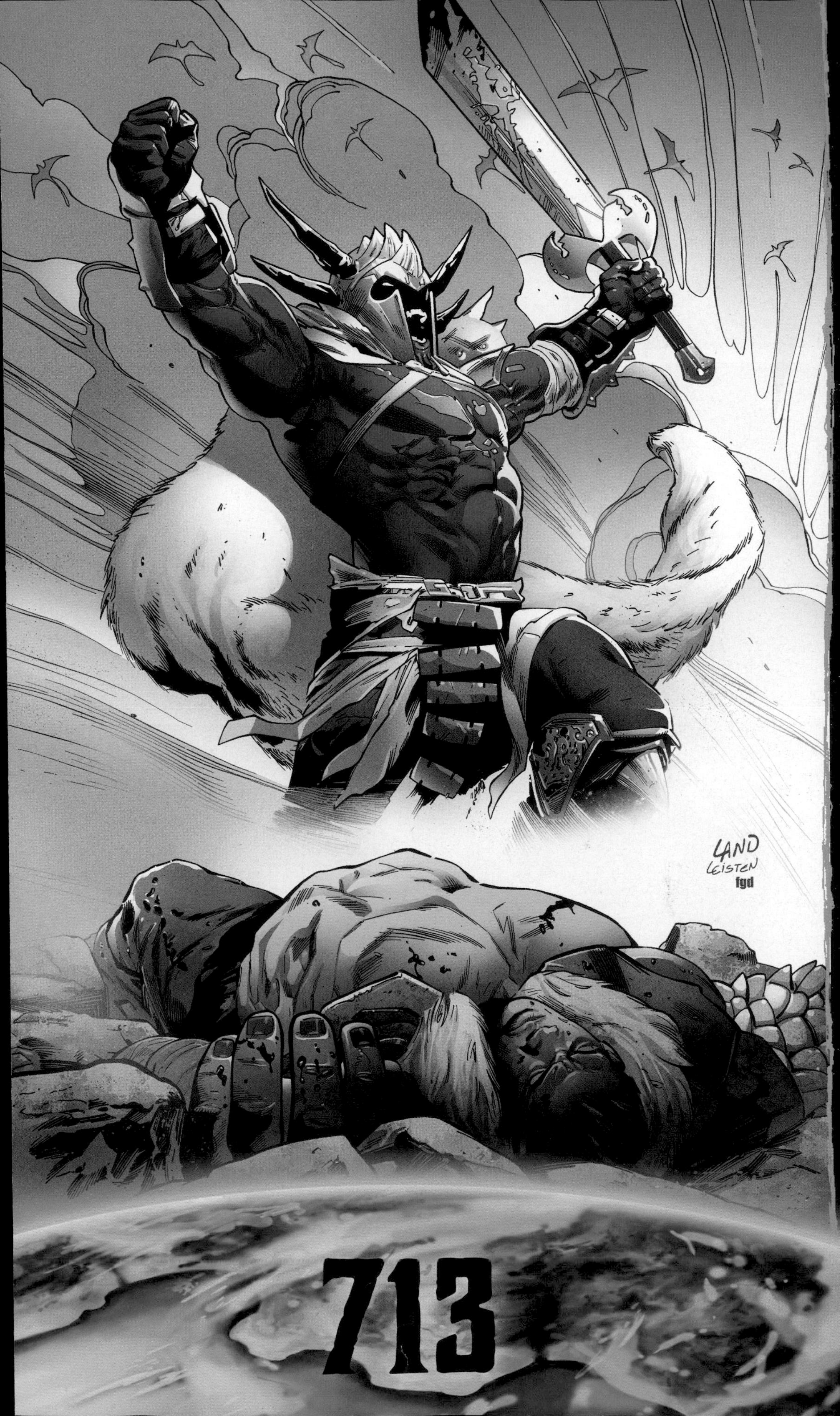
LAND
LEISTEN
fgd
713

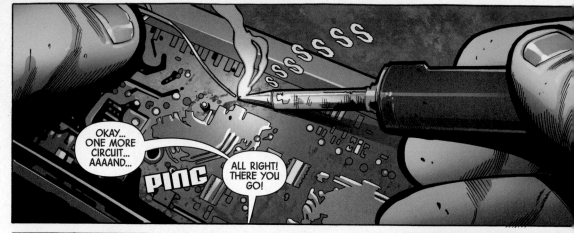

OKAY... ONE MORE CIRCUIT... AAAAND...

PINC

ALL RIGHT! THERE YOU GO!

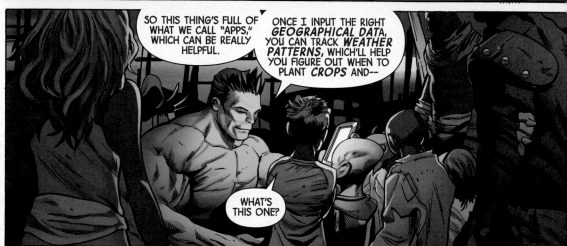

SO THIS THING'S FULL OF WHAT WE CALL "APPS," WHICH CAN BE REALLY HELPFUL.

ONCE I INPUT THE RIGHT *GEOGRAPHICAL DATA*, YOU CAN TRACK *WEATHER PATTERNS*, WHICH'LL HELP YOU FIGURE OUT WHEN TO PLANT *CROPS* AND--

WHAT'S THIS ONE?

OH, THAT? THAT'S CALLED *PAC-MAN*.

OOOH...

WOKKA WOKKA WOKKA

HEH.

AMADEUS...

HUSH, ODINSON. I'M STILL *STITCHING*...

BUT HE SHOULD BE PREPARING FOR *BATTLE*.

YEAH...

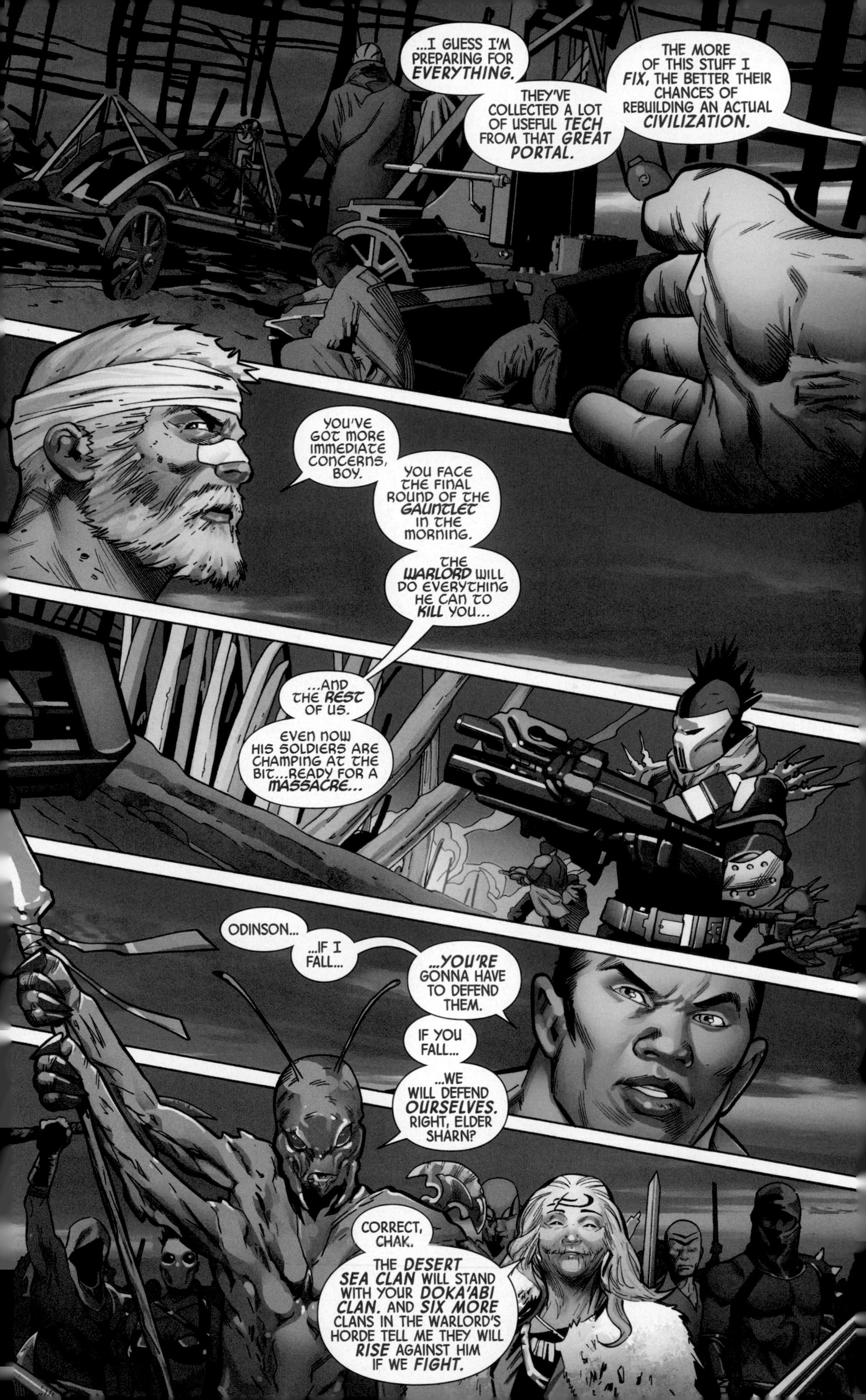
...I GUESS I'M PREPARING FOR EVERYTHING.
THEY'VE COLLECTED A LOT OF USEFUL TECH FROM THAT GREAT PORTAL.
THE MORE OF THIS STUFF I FIX, THE BETTER THEIR CHANCES OF REBUILDING AN ACTUAL CIVILIZATION.
YOU'VE GOT MORE IMMEDIATE CONCERNS, BOY.
YOU FACE THE FINAL ROUND OF THE GAUNTLET IN THE MORNING.
THE WARLORD WILL DO EVERYTHING HE CAN TO KILL YOU...
...AND THE REST OF US.
EVEN NOW HIS SOLDIERS ARE CHAMPING AT THE BIT...READY FOR A MASSACRE...
ODINSON...
...IF I FALL...
...YOU'RE GONNA HAVE TO DEFEND THEM.
IF YOU FALL...
...WE WILL DEFEND OURSELVES. RIGHT, ELDER SHARN?
CORRECT, CHAK.
THE DESERT SEA CLAN WILL STAND WITH YOUR DOKA'ABI CLAN. AND SIX MORE CLANS IN THE WARLORD'S HORDE TELL ME THEY WILL RISE AGAINST HIM IF WE FIGHT.

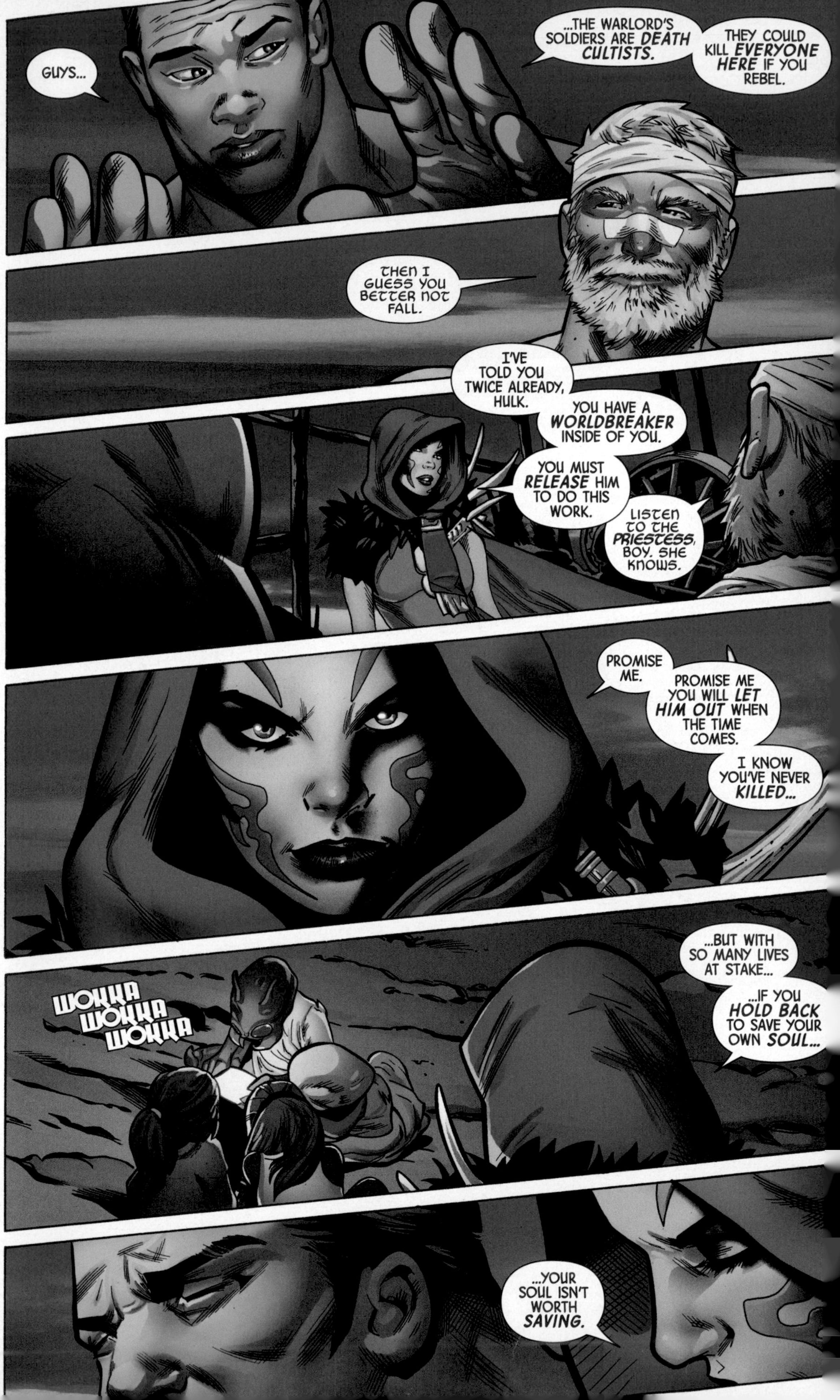
GUYS...
...THE WARLORD'S SOLDIERS ARE DEATH CULTISTS.
THEY COULD KILL EVERYONE HERE IF YOU REBEL.
THEN I GUESS YOU BETTER NOT FALL.
I'VE TOLD YOU TWICE ALREADY, HULK.
YOU HAVE A WORLDBREAKER INSIDE OF YOU.
YOU MUST RELEASE HIM TO DO THIS WORK.
LISTEN TO THE PRIESTESS, BOY. SHE KNOWS.
PROMISE ME.
PROMISE ME YOU WILL LET HIM OUT WHEN THE TIME COMES.
I KNOW YOU'VE NEVER KILLED...
WOKKA WOKKA WOKKA
...BUT WITH SO MANY LIVES AT STAKE...
...IF YOU HOLD BACK TO SAVE YOUR OWN SOUL...
...YOUR SOUL ISN'T WORTH SAVING.

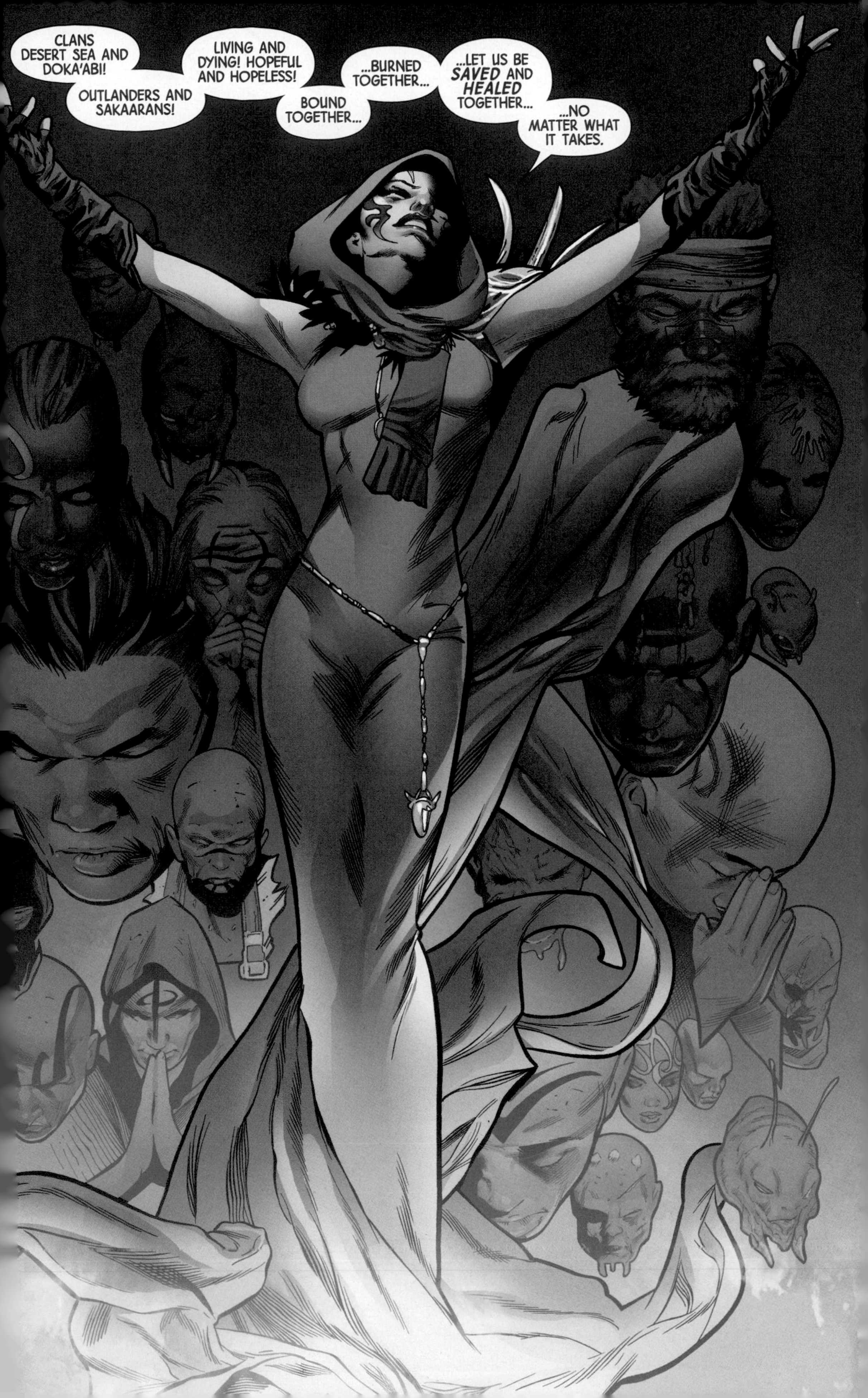
CLANS DESERT SEA AND DOKA'ABI!
OUTLANDERS AND SAKAARANS!
LIVING AND DYING! HOPEFUL AND HOPELESS!
BOUND TOGETHER...
...BURNED TOGETHER...
...LET US BE SAVED AND HEALED TOGETHER...
...NO MATTER WHAT IT TAKES.

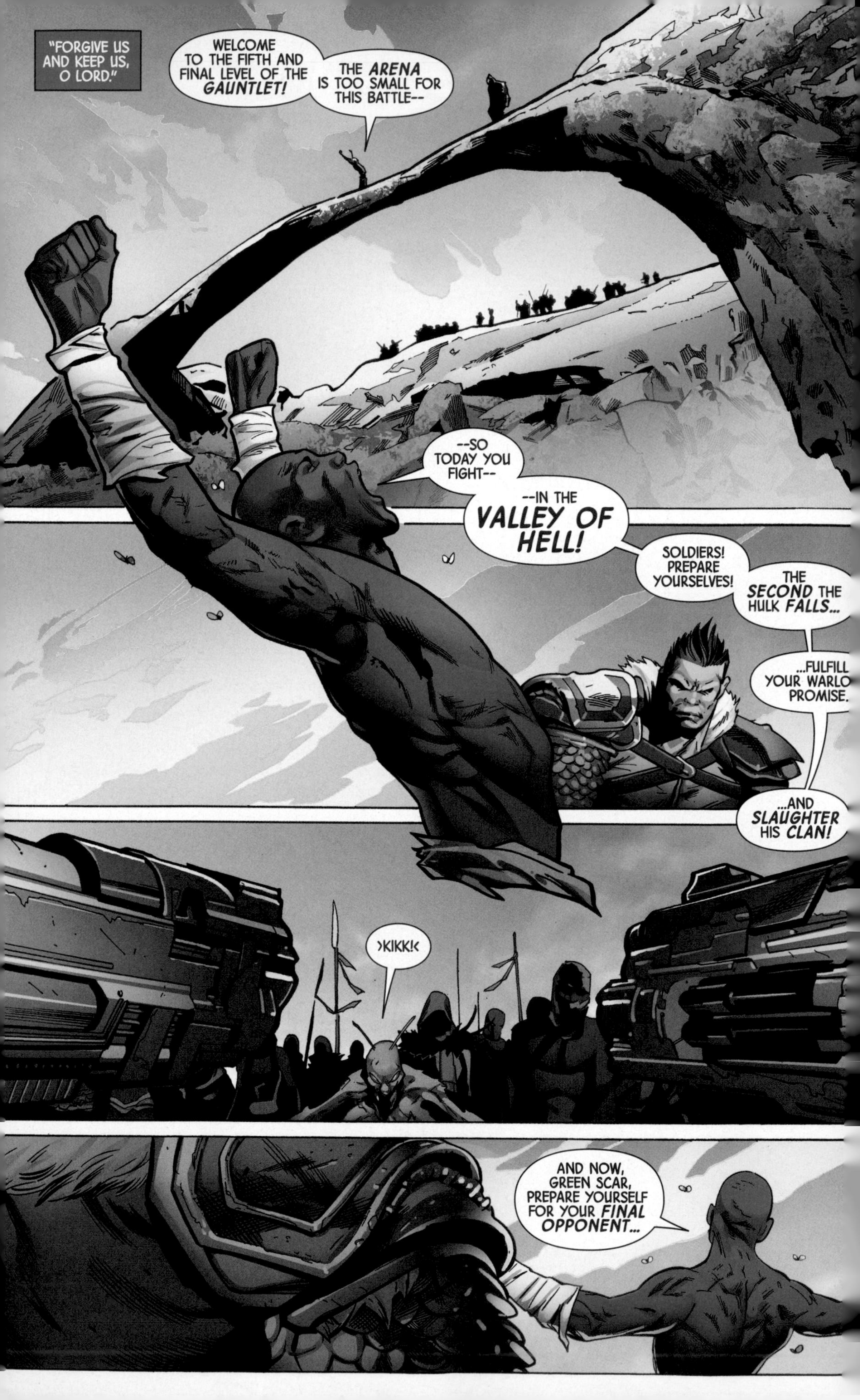
"FORGIVE US AND KEEP US, O LORD."
WELCOME TO THE FIFTH AND FINAL LEVEL OF THE GAUNTLET!
THE ARENA IS TOO SMALL FOR THIS BATTLE--
--SO TODAY YOU FIGHT--
--IN THE VALLEY OF HELL!
SOLDIERS! PREPARE YOURSELVES!
THE SECOND THE HULK FALLS...
...FULFILL YOUR WARLO PROMISE.
...AND SLAUGHTER HIS CLAN!
›KIKK!‹
AND NOW, GREEN SCAR, PREPARE YOURSELF FOR YOUR FINAL OPPONENT...

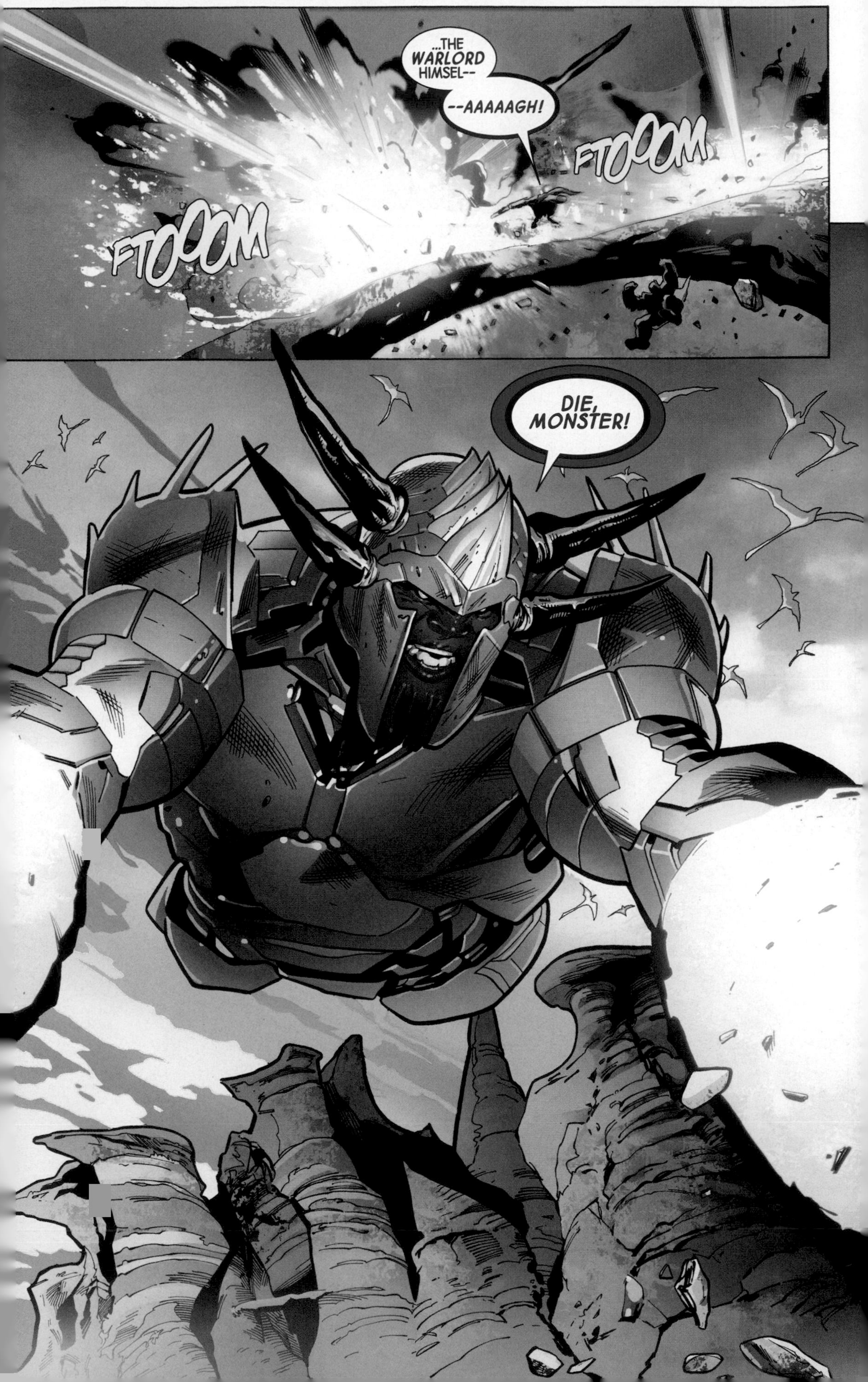
...THE WARLORD HIMSEL--
--AAAAAGH!
FTOOOM
FTOOOM
DIE, MONSTER!

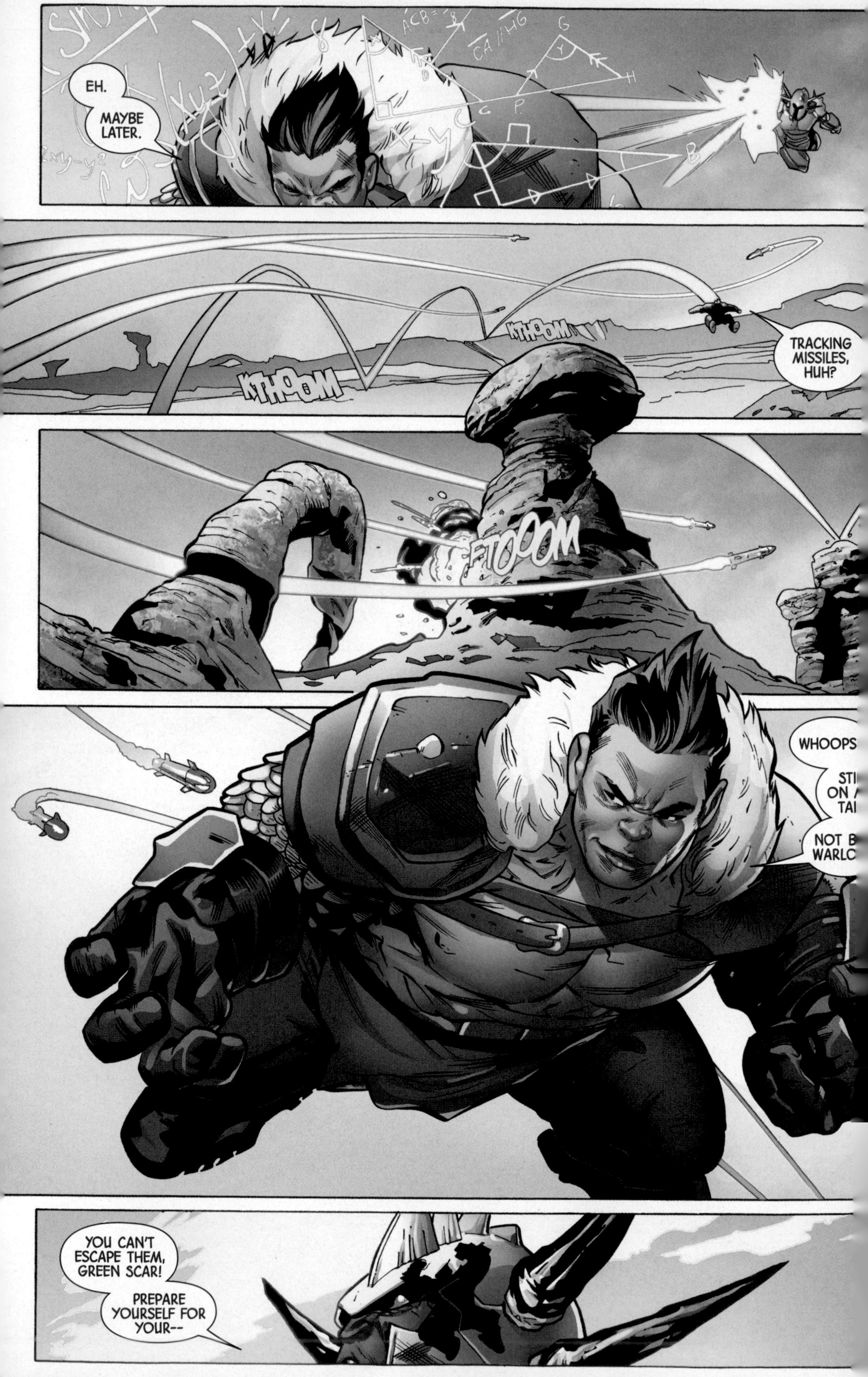
EH.
MAYBE LATER.
KTHOOM
KTHOOM
TRACKING MISSILES, HUH?
FTOOOM
WHOOPS
YOU CAN'T ESCAPE THEM, GREEN SCAR!
PREPARE YOURSELF FOR YOUR--

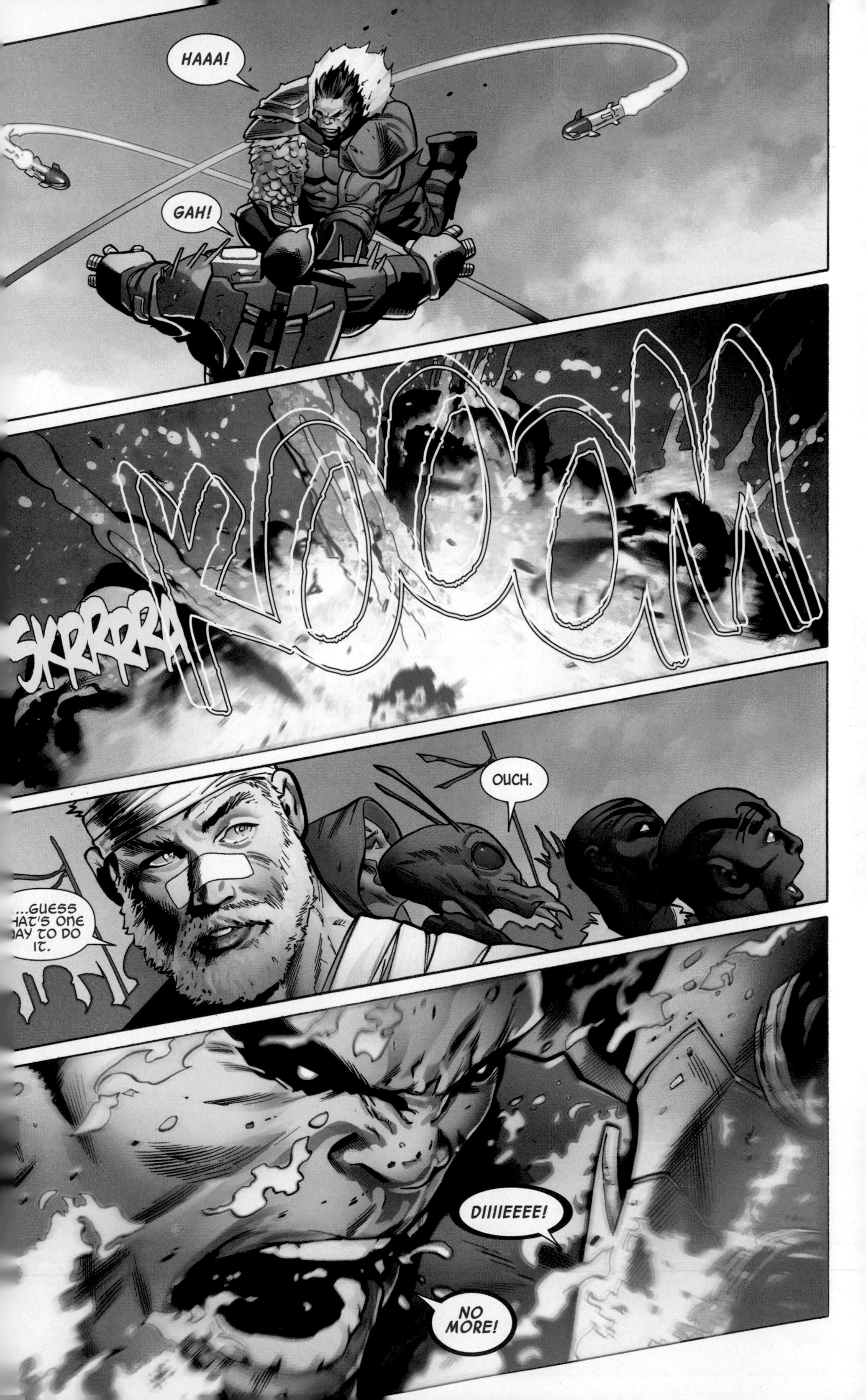
HAAA!
GAH!
SKRRRRA
KROOOOM
OUCH.
...GUESS THAT'S ONE WAY TO DO IT.
DIIIIEEEE!
NO MORE!

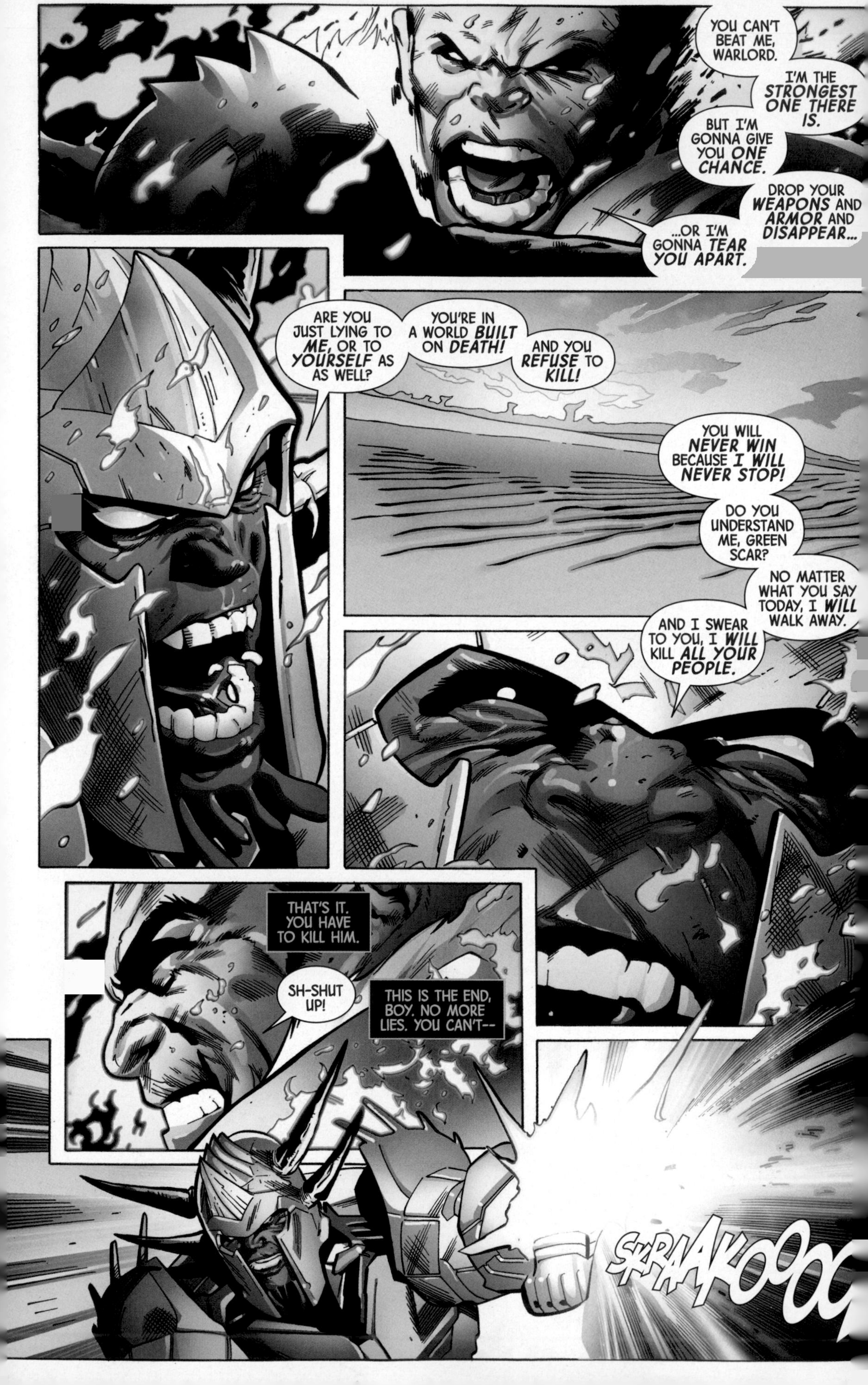
YOU CAN'T BEAT ME, WARLORD.
I'M THE STRONGEST ONE THERE IS.
BUT I'M GONNA GIVE YOU ONE CHANCE.
DROP YOUR WEAPONS AND ARMOR AND DISAPPEAR...
...OR I'M GONNA TEAR YOU APART.
ARE YOU JUST LYING TO ME, OR TO YOURSELF AS AS WELL?
YOU'RE IN A WORLD BUILT ON DEATH!
AND YOU REFUSE TO KILL!
YOU WILL NEVER WIN BECAUSE I WILL NEVER STOP!
DO YOU UNDERSTAND ME, GREEN SCAR?
NO MATTER WHAT YOU SAY TODAY, I WILL WALK AWAY.
AND I SWEAR TO YOU, I WILL KILL ALL YOUR PEOPLE.
THAT'S IT. YOU HAVE TO KILL HIM.
SH-SHUT UP!
THIS IS THE END, BOY. NO MORE LIES. YOU CAN'T--
SKRAAKOOOG

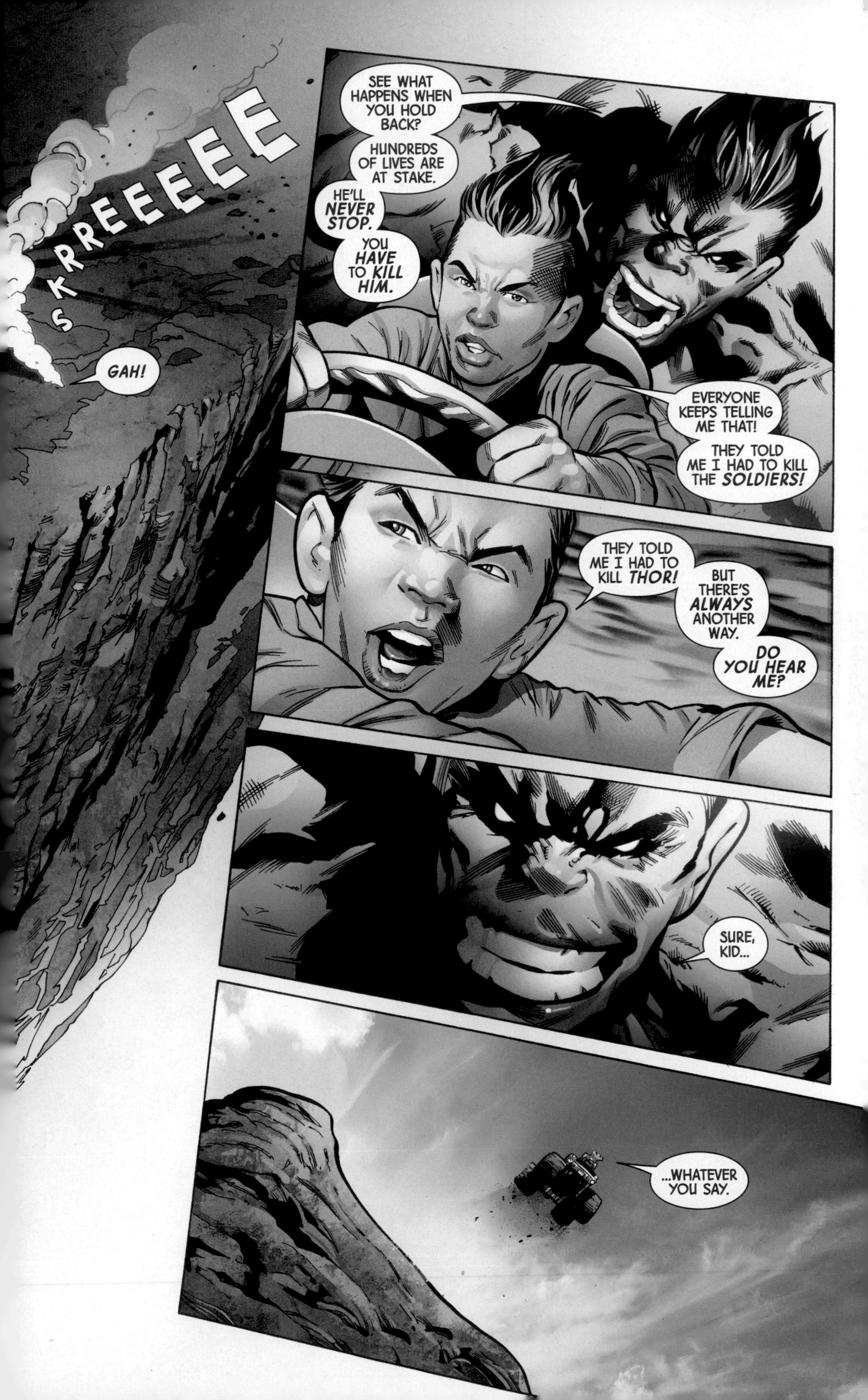
SKREEEEEE
GAH!
SEE WHAT HAPPENS WHEN YOU HOLD BACK?
HUNDREDS OF LIVES ARE AT STAKE.
HE'LL NEVER STOP.
YOU HAVE TO KILL HIM.
EVERYONE KEEPS TELLING ME THAT!
THEY TOLD ME I HAD TO KILL THE SOLDIERS!
THEY TOLD ME I HAD TO KILL THOR!
BUT THERE'S ALWAYS ANOTHER WAY.
DO YOU HEAR ME?
SURE, KID...
...WHATEVER YOU SAY.

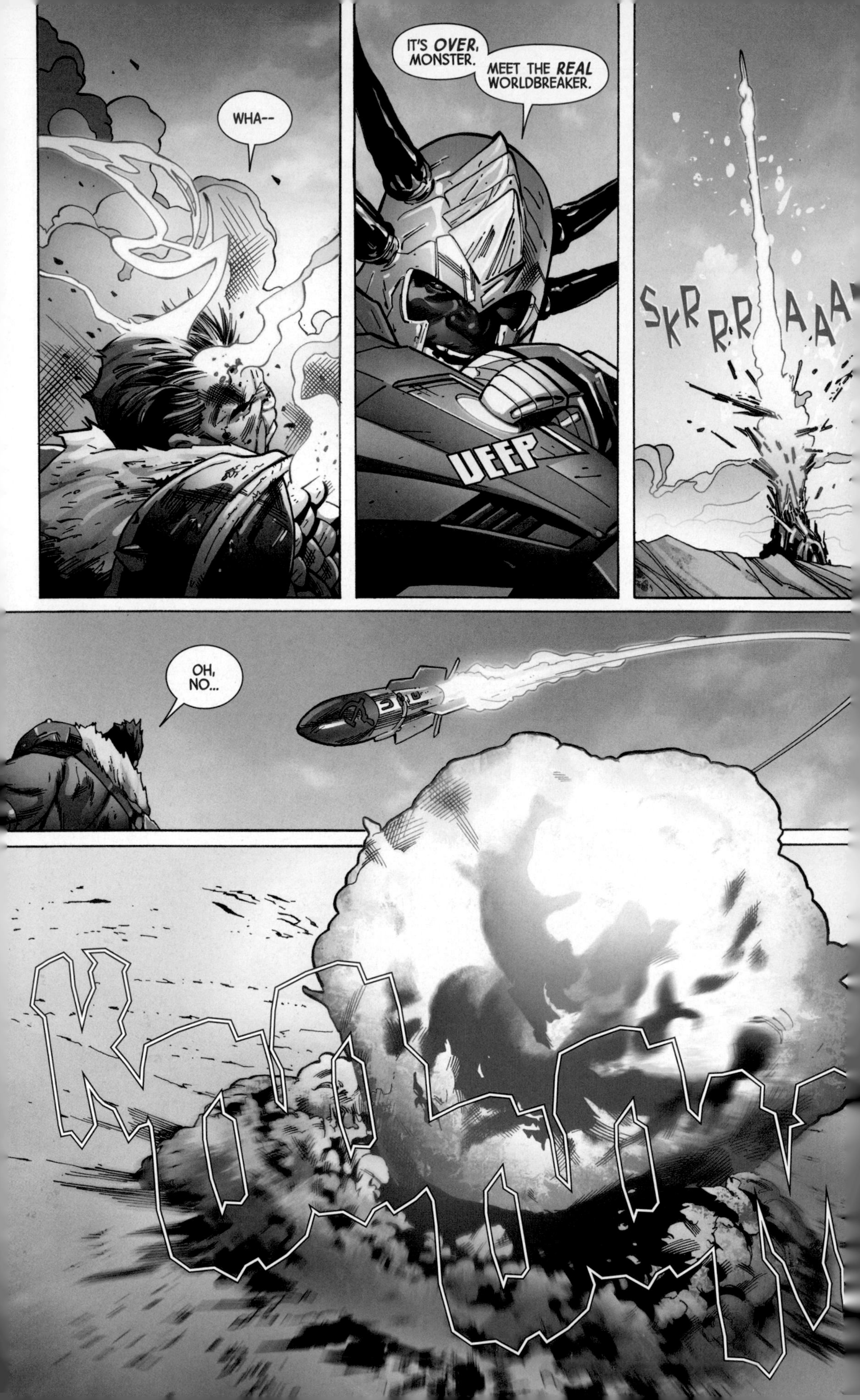
WHA--
IT'S OVER, MONSTER.
MEET THE REAL WORLDBREAKER.
SKRRRAAA
OH, NO...

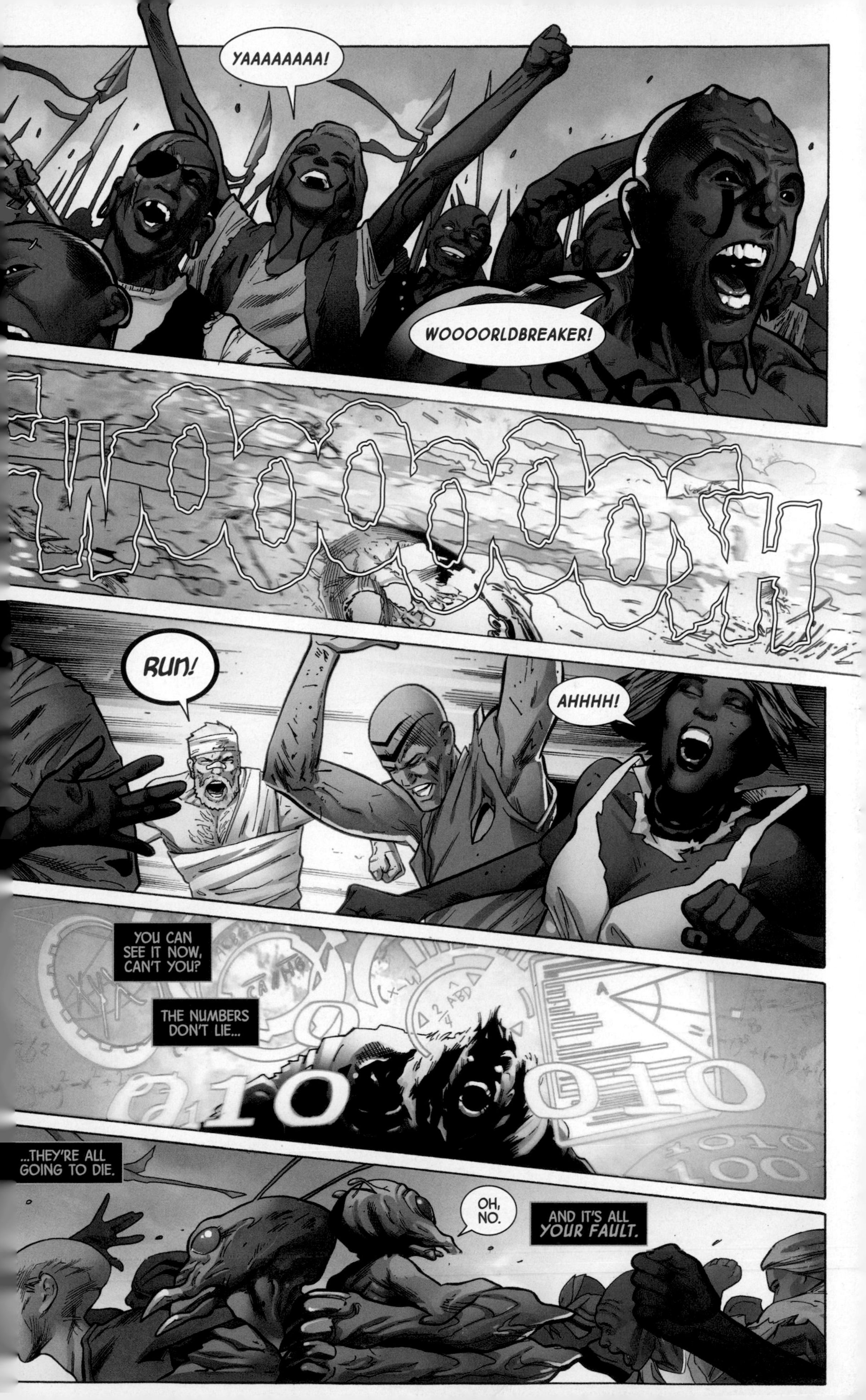

YAAAAAAAA!
WOOOORLDBREAKER!
WOOOOOOOOOH
RUN!
AHHHH!
YOU CAN SEE IT NOW, CAN'T YOU?
THE NUMBERS DON'T LIE...
...THEY'RE ALL GOING TO DIE.
OH, NO.
AND IT'S ALL *YOUR FAULT.*

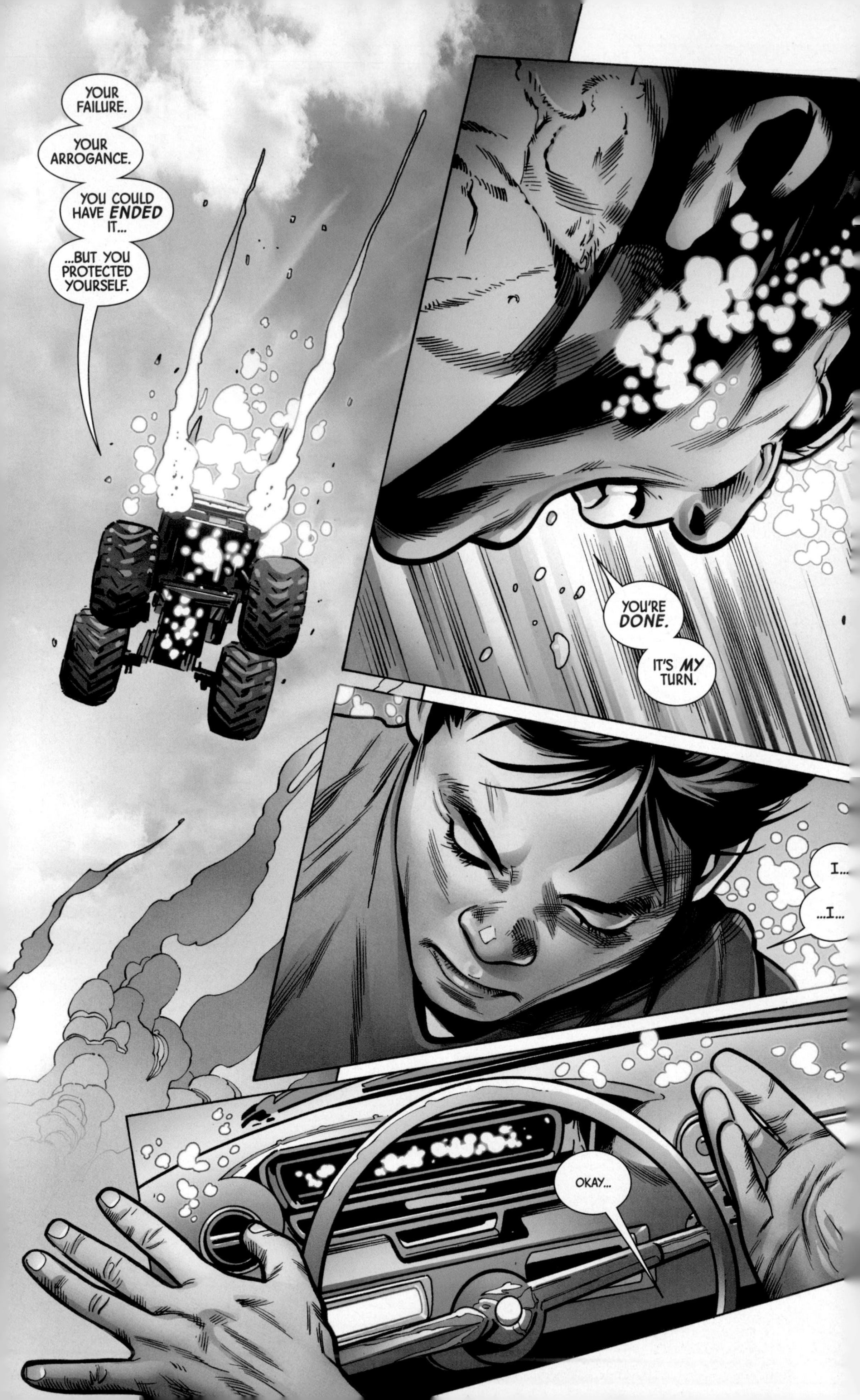
YOUR FAILURE.
YOUR ARROGANCE.
YOU COULD HAVE ENDED IT...
...BUT YOU PROTECTED YOURSELF.
YOU'RE DONE.
IT'S MY TURN.
I...
...I...
OKAY...

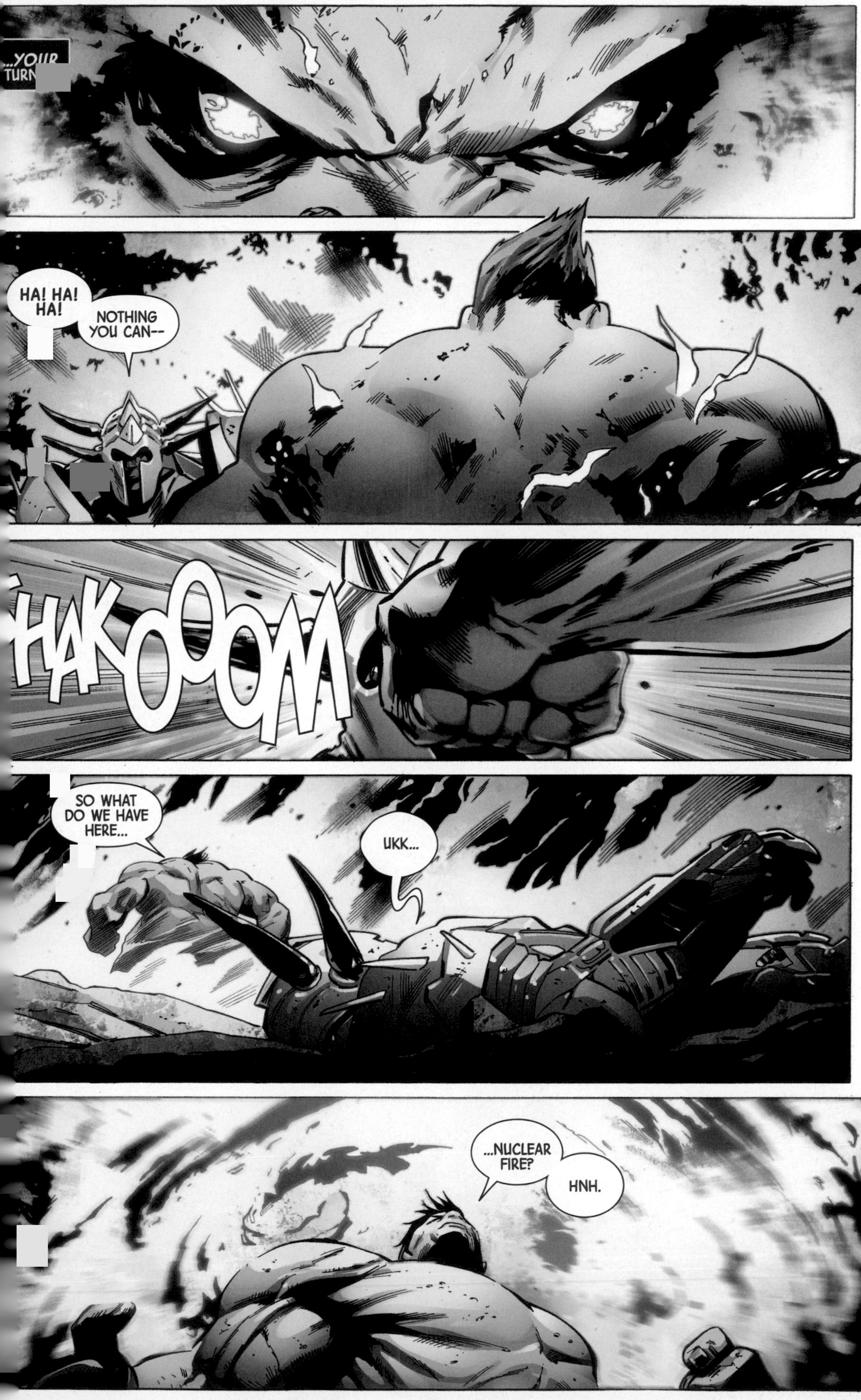
...YOUR TURN
HA! HA! HA!
NOTHING YOU CAN--
SHAKOOOM
SO WHAT DO WE HAVE HERE...
UKK...
...NUCLEAR FIRE?
HNH.

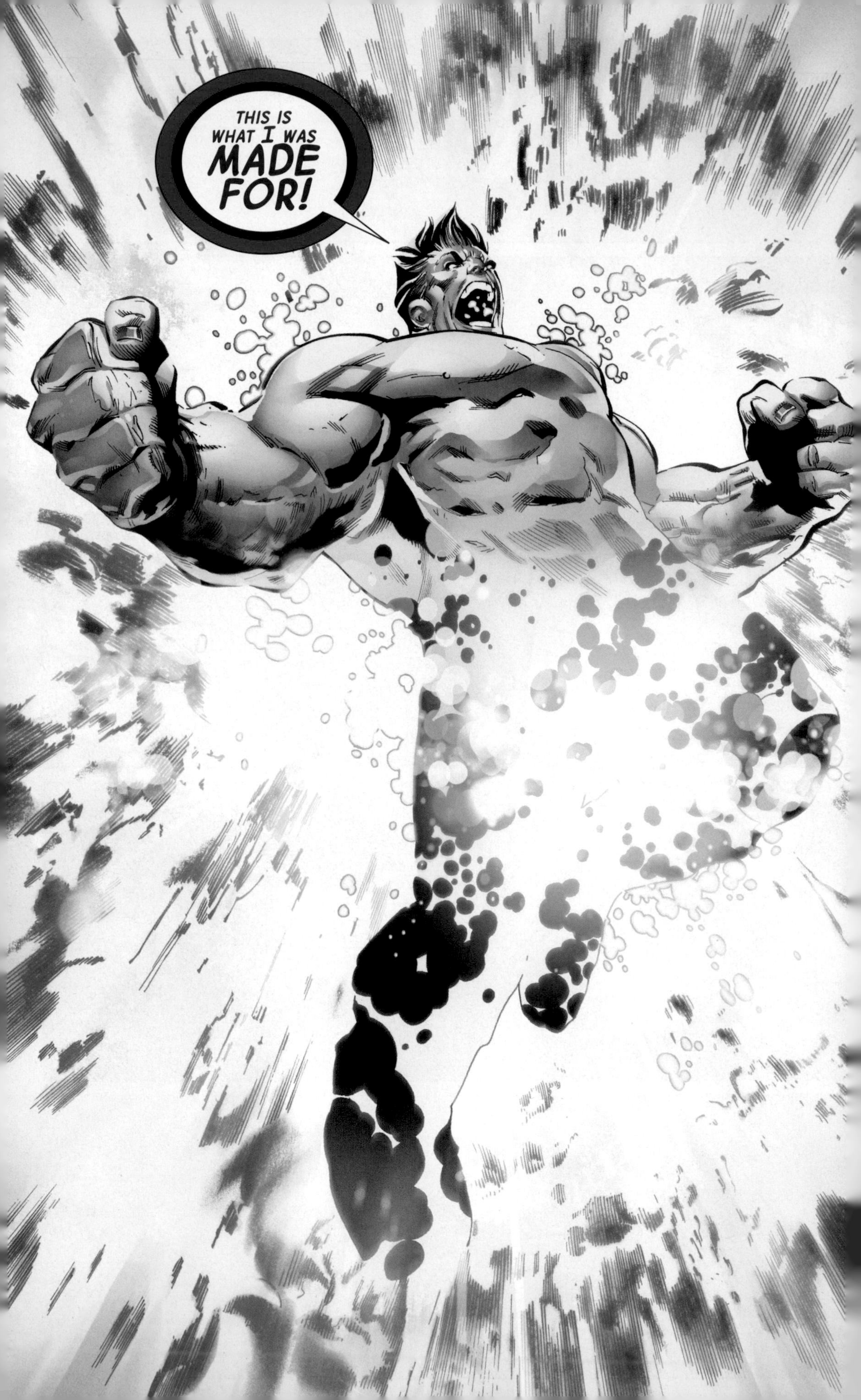
THIS IS WHAT I WAS MADE FOR!

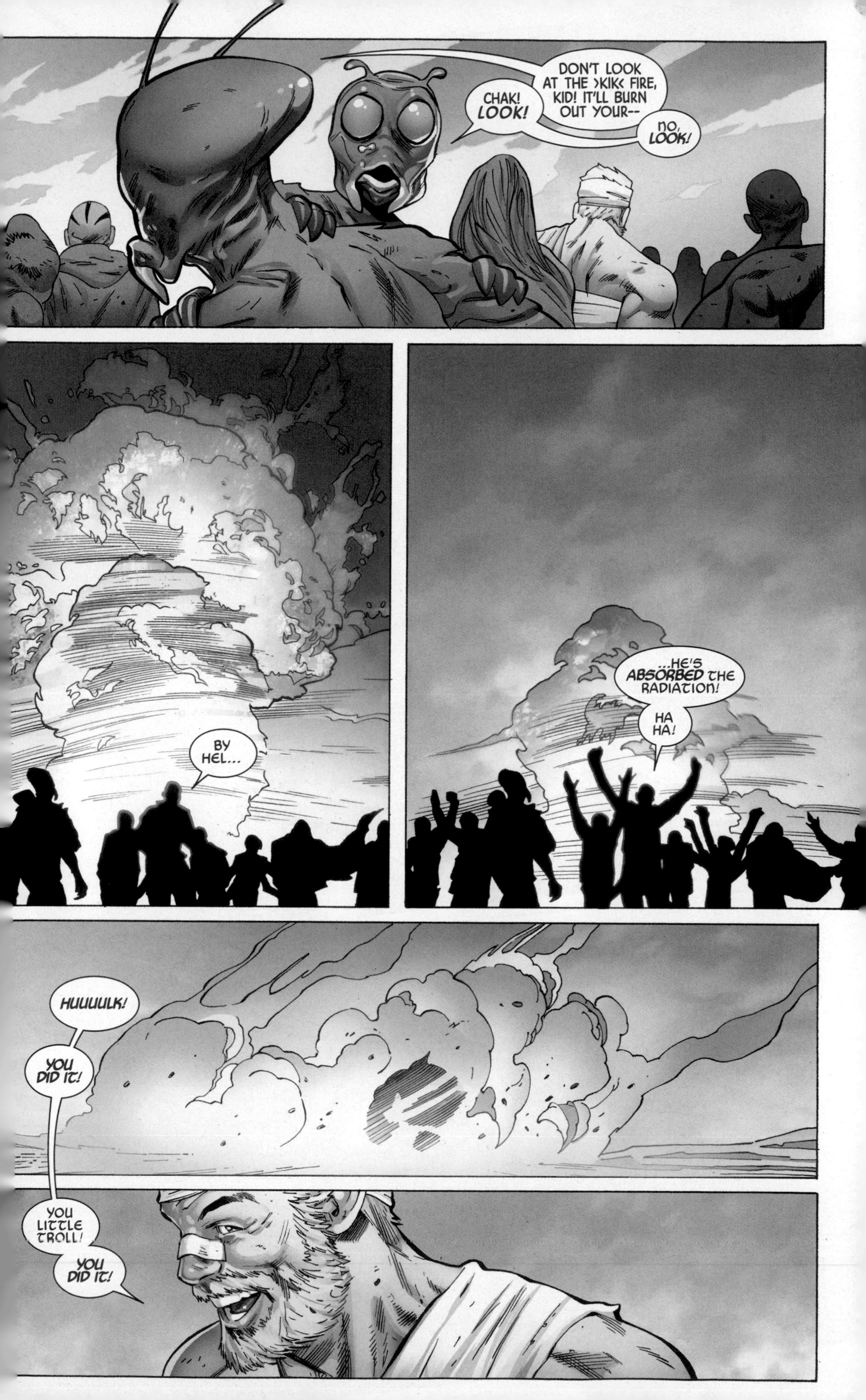
CHAK! LOOK!
DON'T LOOK AT THE ›KIK‹ FIRE, KID! IT'LL BURN OUT YOUR--
NO, LOOK!
BY HEL...
...HE'S ABSORBED THE RADIATION!
HA HA!
HUUUULK!
YOU DID IT!
YOU LITTLE TROLL!
YOU DID IT!

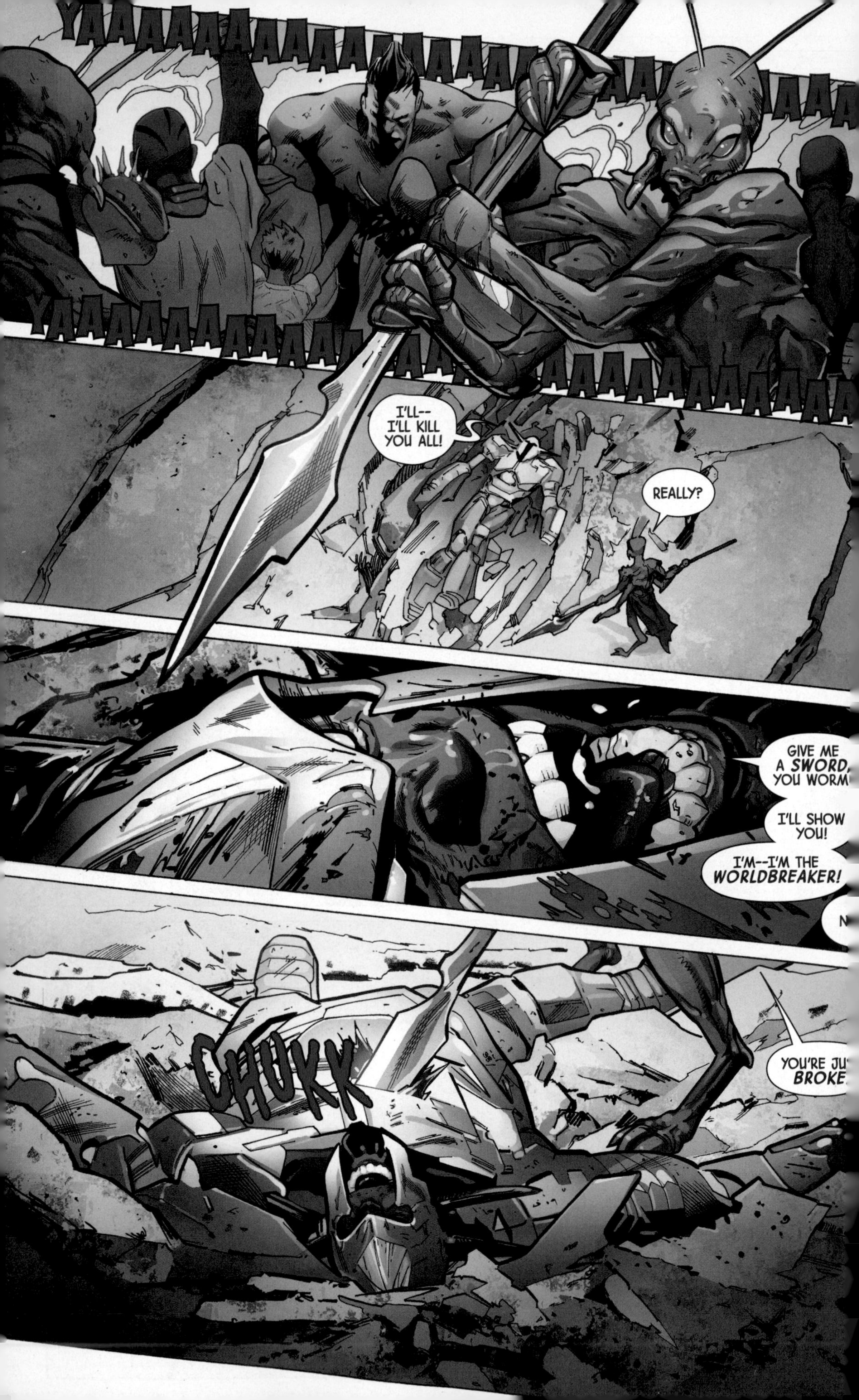
YAAAAAAAAAAAAAAAAAAA
YAAAAAAAAAAAAAAAAAAAA
I'LL-- I'LL KILL YOU ALL!
REALLY?
GIVE ME A SWORD, YOU WORM
I'LL SHOW YOU!
I'M--I'M THE WORLDBREAKER!
CHUKK
YOU'RE JU BROKE

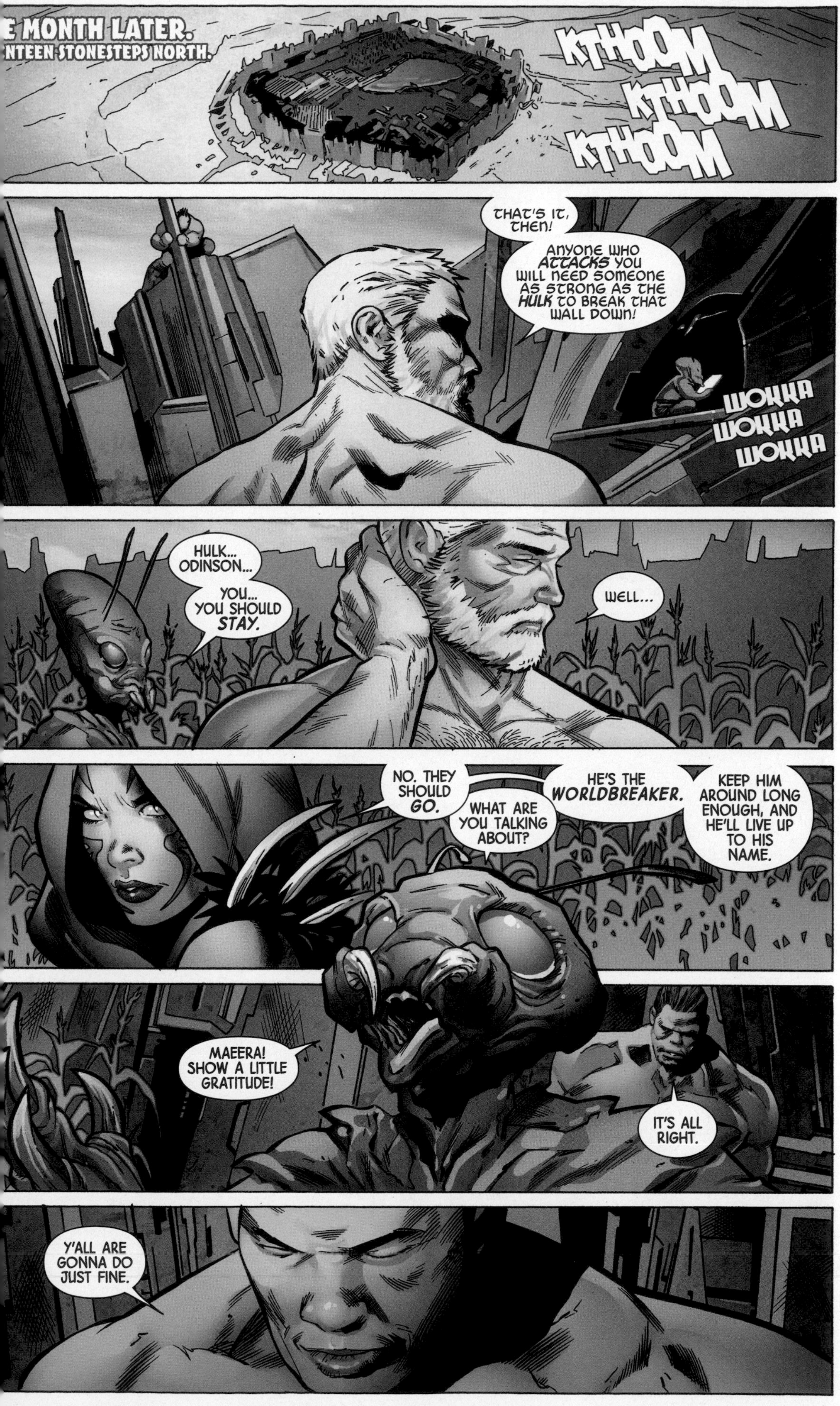

E MONTH LATER.
NTEEN STONESTEPS NORTH.
KTHOOM KTHOOM KTHOOM
THAT'S IT, THEN!
ANYONE WHO ATTACKS YOU WILL NEED SOMEONE AS STRONG AS THE HULK TO BREAK THAT WALL DOWN!
WOKKA WOKKA WOKKA
HULK... ODINSON...
YOU... YOU SHOULD STAY.
WELL...
NO. THEY SHOULD GO.
WHAT ARE YOU TALKING ABOUT?
HE'S THE WORLDBREAKER.
KEEP HIM AROUND LONG ENOUGH, AND HE'LL LIVE UP TO HIS NAME.
MAEERA! SHOW A LITTLE GRATITUDE!
IT'S ALL RIGHT.
Y'ALL ARE GONNA DO JUST FINE.

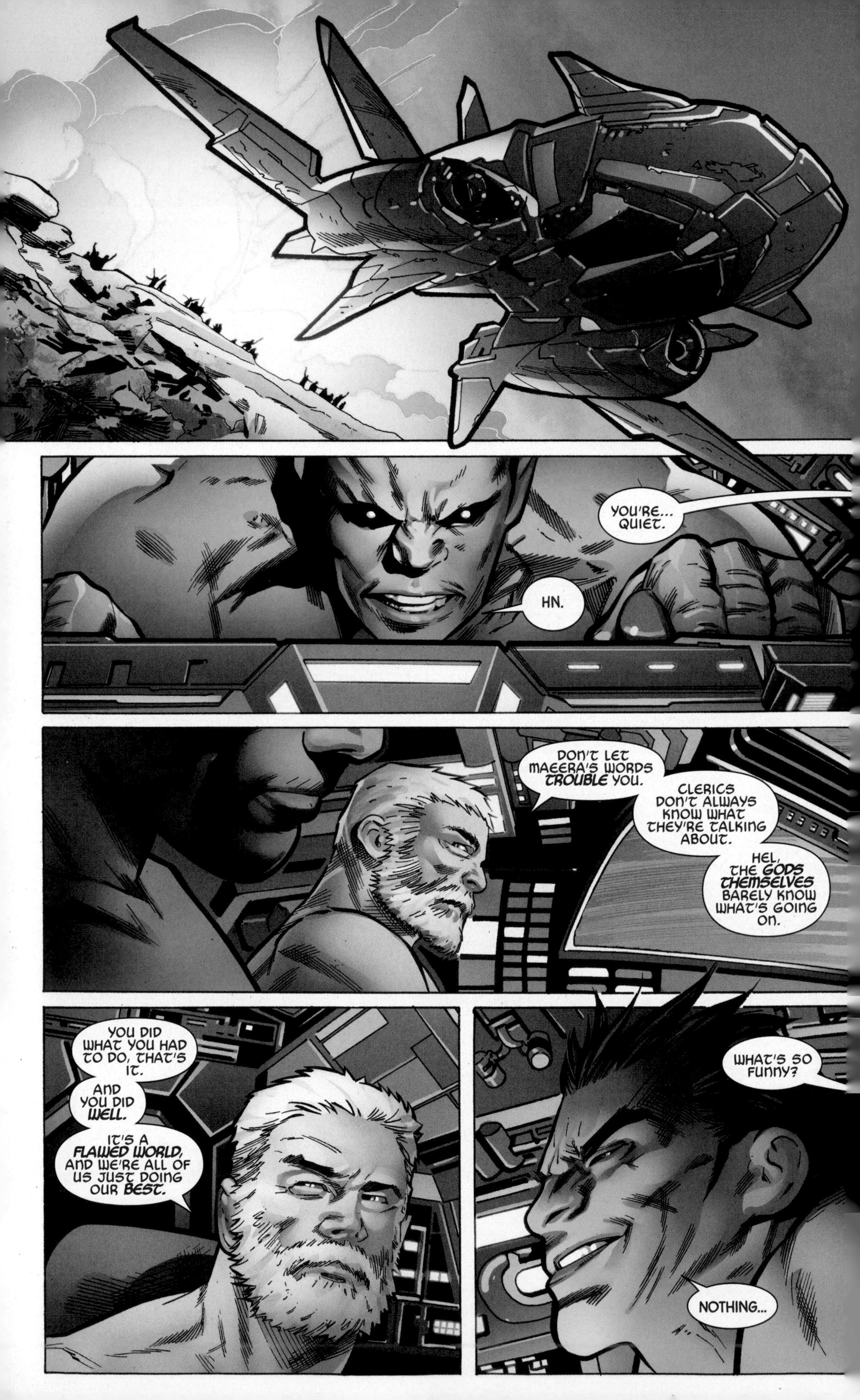
YOU'RE... QUIET.
HN.
DON'T LET MAEERA'S WORDS TROUBLE YOU.
CLERICS DON'T ALWAYS KNOW WHAT THEY'RE TALKING ABOUT.
HEL, THE GODS THEMSELVES BARELY KNOW WHAT'S GOING ON.
YOU DID WHAT YOU HAD TO DO, THAT'S IT.
AND YOU DID WELL.
IT'S A FLAWED WORLD, AND WE'RE ALL OF US JUST DOING OUR BEST.
WHAT'S SO FUNNY?
NOTHING...

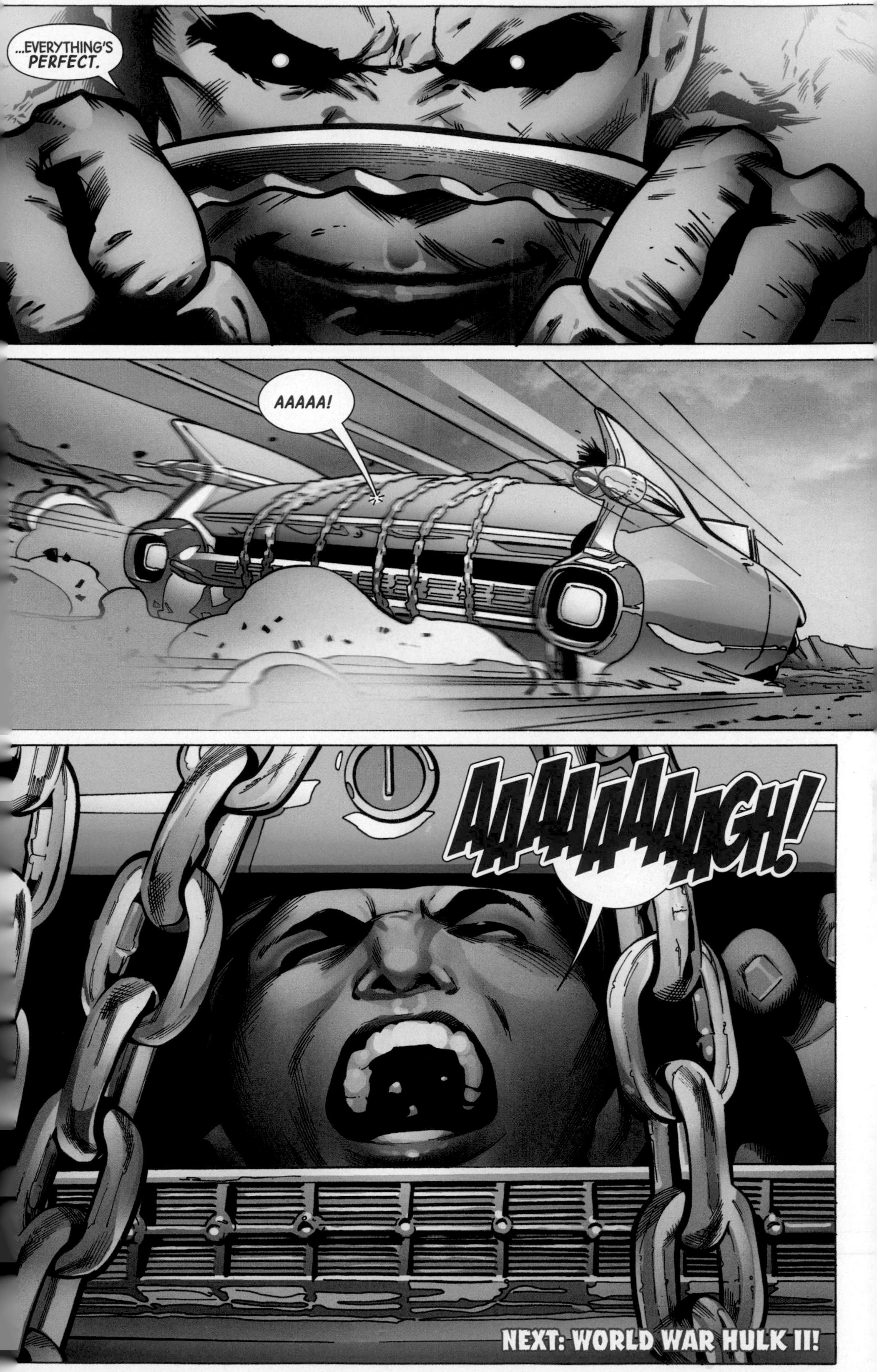
...EVERYTHING'S PERFECT.
AAAAA!
AAAAAAAAAGH!
NEXT: WORLD WAR HULK II!

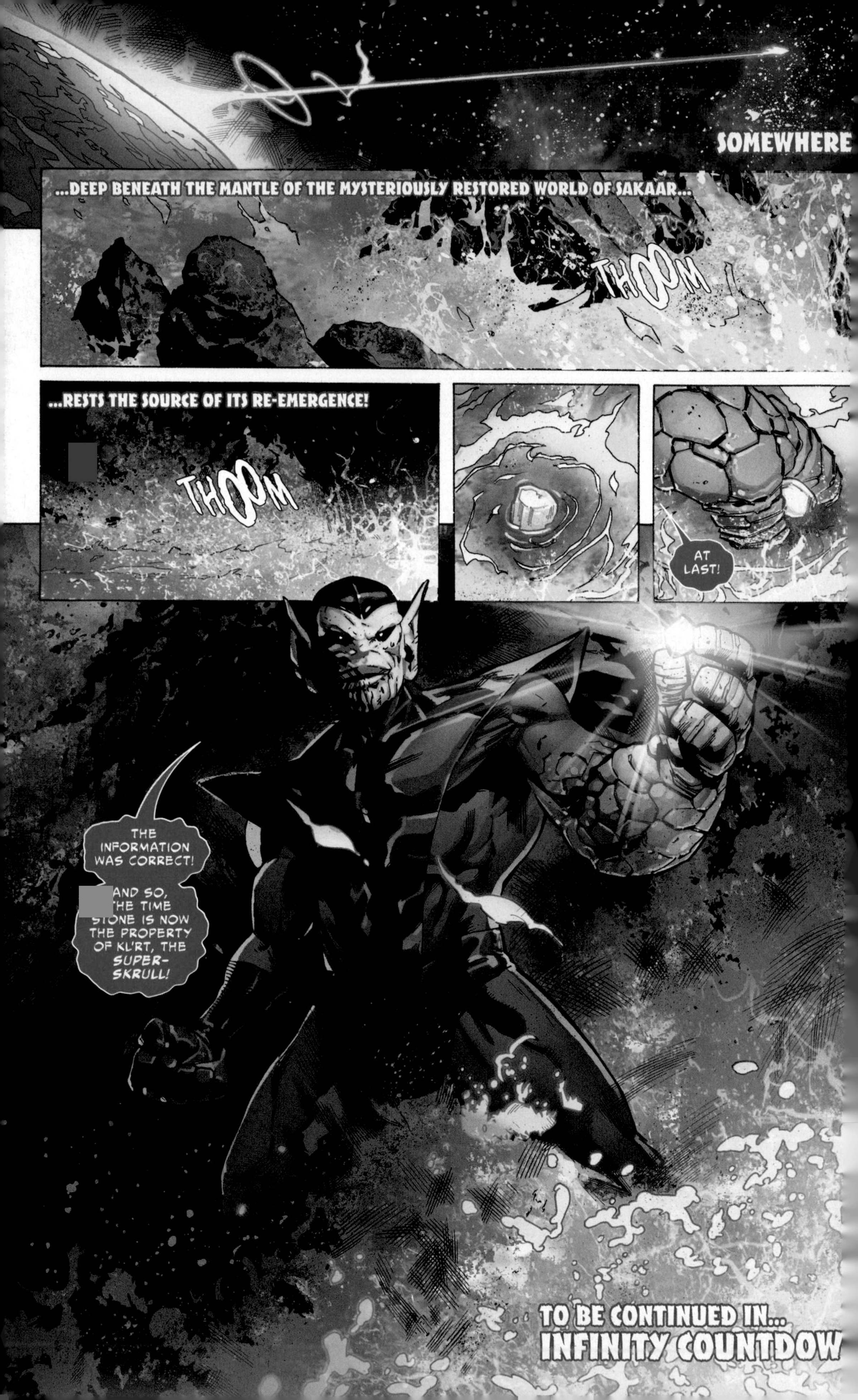
SOMEWHERE
...DEEP BENEATH THE MANTLE OF THE MYSTERIOUSLY RESTORED WORLD OF SAKAAR...
THOOM
...RESTS THE SOURCE OF ITS RE-EMERGENCE!
THOOM
AT LAST!
THE INFORMATION WAS CORRECT!
AND SO, THE TIME STONE IS NOW THE PROPERTY OF KL'RT, THE SUPER-SKRULL!
TO BE CONTINUED IN...
INFINITY COUNTDOW

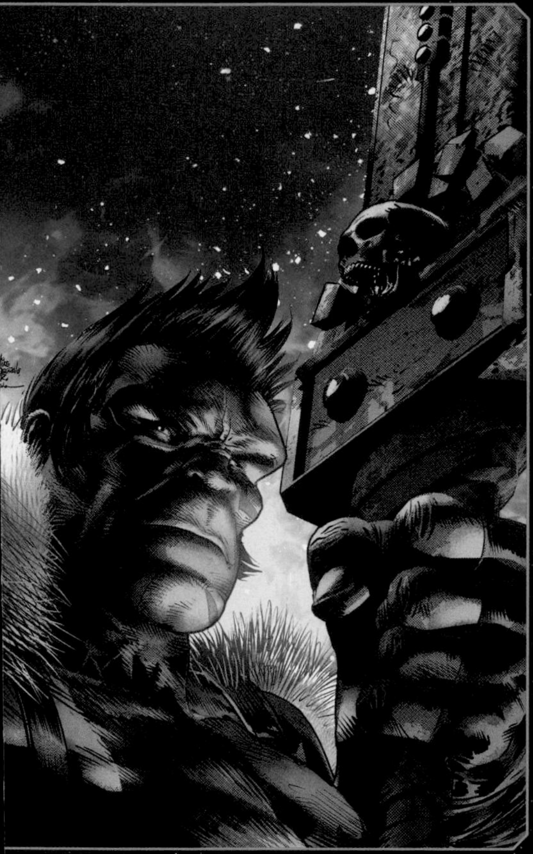

MIKE DEODATO JR. & MARCELO MAIOLO
#709 VARIANT

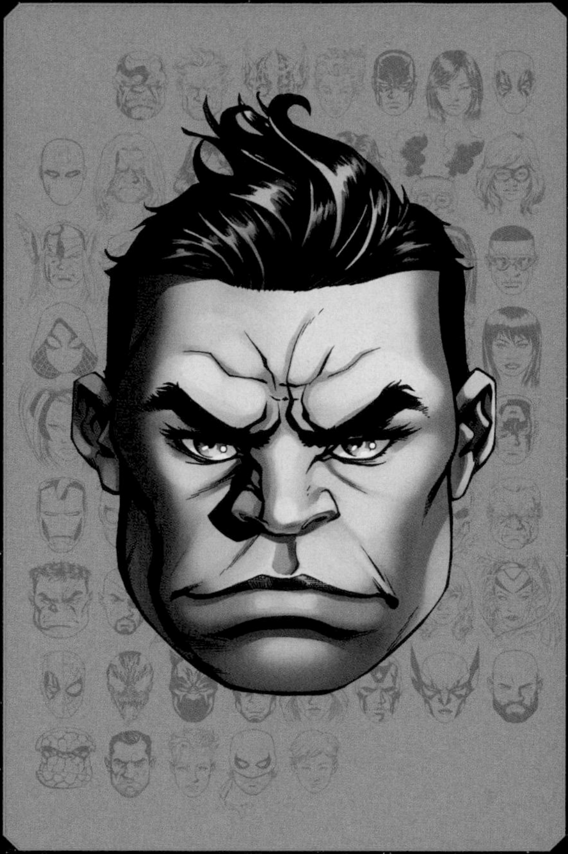

MIKE McKONE & RACHELLE ROSENBERG
#709 LEGACY HEADSHOT VARIANT

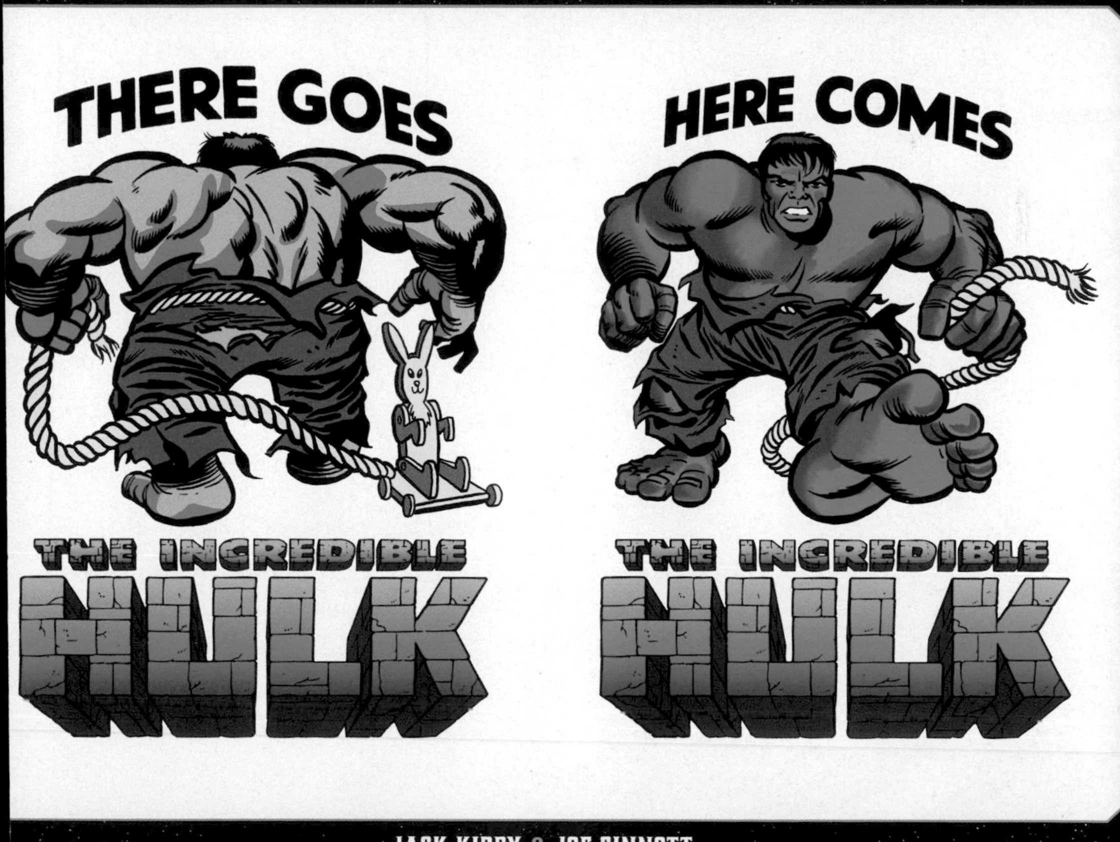
THERE GOES
HERE COMES
THE INCREDIBLE
HULK
THE INCREDIBLE
HULK

JACK KIRBY & JOE SINNOTT
#709 T-SHIRT VARIANT

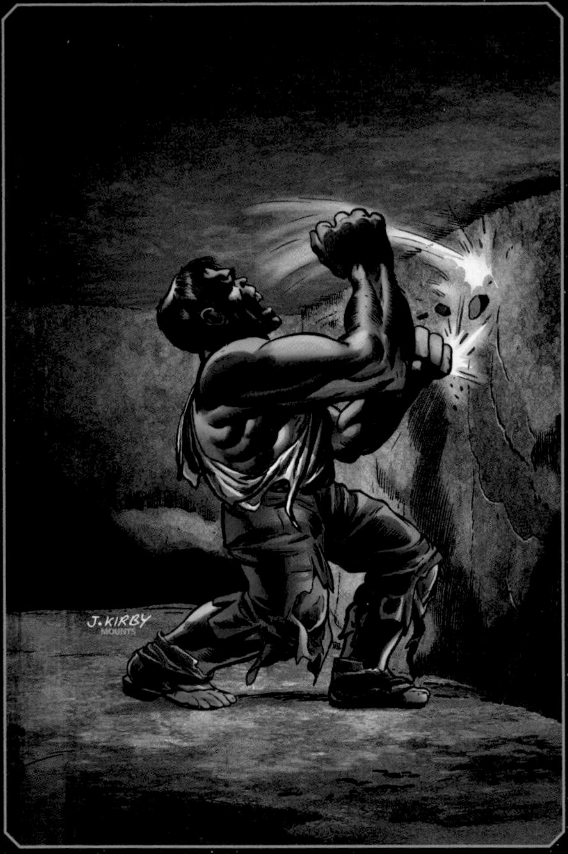
J. KIRBY
MOUNTS

JACK KIRBY, DICK AYERS & PAUL MOUNTS
#710 KIRBY 100TH VARIANT

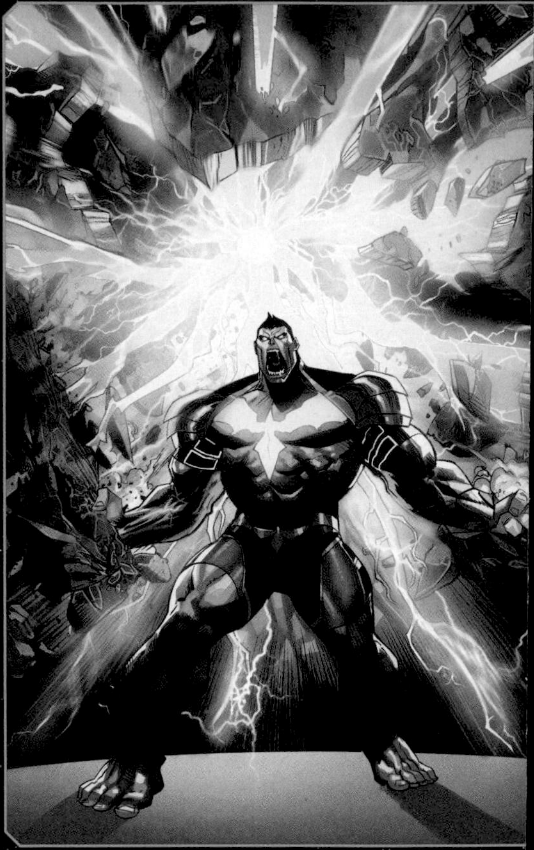

DANIEL MORA
#711 PHOENIX VARIANT

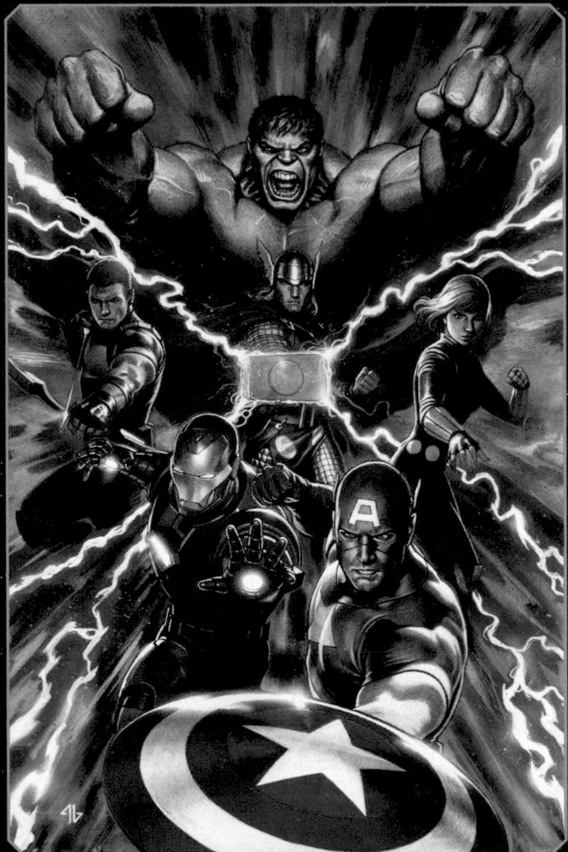

ADI GRANOV
#712 AVENGERS ASSEMBLE VARIANT

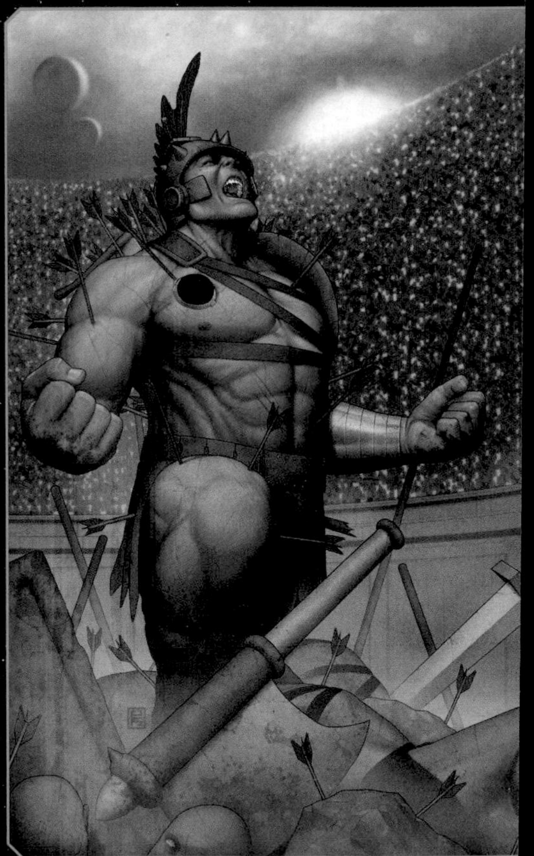

JOHN TYLER CHRISTOPHER
#713 VARIANT